Intelligent skins

Butterworth-Heinemann
Linacre House, Jordan Hill, Oxford OX2 8DP
225 Wildwood Avenue, Woburn, MA 01801-2041
A division of Reed Educational and Professional Publishing Ltd

Ɛ A member of the Reed Elsevier plc group

First published 2002

British Library Cataloguing in Publication Data
A catalogue record for this book is available from the British Library

Library of Congress Cataloguing in Publication Data
A catalogue record for this book is available from the Library of Congress

ISBN 0 7506 4847 3

For information on all Architectural Press publications
visit our website at www.architecturalpress.com

Produced and typeset by Gray Publishing, Tunbridge Wells, Kent
Printed and bound in Italy

Intelligent skins

**MICHAEL WIGGINTON
AND JUDE HARRIS**

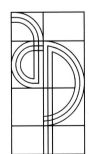

OXFORD AUCKLAND BOSTON JOHANNESBURG MELBOURNE NEW DELHI

Contents

	Acknowledgements	vi
Preface	The origins of this book	vii
	Picture acknowledgements	viii
Chapter 1	Introduction	3
Chapter 2	The environmental context and the design imperative	7
Chapter 3	Buildings and intelligence: metaphors and models	17
Chapter 4	The intelligent skin: the deepening metaphor	27
Chapter 5	Method	36
Chapter 6	Features	39
Chapter 7	The future	43
Chapter 8	The case studies	45
Case study 1	GSW Headquarters *Berlin*	49
Case study 2	Debis Building *Berlin*	55
Case study 3	Commerzbank Headquarters *Frankfurt-am-Main*	59
Case study 4	Stadttor (City Gate) *Düsseldorf*	65
Case study 5	GlaxoWellcome House West *Greenford*	71
Case study 6	The Environmental Building *Garston*	75
Case study 7	Helicon *London*	83
Case study 8	Tax Office Extension *Enschede*	87
Case study 9	Headquarters of Götz *Würzburg*	93

Contents – continued

Case study 10	Phoenix Central Library *Phoenix, Arizona*	99
Case study 11	The Brundtland Centre *Toftlund Sønerjylland*	103
Case study 12	The Green Building *Dublin*	109
Case study 13	Heliotrop® *Freiburg-im-Breisgau*	115
Case study 14	Villa Vision *Taastrup*	121
Case study 15	Business Promotion Centre *Duisburg*	125
Case study 16	School of Engineering and Manufacture *Leicester*	129
Case study 17	SUVA Insurance Company *Basel*	137
Case study 18	Solar House Freiburg *Freiburg*	143
Case study 19	Design Office for Gartner *Gundelfingen/Donau*	149
Case study 20	TRON – Concept Intelligent House *Tokyo*	155
Case study 21	Super Energy Conservation Building *Tokyo*	159
Case study 22	Occidental Chemical Center *Niagara Falls, New York*	163
	Selected bibliography	169
	Definitions	171
	Index	175

Acknowledgements

The authors owe a huge debt of gratitude to the designers, building owners and users associated with each of the case study buildings who have answered questions, and provided guided tours, drawings and photographs for their project, enabling us to portray our ideas of the intelligent building and its envelope – the intelligent skin. Every architect and engineer named in the case studies has contributed enormous effort, and exhibited tremendous patience, as we have sought to ensure the proper, accurate, and full representation of their work. In this sense the book is a co-operative effort, although we ourselves must take the blame for any inaccuracies.

On a personal note, much gratitude is due to our colleagues, who have supported us both through the original research, and through the task of turning the work into a book, as well as our families who inevitably have had to live with the efforts.

The project would not have started without a grant of 'seed funding' by the Higher Education Funding Council or England under the DevR scheme, and we remain very grateful for that original impetus, and to the University of Plymouth for its continued support.

Preface: the origins of this book

This book has its origins in two sets of ideas. The first comes out of research carried out in the early 1980s during the preparation of my book *Glass in Architecture*. In a lecture at the RIBA given in 1985, called 'Glass Architecture and the Thinking Skin', the idea of new building skin technologies assisting in the evolution of responsive buildings was set out as an 'end-piece' to the lecture. This itself was not new, and had been promoted by architects and engineers for some time, in the UK most notably by Michael Davies and others who had realized the potential of the new glasses and control technologies. Work on the technical content of *Glass in Architecture* undertaken during the late 1980s, made evident the worldwide efforts of designers to develop what were named 'complex multiple skins' in my research.

The second origin lay in a 'low energy' Diploma studio taught at the Scott Sutherland School of Architecture in the Robert Gordon University in Aberdeen in the early 1990s. With the assistance of such distinguished engineers as Tom Barker of Ove Arup & Partners, and Max Fordham of Max Fordham & Partners, it became quite clear that, whilst buildings could be devised for very low energy in use, varying diurnal and seasonal conditions made the design of purely passive buildings (that is, buildings which could sit, inert, and maintain comfort, day and night, throughout the year), virtually impossible if 'zero-environmental-energy' was an objective. The demands made upon the building fabric required the proposition of variable envelopes a prerequisite to the creation of a building with very small provision of environmental services, or perhaps no provision of some of these at all. In the project studies forming the Diploma Programme it was evident that, for example, the thermal transmittance of the building skin should have a different value at different times if stable thermal conditions were to be held inside the building without the importing of energy to drive a heating or cooling system: this requirement for a building to 'open up' or 'close down' has obvious relationships in the optical actions of the human eye, which we close when we wish to sleep, and the iris of which 'stops down' the pupil automatically in bright light. The possible absence of a human operator to produce this action, and the sometimes counterintuitive nature of the action, suggested that the building ought to be intelligent enough to know what to do in different circumstances in order to maintain its 'metabolism' at levels consistent with comfort for its human occupants.

Consideration of these two study programmes provided the basis for a research programme devised in 1995 named the Intelligent Façade Programme. This was a 10-stage programme intended to investigate the feasibility of the intelligent façade, this being defined as a façade incorporating variable technology which would amend itself to provide comfort conditions inside the building whatever the external environmental conditions might be, in any particular building location. It was accepted at the outset that this would have to be 'demonstrated' to be economically viable, and it was based philosophically on the principle that buildings for much of the twentieth century had developed design paradigms such that the morphology and construction of a building was designed to suit a set of functional and aesthetic objectives, often not environmentally driven, only for engineers to be asked to correct the environment by the incorporation of environmental systems, which themselves required large and unnecessary amounts of energy.

Considerations of an 'intelligent building' thus offered the potential for the development of buildings where variable building fabric, integrated with good 'passive' design, could redistribute investment cost from building services into building fabric, and thus reduce energy costs in use, and (it was hoped), total life-cycle costing.

While the 10-stage programme was intended to include studies of modelling, prototype evaluation, and a variety of other activities, the first appropriate task was considered to be a case study review.

Funding was provided for this by the University of Plymouth when I became Head of the School of Architecture in 1996. This enabled Jude Harris to join the research team working on the newly conceived programme, and this book is the outcome.

Interest in the subject area has grown, partly as a result of the dissemination of the work we have done since the programme started. The European Union research programme known as 'COST C13: Glass and Interactive Building Envelopes', is a four-year international programme, started in October 2000, involving 16 nations so far, including the USA represented by Lawrence Berkeley Laboratories. The Management Committee, on which I serve, is progressing the search for useful and viable interactive façade design. The Committee includes architects, building physicists, and engineers, including representation from most of the important national research centres in Europe. This effectively moves the idea of the intelligent façade out of the world of fantasy and into the world of real building. The search for the intelligent skin is on.

Michael Wigginton
Plymouth

Picture acknowledgements

The authors and publisher are grateful to the following for permission to reproduce material in this book. Every effort has been made to contact copyright holders and any rights not acknowledged here will made in future printings if notice is given to the publishers.

Chapter 1
Drawing by Petzinka Pink und Partner, Dusseldorf (p. 2)
Occidental Chemical Center: Barbara Elliott Martin/Cannon Design (p. 3)

Chapter 2
View of Paris smog: Sunset/FLPA – Images of Nature (p. 6)
The Dordogne: Michael Wigginton (p. 6)
Oil refinery: Michael Wigginton (p. 7)
Wind turbine: Michael Wigginton (p. 8)
Chicago office buildings: Michael Wigginton (p. 11)
Thai village house: Michael Wigginton (p. 11)
SUVA Building (Case Study 17) Before: Herzog & de Meuron/Ruedi Walti (p. 13)
SUVA Building (Case Study 17) After: Herzog & de Meuron/Ruedi Walti (p. 13)

Chapter 3
The Sky Lab: NASA/Michael Wigginton (p. 16)
Control thermometer: Robert Gray (p. 18)
Fridge/freezer controls: Michael Wigginton (p. 19)
City Place: Skidmore Owings & Merrill (SOM), Chicago (p. 21)
Deer: Corel (p. 23)
Plants: Corel (p. 23)
Human shoulder: Michael Wigginton (p. 24)

Chapter 4
Tennis player (Tim Henman): Birmingham Photo Library (p. 26)
Human skin: Science Photo Library (p. 28)
Human eye: Michael Wigginton (p. 29)
Chiddingstone Street with blind/curtains: Michael Wigginton (p. 30)
House for the Future: National Museums & Galleries of Wales (p. 32)
Roof-mounted photovoltaics (SUVA Building, Basel): Jude Harris (p. 33)

Chapter 6
Case Study 6: Dennis Gilbert/VIEW (p. 39)
Case Study17: Herzog & de Meuron/Ruedi Walti (p. 40)
Case Study 19: Firma Gartner/Pancho Balluveg/Karsten de Riese/Werkfoto Gartner (p. 40)
Case Study 12: Murray O'Laoire Architects (p. 40)
Case Study 4: Jude Harris (p. 41)
Case Study 11: KHR AS Arkitekter/Bruntland Center Danmark (p. 41)
Case Study 16: Alan Short (p. 41)
Case Study 22: Barbara Elliott Martin/Cannon Design (p. 41)

Chapter 7
Photovoltaics on the Space Shuttle: NASA/Michael Wigginton (p. 43)

Case Study 1
Photos: Annette Kisling, Berlin; Butter + Bredt, Berlin; Kisling und Bruns, Berlin.
Drawings: Sauerbruch Hutton Architects

Case Study 2
Photos: M Denancé; E Cano; V Mosch; Berengo Gardin. Drawings: Renzo Piano Building Workshop

Case Study 3
Photos: Ian Lambot; Jude Harris. Drawings: Foster & Partners

Case Study 4
Photos: Jude Harris; Petzinka Pink und Partner. Drawings: DBZ/DS Plan

Case Study 5
Photos and drawings: RMJM.

Case Study 6
Photos: Dennis Gilbert/VIEW; Jude Harris. Drawings: Feilden Clegg Architects; Building Research Establishment

Case Study 7
Photos: Sheppard Robson; Peter Durant. Drawings: Sheppard Robson

Case Study 8
Photos: Ooerlemans van Reeken Studio/Robert Ooerlemans; Buro Solo Delft. Drawings: Ruurd Roorda

Case Study 9
Photos: Andreas Lauble; Jude Harris. Drawings: Webler + Geissler

Case Study 10
Photos: Bill Timmerman

Case Study 11
Photos: KHR AS Architekter; Bruntland Center Danmark. Drawings: KHR AS Architekter

Case Study 12
Photos: Murray O'Laoire Associates. Drawings: Murray O'Laoire Associates

Case Study 13
Photos: George Nemec, Merzhausen; Jude Harris. Drawings: Rolf Disch

Case Study 14
Photos: Dansk Architektur Center; Gammel Dok; Flemming Skude. Drawings: Flemming Skude and Ivar Moltke

Case Study 15
Photos: Dennis Gilbert/VIEW. Drawings: Foster & Partners; John Hewitt

Case Study 16
Photos: Alan Short (Short Ford & Associates); Jude Harris. Drawings: Short Ford & Associates

Case Study 17
Photos: Schmidlin; Herzog & de Meuron; Ruedi Walti; Jude Harris. Drawings: Herzog & de Meuron; Schmidlin

Case Study 18
Photos: A Berghoff; Fraunhofer Institute for Solar Energy Systems ISE. Drawings: Hölken & Berghoff

Case Study 19
Photos: Firma Gartner; Sigrid Neubert; Pancho Balluveg; Karsten de Riese; Werkfoto Gartner; Jude Harris. Drawings: Hölken & Berghoff

Case Study 20
Photos: Ken Sakamura. Drawings: TRON Intelligent House

Case Study 21
Photos and drawings: Ohbayashi Corporation

Case Study 22
Photos: Barbara Elliott Martin; Cannon Design; Michael Wigginton. Drawings: John Hewitt

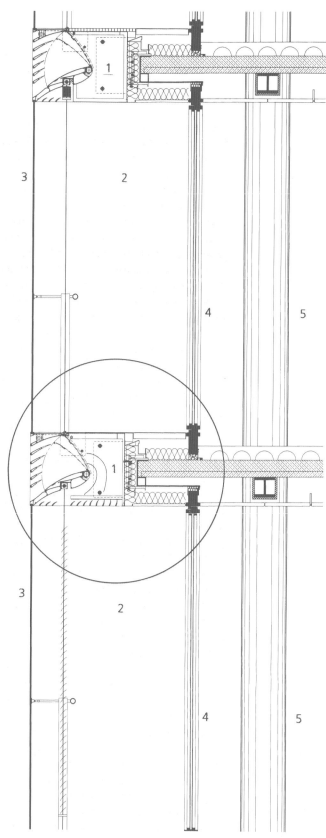

▲ External wall section, Stadttor, Dusseldorf, Germany, by Petzinka Pink und Partner, Case study 4.

Introduction

The idea of the 'intelligent building' has achieved a certain currency in the past few decades. With concepts such as 'smart materials' it represents the introduction into design principles of ideas related to self-adjustment and responsiveness, made possible by new technologies in general, and information technology in particular. Not all applications of such terminology have equal legitimacy, and there are as many uses which are based on professional promotion as are based on true applications of a rigorously applied concept. However, underpinning this marketing rhetoric lies a concept of genuine potential use, and great architectural and tectonic significance.

In this book it is assumed that the intelligent building is based on a very different paradigm to that which is conventionally understood. The conventional paradigm relates to the use of more or less complex building management systems, to provide a building with active systems and controls that allows the motorized action of what might be called subordinate functions and appliances. These are useful and important aspects of the evolution of building services control and management. Typical systems are related to security and the automatic or remote activation of appliances. The Intelligent Skin Study, which is part of a broader Intelligent Building Programme, is related to its responsive performance, sometimes but not always in relation to the environmental performance of the whole building, and bears a much closer comparison with the biological idea of intelligence and response, such as is seen in the 'natural intelligence' of the human skin, and the science of artificial intelligence. This aspect of the work is more fully covered in Chapter 3.

Seen in this context, the 'intelligent skin' forms part of the intelligent building, and refers to the element of a building that performs the function of enveloping the inhabited interior, the design and construction of which forms the single greatest potential controller of its interior environment, in terms of light, heat, sound, ventilation and air quality.

The façade of a building can account for between 15% and 40% of the total building budget,[1] and may be a significant contributor to the cost of up to 40% more through its impact on the cost of building services.

In complex buildings, the mechanical and electrical services can account for 30–40% or more of the total building budget. Associated research being carried out on the programme suggests that between 30% and 35% of the capital cost of a well-serviced, high-specification office building is attributable to building services, with 13–15% being attributable to what might be called environmental services: those services devised to control the internal thermal and ventilation environment.[2] To these costs are eventually added the lifetime costs of the systems involved, including maintenance, replacement and energy costs.

The propositions presented in this book are predicated on the assumption that the effect of responsive building fabric, to complement, reduce, and in some cases render unnecessary, mechanical and electrical environmental systems, may result in the effective redeployment of a building's construction budget.

It is the application of the biological metaphor of the human skin that makes it seem more appropriate to describe this enveloping membrane as the 'intelligent skin', emphasizing its close relationship with the human epidermis.

▲ The Occidental Chemical Building of 1981, originally known as the Hooker Building at Niagara Falls, New York by Cannon Design was one of the first buildings to incorporate intelligent response in its skin. The large aerofoil solar protecting louvres tilt automatically to keep the sun's direct beams from striking the internal glass wall, by the action of a solar cell on the rear edge of one louvre on each bank.

This book describes the context within which the need for variability in building skin performance has arisen, and goes on to demonstrate how such dynamic response mechanisms have been incorporated into the design and construction of a number of buildings over the past 20 years.

The case study work has made it clear that none of the buildings studied during this early stage in the evolutionary process of the Intelligent Building Programme can be regarded as truly intelligent, in the terms proposed by the programme. A conclusion has been drawn that the buildings studied provide clues to what might be called the 'genetic' make-up of this new generation of buildings. This genetic model has helped in determining the method of consideration of the buildings studied, in considering the range and variations in function of the different technologies used to moderate energy and material flows through the building envelope, and thus maintain and enhance the environment of the building interior.

Most buildings today are equipped with increasingly advanced technologies, but few seem to be exploiting the true potential that this 'environmental intelligence' has to offer. The intention of this study is to take the idea of the intelligent building a few steps further towards realizing the benefits of reduced energy consumption, and increased occupant comfort and control.

The emphasis is on the *active* and *automatic* control of the functions performed by the building envelope. This is very different to the conventional *passive* architectural approach which seems (quite understandably and properly) to have prevailed in the environmental design of buildings. 'Passive' architecture has evolved in response to concerns about the implications of mechanical provision, related to the problems of complexity, cost, servicing, and the increasing dependency on technology, rather than independence from it, and remains of fundamental importance for the architecture of the future. However, the passive approach cannot provide answers to all the problems of climate control, and this has led to a search for means of making the building dynamic and responsive. Responsive building fabric itself requires technology, and the reason for the tentative evolution from passive to active seems largely to do with lack of precedent, combined with natural and proper concerns about costs and effectiveness, and issues of maintenance.

Other parts of the Intelligent Façade Programme referred to in the preface, currently underway, are examining these aspects of the proposition. Meanwhile, the buildings included in the case studies incorporate systems and mechanisms providing variability in the building envelope, necessary to achieve required internal conditions whatever the external climate may present. As such, these buildings incorporate the first steps in the evolution of the intelligent building.

The case studies were selected in accordance with the method set out in Chapter 5, and represent the identification of a small percentage given the more than 300 buildings from across the world reviewed at the start of the programme. Each of them is considered in some way to provide what has been termed in this book the 'genetic material' for the intelligent building. As is made clear in Chapter 5, the case study work could not enter into monitoring and analysis of the buildings concerned, since this would require agreements between the researchers, clients, and design teams, together with project-by-project research, on a much larger scale. It would also have been difficult, if not impossible, to ensure accurate data suitable for proper comparison. For this reason the reports are purely descriptive in format, providing some details of the current 'state of the art' in built projects, across the world. Drawings and data are included in the state they were provided by each building's authors, usually tested by personal interview.

The case studies presented are generally individual examples of initiative, where the expertise and technique involved is in the ownership of the consultants and manufacturers involved in a single project. The objective of the case study, as set out in this book, is to establish the criteria, mechanisms and design methods related to the newly defined intelligent skin. At this stage in the programme, which identifies and promotes the concept of the 'intelligent skin', it is hoped that some of the ideas and 'genetic characteristics' will be disseminated into the architectural and allied professions, to assist in the continued evolution of the concept, to form an economically and functionally viable proposition, which contributes to the development of very low energy, and intelligent, architecture, and perhaps new morphologies.

References

1 Andrew Hall of Arup Façade Engineering, speaking at RIBA Advances in Technology Series, 'Advances in Cladding', Monday 7 July 1997.
2 Michael Wigginton and Battle McCarthy: 'The Environmental Second Skin'. Research carried out for the UK Department of the Environment Transport and the Regions (first published at www.battlemccarthy.demon.co.uk/research/environmentalsecondskins).

▲ Two images of France: Paris has recently been subject to traffic restrictions resulting from the pollution generated by its urbanization. The contrast with the rural scene in the Dordogne could not be more stark.

6   The environmental context and design imperative

Introduction

The origin of the Intelligent Façade Programme lies in the environmental imperatives which emanate from building energy use considerations. These are well established, but are summarized below, not least because they formed the legitimizing rationale behind the research programme, but also because in understanding the quantitative basis of energy and the impact of its use, we can understand the measure of the necessary solutions.

The major global environmental problems facing us at the beginning of the twenty-first century are dominated by the potential and impending risk posed by the greenhouse effect and the resulting impact of climate change. There are also concerns about the damage being inflicted on fragile ecosystems by increasing development and resource extraction, and the depletion of the ozone layer, which allows harmful ultraviolet radiation to penetrate the lower atmosphere. In parallel with these often imperceptible effects there has been a general deterioration in air quality, most striking in urban areas. It is well established that buildings place a major burden on the environment, both directly and indirectly, and it is clear that they have a major role to play in the collective efforts required to avoid significant and possible catastrophic environmental degradation.

The energy context

Global impact: energy use and the greenhouse effect

Humanity's thirst for energy has increased extraordinarily since the industrial revolution, particularly after the realization of the exploitative benefits of electricity which led to the construction of the first power stations in the final quarter of the nineteenth century. Mechanized transport added to the already burgeoning use of energy early in the twentieth century, itself fuelled by the discovery of the immense potential of oil, which was accompanied by the realization of the benefits of natural and artificial gas.

The resource, and emissions, implications of this rapidly expanding use of energy was ignored for three-quarters of a century. The potential for nemesis in energy use and resource depletion, as in many other aspects of human activity, was brought to light very clearly in the Club of Rome's Report *The Limits to Growth*, published in 1972.[1] The degree of dependency of the developed world, in particular, on the availability and price of energy was realized at about the same time, with the oil embargoes applied by some oil-producing nations in 1973 and 1974. The oil crises of the 1970s served to heighten concern over the long-term viability of reliance on fossil-based fuels for energy, but this was more through concern for price and security of supply than for any wish to conserve the environment.

◀ While oil does not play as great a role in the UK as coal and gas in the creation of electrical power, it remains at the heart of the global issue of energy consumption and pollution. It is a major driver of the politics of energy, as well as having major significance in relation to energy and sustainability.

▲ Our thirst for electrical power is a major driver of emissions. Buildings use about 65% of the electrical power generated in the UK. The power output of this token wind turbine is a tiny fraction of the output of the major fossil-fuel power station behind it.

The greenhouse effect was formally recognized as a problem in 1988 by the establishment of the Intergovernmental Panel on Climate Change (IPCC). The panel was set up jointly by the World Meteorological Organization and the United Nations Environment Programme. The greenhouse effect relates to the build-up of so-called greenhouse gases in the earth's atmosphere, which form a protective layer and are relatively transparent to incoming short-wave radiation from the sun. The gases forming the atmosphere are relatively opaque to longer wave radiation which is emitted back from the warmed surface of the earth. This phenomenon is similar to the way that glass behaves in relation to radiation transmission, and this provides the greenhouse analogy. The naturally occurring greenhouse effect is fundamentally benign, and serves to sustain life on our planet by balancing incoming solar radiation with radiation losses from the earth in such a way as to maintain what we know as habitable temperatures, the temperatures which animal life has evolved to tolerate and be comfortable in. This thermal environment at the earth's surface is very sensitive to the balance of the greenhouse effect; the temperature at sea level would be 33°C lower without the naturally occurring layer of insulating greenhouse gases.[2] The increased concentrations of greenhouse gases generated by human activity, which inhibit long-wave radiation transmission, have upset this balance, and are widely believed to be responsible for the gradual warming of the earth's surface.

The implications of global warming have been widely debated, but the current scientific consensus concludes that there could be significant changes in the planetary climate. Increased temperatures will lead to the thermal expansion of the world's oceans (which constitute 70% of its surface) and the melting of polar ice deposits, the combined effect of which will cause sea levels to rise across the globe. The effect of this in certain parts of the world, where large populations inhabit land which has a topography close to sea level, will be disastrous. In places as far apart as Bangladesh and the UK we are seeing predictions of significant changes in the coastline. In England this refers particularly to East Anglia and other low-lying parts of the country. Independently of this effect on the world's oceans, there is growing evidence of major shifts in weather patterns established on record over many centuries. Changing ocean currents, which play a vital role in stabilizing weather systems, may further disrupt climate patterns. There may also be implications for crop growth, and the regional distribution of pests and diseases.

The main greenhouse gases are carbon dioxide, methane, chlorofluoro-carbons (CFCs), nitrous oxides, tropospheric ozone, and water vapour. Carbon dioxide (CO_2) is considered to have the most significant effect on global warming, followed by methane. The main anthropogenic source of greenhouse gases is the combustion of fossil fuels, such as oil, coal and gas, largely for energy and transportation. An increasing world population, and the proportional rise in energy and resource consumption, increasing industrialization, and an intensification of agriculture are all exacerbating the greenhouse effect. The problem is made worse by the destruction of carbon dioxide 'sinks' caused by mass deforestation, most notable in the tropical rain forests.

Recent concern in relation to climate and the whole environment has arisen through increasing attention to global sustainable development, which is concerned to a significant degree with buildings and energy. The United Nations World Commission on Environment and Development, under the chairmanship of the then prime minister of Norway, Gro Harlem Brundtland, produced its report, *Our Common Future*, in 1987.[3] In September of the same year attempts to reduce the depletion of the ozone layer by limiting the use of damaging substances such as CFCs and HCFCs were tackled by the Montreal Protocol.[4] The United Nations Conference on Environment and Development (The Earth Summit) at Rio de Janeiro in 1992 published one of the most comprehensive documents concerned with the implementation of sustainable development.[5] At the summit there were also pledges given by world leaders to reduce carbon dioxide emissions (by maintaining 1990 levels), to protect the rain forests, and maintain the biodiversity of the planet. The UK may be one of only a few OECD countries to meet these targets for reduction.[6] The British government also has a domestic goal to cut the UK's emission of carbon dioxide by 20% below 1990 levels by 2010.

In December 1997, at the Kyoto Summit, governments signed a legally binding protocol[7] that stipulated an aggregate 5.2% reduction in the 'basket' of greenhouse gases[8] by 2008–12. The third conference of the parties to the United Nations Convention on Climate Change succeeded in producing an international agreement to combat climate change after 10 days of intense negotiations.

As part of this agreement, the European Union is committed to reducing greenhouse gas emissions to concentrations 8% lower than levels recorded in 1990 by the year 2010. The UK has agreed to cuts of 12.5%[9] as part of a burden-sharing agreement among member states. The United States and Canada agreed to reduce their greenhouse gas emissions by 7% and 6%, respectively, and Japan agreed to reductions of 6%. For the first time in history, most industrialized nations (except Australia, New Zealand, Norway, Iceland and Russia)[10] are now legally bound in principle to reduce the global emissions of greenhouse gases.

There is some scepticism about clauses within the protocol which provide a number of 'flexibility mechanisms' intended to reduce the cost of implementation, which are potentially open to abuse. The targets set also fall a long way short of the reductions of between 50% and 70% recommended by scientists as necessary to prevent or mitigate the worst impact of climate change. However, the outcome from Kyoto is clearly a move in the right direction (although it should be noted that the United States' Senate has shown no signs of ratifying the Treaty and the new Bush administration seems to be rebutting it). The USA is the biggest supporter of 'emissions trading', where quotas for emitting harmful gases can be sold on the open market.

The UK government has proposed a 'three-pronged approach' for the abatement of greenhouse gases in the UK.[11] Transport is the next major consumer of energy after buildings, and an integrated transport strategy is considered essential in meeting reduction targets. It is also proposed that the generation of electricity from renewable energy sources, and the increased use of combined heat and power systems, can serve to reduce the emissions produced by the generation of electricity, which has been dominated hitherto by the relatively inefficient combustion of fossil fuels.[12] Finally, it is believed that an extension of the government's energy-efficiency programme will contribute significantly to reducing the profligate consumption of energy in buildings. It has been estimated that buildings can contribute up to one-third of overall targeted reductions. One of the most significant contributions buildings can make to the environment is to reduce their reliance on the consumption of non-renewable resources, by the more efficient use of energy, in their construction, operation and maintenance. In the UK the energy use in buildings is increasingly becoming a matter for control under the Building Regulations, and consultation documents are currently circulating regarding proposed revisions to Part L (Conservation of Fuel and Power) which include

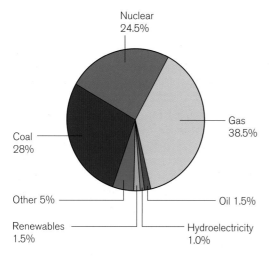

Nuclear
24.5%

Gas
38.5%

Coal
28%

Oil 1.5%

Other 5%

Renewables
1.5%

Hydroelectricity
1.0%

▲ Electricity generation by fuel source. Source: *UK Energy in Brief 2000*, Department of Trade and Industry (DTI), July 2000, Government Statistical Service.

measures that will significantly raise performance standards for insulation and air-tightness of building fabric and heating system performance.

Fuels

The principal fuel sources for final energy consumption across much of western Europe are presently petroleum, natural gas, electricity, nuclear, coal, and other solid fuels. Conversion efficiencies from primary fuel to delivered energy consumption can be very low: as little as 30% in the case of electricity, with the remainder lost in the conversion of the primary fuel and transmission losses across the grid.

The fuels used to generate electricity in the UK in 1999 were coal (28%), nuclear power (24.5%), natural gas (38.5%), oil (1.5%), and other fuels (6.5%, including renewables), and hydroelectric generation (1%).[13] Buildings use about two-thirds of the electricity consumed in the UK, and consequently are responsible for a large proportion of primary energy use. The other principal energy source for buildings is natural gas (direct heating). This means that buildings are directly and indirectly producing more than half of the UK's carbon dioxide emissions.[14]

In spite of improving energy efficiency in buildings over the past 30 years, energy consumption levels have remained relatively static at about 150 million tonnes of oil equivalent (mtoe) per year, distorted in recent years by periods of exceptionally cold weather.[15] Increasing efficiencies in power generation have been largely offset by an increase in the proportion of electricity supplied overall, which has increased by more than 58% since 1970.[16]

The opportunities for conservation clearly lie in attempting to reduce energy consumed for space heating and cooling, water heating, and electric lighting within buildings.

Transport

The next major consumer of energy after buildings is transport, which accounts for over 34% of total energy consumption.[17] It is inextricably linked to the built environment in that location affects car use, and movement between buildings consumes the largest proportion of transportation energy. The trend for urban dispersal has exacerbated the problem, and this may result in increased density of settlement in the future. The pollution from increased traffic levels is partly to blame for the increased demand for air-conditioning systems (high consumers of energy) in buildings located within urban centres. Air conditioning is even becoming a standard fixture in many new cars, leading to increased fuel consumption. However, fuel consumption itself is becoming an increasingly important marketing feature, and hybrid cars are now becoming available. Integrated transport systems, and the development of zero- or low-emission vehicles, are both as important as tackling the burden of our buildings on the environment.

The developing world

Energy consumption figures differ significantly between those of economically advanced nations and the developing world by a factor of up to 100. The US president acknowledged in 1997 that the USA constitutes 5% of the world's population, while owning 22% of the world's wealth, and producing 25% of global pollution.[18] On a per capita basis, US citizens account for nearly

80,000kWh per person per annum, when figures in the developing world can be as low as 800kWh per person each year.[19] To give an idea of this in terms of quantity, a typical household in the UK might have an annual energy consumption of 35,000kWh, or about 9000kWh per person for a four-person household. This is only domestic consumption, and such a family can be relied on to be using energy in employment, education, travel, leisure, and the multitude of other energy-consuming activities. In comparison with the US figure of 80,000kWh, UK citizens consume 45,800kWh each year, compared with an average for Europe (including the European parts of the former Soviet Union) of 36,400kWh per capita. The North American average (including Canada and Mexico) equates to 73,300kWh per person per annum, compared with an annual average for the rest of the world (excluding North America, Europe, and the former Soviet Union) of 799kWh per capita. The world average consumption is 16,700kWh per person.[20] The issues raised by these figures are not just those of global equity.

If we begin to allow for a relationship between aspiration and energy consumption, we can quickly see the problem generated by the relentless increase of energy consumption in the developing world (which includes the People's Republic of China), as its population strives to live at the same level of consumption as the present developed world. There is a clear and established correlation between energy consumption levels and economic activity and world-wide demand for energy is currently increasing at a rate of 2% each year.[21] The implications associated with rising consumption levels in the developing world are matters for grave concern, and any future global strategies must allow for the increased use of energy by developing countries, and the development and dissemination of appropriate technologies, which rely on low emission energy supply using renewable sources.

Energy costs

The present costs of energy as delivered are not truly reflective of the negative externalities and social costs associated with its production. The prices for gas, electricity and coal in 1999 were said to be at their lowest since records began in 1970.[22] At the time of writing a barrel of oil sells for about 13p per litre (between 10.14p and 15.39p during the first half of 2001)[23] and one of its principal by-products, petrol, sells for about 25p per litre in the USA (compared with over 80p per litre in the UK).

The comparison between the Chicago office buildings and the Thai village house is not simply a contrast between so-called advanced technological architecture and primitive building. It is also a contrast between the profligate use of energy, constructed with resources from all around the planet, and the use of materials procured locally to produce buildings which solve problems of heavy rainfall, sun shading and natural ventilation using construction techniques of very low embodied energy.

While we may not be able to return to the culture of low density, low technology, indigenous construction, we have to learn its lessons.

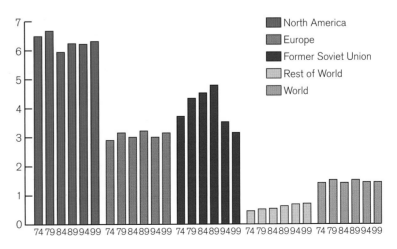

► World energy consumption per capita. Source: *BP Amoco Statistical Review of World Energy 2000*, BP Amoco, June 2000.

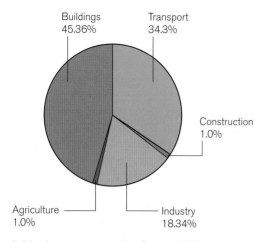

▲ Inland energy consumption. Source: *UK Energy in Brief*, Department of Trade and Industry (DTI), July 2000, Government Statistical Service.

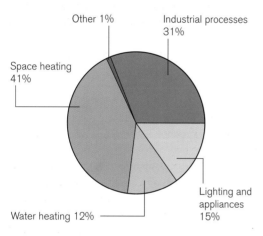

▲ Energy consumption for non-transport uses. Source: *Energy Consumption in the United Kingdom,* Energy Paper 66, DTI, Stationery Office, 1997.

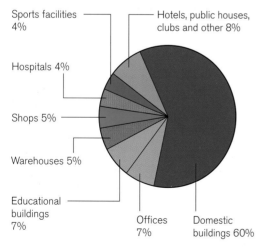

▲ Energy consumption by building type. Source: *Environmental Issues in Construction*, CIRIA Publications, No. 94, 1993.

The 'real' price of energy, which might include the costs of maintaining the biosphere's balance (an imponderable cost) and anti-pollution measures, is not established. Meanwhile decreasing or low energy prices weaken the case for the economic justification for energy conservation. In commercial buildings energy costs represent only a small percentage of total annual costs to the enterprises which occupy them, with salary costs typically being an organization's biggest liability.[24] The buildings themselves account for the next biggest capital cost. However, the high cost of the salary bill contributes to the considerations of energy use, given the increased productivity which results from improved comfort levels, particularly those delivered from natural sources, such as daylight, and naturally introduced fresh air.

The factor four effect

It has been said that the best opportunity for reducing energy consumption lies in the conservation of energy. The recently described 'factor four effect' set out by Amory Lovins and others suggests that it is possible for us to become much more efficient with today's technologies, by improving the efficiencies of power stations and transport.[25] If buildings were able to benefit from improvements such as those seen in the computer industry in terms of performance and price (such as with photovoltaics and other solar electricity generation devices), their burden on the environment could be significantly reduced. Similarly, advances in areas such as biotechnology make the building industry appear extremely slow to evolve by comparison.

The role of buildings

Low energy design

Historically, there has long been an awareness of the effect that buildings have on the environment, dating from the writings of Vitruvius, through to William Morris' concern about environmental damage resulting from the pace of urbanization and industrialization in the late nineteenth century. The potential in building design for the reduction of energy consumption, and for the introduction of benefits of solar power (for example) became evident early in the twentieth century, and evolved significantly in the 1930s. The ecological aspects of the impact of buildings became more widely debated during the 1960s and 1970s, which also marked the beginnings of ecological design as we know it today.

It has been observed by Donald Watson, a US professor of architecture, that we are now 'high on the learning curve' of environmental architecture, as architects have been seeking to practise it since the early 1970s.[26] In the UK, this has been translated into common design approaches, such as using thermal mass, natural ventilation, external shading and limiting internal heat gains (using natural or high-efficiency lighting, and low-power domestic electrical appliances, for example).

It is well established that buildings now account for nearly half of all delivered energy consumption across most of the developed world. The other dominant consumers are transport and industry, whose activities are closely associated with buildings and their location. Among the principal final users, it is difficult to state exactly what constitutes building energy use, and what is more accurately described as process energy use. In the domestic and service sectors it is accepted that the energy used is primarily consumed in buildings. For the transport and agricultural sectors it is known that most of their energy is used for other purposes. The industrial process of construction itself is estimated to constitute up to 1% of total energy consumption.[27] With these assumptions, buildings accounted for 45.36% of energy consumption in the UK in 1999, equating to 70.1 mtoe, or nearly 850,000 million kilowatt hours per annum.[28]

Energy consumption for non-transport uses is principally attributable to buildings, and is used for space heating (41%), water heating (12%), lighting and appliances (15%), with the remaining 31% being used for industrial processes.[29] Another major consumer of energy is cooling, which is becoming a more significant energy load in buildings with the increased use of automated office equipment and a rise in the prestige associated with air conditioning, accounting for up to 6% of the energy consumption in the services sector.[30] Energy consumption by building type in the UK is dominated by the domestic sector, which accounts for 60% of energy use, followed by offices (7%), educational buildings (7%), warehouses (5%), shops (5%), hospitals (4%), sports facilities (4%), and hotels public houses, clubs and other buildings (8%).[31]

To summarize, it can be seen that buildings account for more than half of the UK's carbon dioxide emissions arising from the combustion of fossil-based fuels,[32] and also the depletion of non-renewable reserves. Buildings can be seen as major contributors to both ozone depletion and the greenhouse effect. They are also largely responsible for the extraction and consumption of a large array of non-renewable resources used in their construction and operation.

Embodied energy

It is not only the daily consumption of fossil-fuel-derived energy use in buildings, and the transportation of people and goods between buildings and settlements, which generates this energy use. It is also the combustion of fossil-based fuels for the extraction and production of building materials, and the transportation of these materials to their construction sites. A completed building will have acquired a positive balance of 'embodied energy' before it is occupied and joins the ranks of energy consumers, and this will usually increase throughout the occupied operation and maintenance cycle of its lifetime (as materials appear as part of building refits) and further during its demolition. Applying the 'life-cycle costing' principle, the full extent of the influence that buildings have on the environment becomes clearer, and the role that they have to play in reducing the environmental burden they impose is accentuated.

Existing building stock

If a significant change in energy consumption trends is to be implemented, there must also be consideration of the existing building stock. New buildings only add somewhere between 1% and 5% to the total building stock each year. It is therefore essential to consider not only low-energy strategies for new buildings, but also how energy saving strategies can be applied to existing buildings in refurbishment. The incorporation of intelligent technologies does not have to be confined to new building design. This is demonstrated by the inclusion of a case study building in this book which has been refurbished and overclad with a new 'intelligent' skin (Case study 17, SUVA Insurance Company).

The role of the design team

Many believe that there is a moral imperative for architects and engineers involved in the design process to ensure that buildings reduce the

▲ As well as considering the energy performance in the design of new buildings it is also important to address the existing building stock. The SUVA Insurance Company (Case Study 17) in Basel was an existing stone-clad building, which has now been overclad with an 'intelligent' glazing system by Herzog & de Meuron Architects. This new actively controlled 'skin' has resulted in a greatly enhanced energy performance for the building.

environmental burden they impose on the planet. One of the most significant contributions that can be made is to reduce building energy consumption. This does not only involve low-energy strategies for the building operation, but also consideration of the more widespread urban issues that influence fossil fuel use for buildings and transportation. There should also be an awareness of the contribution that both 'embodied energy' and life-cycle energy in use, contribute to harmful emissions and resource depletion.

A European Charter published in 1996 included a statement by the Renewable Energy in Architecture and Design (READ) Group that 'in future architects must exert a far more decisive influence on the conception and layout of urban structures and buildings and on the use of materials and construction components, and thus on the use of energy, than they have in the past'.[33]

No longer should buildings, and what have been called their 'exclosures',[34] be designed in the same way from Austria to Zimbabwe, safe in the knowledge that building services and control engineering can strive to overcome the impacts of uncomfortable climate. Instead we should 'design with nature', regarding it as an 'ally and a friend' as was so eloquently set out by Ian McHarg over 30 years ago.[35] We can learn a great deal from the responsive and adaptive examples that we see in nature and produce intelligently designed 'enclosural' building morphologies which can reduce the need to import energy for cooling, lighting or heating to a figure close to zero, and possibly even negative, as the building becomes an energy generator.

The ecological goal

The ecological goal in building design should be to strive for a reduction in the total primary energy needs to a minimum, and ideally down to zero, by using only renewable resources and incidental heat gains to 'drive' a building's comfort system, and with the minimal use of continual importing of energy to maintain comfort. By utilizing the building fabric itself (the 'skin'), artificial heating, cooling, lighting, and other energy importing systems can be minimized, or avoided altogether. Ideally, a building is a power station in its own right.

This objective was built into the professional and ethical objectives for architects some years ago, when the 1993 Congress of the UIA/AIA stated:

> 'Buildings and the built environment play a major role in the human impact on the natural environment and on the quality of life; a sustainable design integrates consideration of resource and energy efficiency, healthy build-ings and materials, ecologically and socially sensitive land use, and an aesthetic sensitivity that inspires, affirms, and ennobles; a sustainable design can significantly reduce adverse human impacts on the natural environment while simultaneously improving quality of life and economic well-being'.[36]

The intention embodied in this early statement has been broadly adopted as policy in many nations, including proposed revisions to the Royal Institute of British Architects' Code of Conduct in the UK.

References

1 Meadows, D.H., Meadows, D.L., Randers, J. and Behrens, W.W. III, *Limits to Growth*. Earth Island, 1972.
2 Scullion, M. ed. *Digest of United Kingdom Energy Statistics 2000*, A National Statistics Publication, The Stationery Office, 2000.

3 *Our Common Future*, World Commission on Environment and Development, Oxford University Press, Oxford, 1987.

4 *The Montreal Protocol*, Foreign Office Command Paper, Treaty Series No. 19, HMSO, 1990.

5 *Report of the United Nations Conference on Environment and Development*, Rio de Janeiro, 3–14 June 1992, Volume One: Resolutions Adopted by the Conference, United Nations, New York, 1993.

6 *The Energy Report: Market Reforms and Innovation 2000*, DTI, The Stationery Office, 2000.

7 *Kyoto Protocol to the United Nations Framework Convention on Climate Change*, sourced from the Internet.

8 Basket of greenhouse gases: carbon dioxide, methane, nitrous oxide, hydrofluoro-carbons, perfluorocarbons and sulphur hexafluoride.

9 *The Energy Report: Market Reforms and Innovation 2000*, DTI, The Stationery Office, 2000.

10 Australia – 8% increase; New Zealand and Russia – 0% static levels; Norway – 1% increase; and Iceland – 10% increase.

11 A presentation made by Dr Joanne Wade at the Energy Matters Conference, RIBA, 2 December 1997.

12 *The Energy Report: Market Reforms and Innovation 2000*, DTI, The Stationery Office, 2000.

13 *UK Energy in Brief 2000*, Department of Trade and Industry (DTI), July 2000, Government Statistical Service, p.18.

14 Shorrock, L.D. and Henderson, G., *Energy Use in Buildings and Carbon Dioxide Emissions*, Building Research Establishment Report, Watford, 1990.

15 *Energy Consumption in the United Kingdom*, Energy Paper 66, DTI, The Stationery Office, 1997.

16 *UK Energy in Brief 2000*, Department of Trade and Industry (DTI), July 2000, Government Statistical Service, p.19.

17 *Ibid*, p. 9.

18 Television speech: President Bill Clinton, 22 October 1997.

19 *Sol Power: The Evolution of Solar Architecture*, Stefan and Sophia Behling, Prestel, 1996.

20 *BP Statistical Review of World Energy 1997*, British Petroleum, 1997, p. 40.

21 *The Energy Report: Market Reforms and Innovation 2000*, DTI, The Stationery Office, 2000.

22 *UK Energy in Brief 2000*, Department of Trade and Industry (DTI), July 2000, Government Statistical Service, p. 23.

23 *The Sunday Times Databank*, Business Section, 10 June 2001 (assumes £1=$1.40).

24 According to Paul Morrell of DLE, salary costs can represent up to 86.5% of a client's total costs.

25 Von Weizsäcke, E., Lovins, A.B. and Lovins, L.H. *Factor Four: Doubling Wealth, Halving Resource Use*, Earthscan, 1997.

26 Watson, D. (1991), *Progressive Architecture*, 3/91, March 1991.

27 *The Energy Report: Shaping Change*, Volume 1, DTI, The Stationery Office, 1997, p. 252.

28 *UK Energy in Brief 2000*, Department of Trade and Industry (DTI), July 2000, Government Statistical Service, p. 9.

29 *Energy Consumption in the United Kingdom*, Energy Paper 66, DTI, Stationery Office, 1997.

30 *The Energy Report: Shaping Change*, Volume 1, DTI, The Stationery Office, 1997, p. 260.

31 *Environmental Issues in Construction*, CIRIA Publications, No 94, 1993, p. 32.

32 Shorrock, L.D. and Henderson, G. *Energy Use in Buildings and Carbon Dioxide Emissions*, Building Research Establishment Report, Watford, 1990.

33 *European Charter for Solar Energy in Architecture and Urban Planning*, Berlin, March 1996.

34 The term 'exclosure' was used by John Perry of Arup Façade Engineering at ICBEST 97.

35 McHarg, I.L. *Design with Nature*, Doubleday/Natural History Press, New York, 1969.

36 *Declaration of Interdependence for a Sustainable Future*, UIA/AIA World Congress of Architects, Chicago, 18–21 June 1993.

▲ Sky Lab exemplifies our ability to create enclosures that are autonomous and which demonstrate quasi-intelligence. The space vehicle's 'brain', its controlling computers, are divided between the ground and vehicle itself. Because of its distance from its ground controllers, most of its actions have to be preprogrammed and electrically or electronically generated, with its computers having control.

16   Buildings and intelligence: metaphors and models

Buildings and intelligence: metaphors and models

The idea of the intelligent building has, for many people come to mean the use of information technology and control systems to make the functioning of the building more useful to its occupants, in relation to its management, or in respect of the building's operational purposes. The 'intelligent home' is often thought of as a dwelling in which many of the normal domestic functions, from the drawing of curtains to the remote operation of the oven, are controlled automatically, often by computer. As was explained in Chapter 1, the Intelligent Skin Programme is based on a different paradigm, related to the environmental performance of the whole building, and bears a much closer kinship with the biological phenomena of intelligence and response. In relation to the concepts set out in the programme, the word 'intelligence' is used to suggest the aspects of living responses characterized by the quiet, and autonomic, maintenance of life. To make clear the conceptual basis of this idea, it helps to set out how the word 'intelligence' has come to be used in architecture and building

Introduction: concepts of intelligence

'Intelligence' relates to the possession of intellectual faculties, which provide a capacity for understanding. There is an inferred ability to perceive and comprehend meaning, and apply this acquired knowledge, through the thinking processes of reasoning. The word has its origins in fourteenth-century Latin, and is derived from the word *intelligentia*, which comes from *intelligere*, meaning to discern or select. Etymologically, the word has its origins in ideas of choosing between, derived from *inter* (between) and *leger* (to choose).[1] When using a term such as intelligence to describe inanimate mechanisms, great care must be taken to ensure that its metaphorical use is understood, and not confused with the inappropriate transferring of terminology. Any discussion of the intelligent building must be prefaced by an explanation of why terms are being used, if only to try to justify them, or at least set out the definition being used. With this in mind it is necessary to distinguish between so-called 'artificial intelligence', and the immensely complex, and only partially understood, intelligence of the human brain, and the difference between cognitive reasoning, and autonomic response.

Artificial intelligence

The devising of 'intelligent' systems for inanimate mechanisms has been concerned with the development of what is called 'artificial intelligence' (AI). With AI, objects are provided with the capacity to perform similar functions to those that characterize human behaviour, by emulating the thought process of living beings. Artificial intelligence has been used to mimic the human capacity to process information by learning, inferring, and making and acting on decisions. The science is sufficiently advanced to make it possible to program computers to deal with the logic of language structures – syntax. However, it is much more difficult to program rules for understanding and meaning – semantics. More complex computer programs have now advanced beyond simple programming, where decisions are based on rule-based inference. With such 'expert' systems, data are processed according to a predetermined rule system. Despite their obvious sophistication, these processes still do not approach the true complexity of intelligent, cognitive thought, let alone the autonomic sensory, comfort and life-preserving reactions, such as the dilating of a pupil or the changes of blood flow to the skin.

Artificial neural networks

The prospect of true intelligence is brought closer to reality with artificial neural networks (ANNs), which are able to deal with more complex problems that cannot simply be described by a set of predefined rules or behaviour patterns. The neural network attempts to recreate biological networks by mimicking the information processing functions of brain cells, such as those of generalization and error tolerance. The network is a collection of artificial neurons that perform summation and activation functions to determine their output. Inputs are filtered and modified by inter-connections, and a series of weighting factors, which serve to amplify or attenuate the output signal. The neural network provides artificial systems with abilities such as learning and generalization, the ability to filter irrelevant data, the dexterity to cope with minor errors or incomplete inputs, and most importantly to adapt solutions over time to compensate for changing circumstances.[2]

Natural intelligence

There are clear analogies between artificial intelligence, and the reasoning of the brain. However, considerations of the whole reactive and cognitive actions incorporated into animals suggests that a larger model might be useful in considering 'building intelligence'. The idea of intelligence relates to aspirations of appropriating or devising faculties found in living beings, and the biological capacity for what might be called 'natural intelligence' (to distinguish it from AI) provides a useful analogy. This is exemplified by the various naturally responsive systems seen in nature, such as the thermoregulatory powers of the human skin, the seasonal changes of coat in many mammals, and the opening and closing of flowers in response to sunlight.

One of the closest biological comparisons for the intelligent building is that of the human body, the skin of which provides the common metaphor for the cladding of a building. The installed 'senses', or sensors, of a building are able to detect fire and intruders in the same way that our own senses detect danger. The circulation of fresh air bears a very close resemblance to our own breathing and respiratory systems. For all the characteristics which constitute our physical environment, sensor systems exist, or can be imagined, which replicate the human and animal senses, from the establishing of a level of illumination to the presence of pollution in the air.

Autonomic and somatic

In order to distinguish between this self-adjusting, responsive 'natural intelligence', and the more conventional response and control 'intelligent systems' exemplified by the smart refrigerator, it helps to understand the difference between the human body's neural systems. The human nervous system is divided into the 'somatic' and the 'autonomic'. The former provides for voluntary, and often reasoned control over skeletal muscle, whereas the

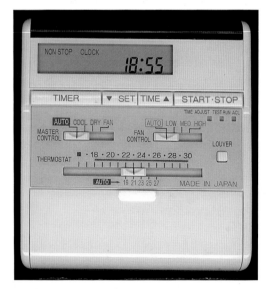

▲ The nature of heat, with its presence or absence signified by temperature, combined with the physical response of materials to their own temperature and the temperatures around them, make thermal control comparatively simple. However, the response is generally 'on' or 'off', and other comfort characteristics are more complex to perceive and control.

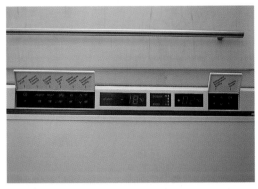

▲ The conventional household fridge/freezer calls out to you when the temperature is too high inside.

latter accounts for the involuntary movements of the cardiac and smooth muscles and glands. If this analogy is applied to buildings, the sort of intelligence considered in this book could be said to involve autonomic responses, where somatic responses might be those exercised by users, e.g. opening a window. Most examples of so-called intelligent buildings that were considered in this study were better able to demonstrate automatic responses than what has been called natural autonomic, intelligent reactions, which may be appropriate for the truly intelligent buildings of the future.

The need for intelligent buildings

Buildings have been constructed and occupied for millennia without the introduction of concepts of intelligence, and it can justifiably be asked why these concepts should be relevant now. The case for the 'intelligent building' lies in the increasingly sophisticated demands for comfort which have accompanied the development of complex building forms and contents, with the consequent burgeoning of energy demand. A conventional building, without the environmental services systems now usually incorporated within it, is a static, inanimate object. It moves only slightly in response to structural and thermal stresses. Its inert nature creates internal environmental conditions which vary with the changes of the external environment, modified by its mass and constructional configurations. The climatic conditions which provide its environmental context in any geographical location vary between morning and afternoon, between day and night and between the seasons. There are also marked differences in climate between different locations around the globe, and these may become more pronounced as a result of global warming. One of the primary functions of buildings is to protect occupants from the extremes of climate, and as such they act as moderators between internal and external conditions. Buildings must 'damp' the extremes of climate to produce internal conditions which vary only within bounds deemed comfortable by occupants.

This moderation action is complicated by the fact that buildings themselves incorporate systems which introduce loads, and thus contribute to the environmental equations which determine internal conditions.

The inability of the passive inert building to provide comfortable conditions is the cause for the provision of environmental services systems, introduced to overcome the inadequacy of the static building. It is the amount of this servicing which provides the greatest justification for the intelligent building. Intelligence can be used to improve the performance of the building fabric by making it more capable, so as to reduce the need for imported energy for heating, cooling, lighting and ventilation. A combination of automatic control and pseudo-instinctive responses to these varying conditions may serve to improve occupancy conditions and operational efficiency in energy terms, bringing the notion of the zero energy building closer to reality.

Occupancy patterns

The environmental control task of buildings is complicated further by their occupancy patterns. As a generalization, it can be assumed that most buildings remain unoccupied for approximately half of the time: places of work during the night and homes during the day. Occupation has two significant impacts on the performance demands of a building. The presence of people makes environmental comfort (including adequate light and ventilation, for example) essential (a constraint that does not necessarily apply when buildings are empty), and the presence of occupants creates the incidental environmental loads implied by their presence: respiration products, heat, and the loads generated by equipment, for example. All of these factors support the case for variability, sometimes to reverse the inertia of buildings, by giving them the capacity to respond dynamically to the variations of climate, occupancy and time.

Increased occupant control

The case for the intelligent building is further reinforced by a variety of considerations, including more precise and predictive maintenance programmes, the optimization and minimization of energy use, and automatic control of increasingly complex building systems. Very significant is the conventionally perceived requirement for increased user control. Occupants of buildings are placing greater emphasis on the need for individual control of their own local environments. This can often be to the detriment of the building environment as a whole. The dropping of a blind to prevent glare can exclude the valuable solar penetration which warms the building, just as the opening of a window to suit an individual's desire for fresh air can undermine a building's overall thermal balance. Maintaining the balance between momentary perceived comfort, and maintenance of comfort diurnally, is one of the tasks of the intelligent skin.

Intelligent buildings: the evolving models

The term intelligent has been applied (and misapplied) to numerous inanimate objects, to describe behaviour purporting to resemble that of living beings. We see everyday objects such as cars with 'intelligent' brakes that progressively increase their action in an emergency, and an 'intelligent' fridge that determines when food has passed its sell-by date and re-ordering of replacement provisions as required.

The word 'intelligent' was first used to describe buildings at the beginning of the 1980s, and its use has been accompanied by the American term 'smart', used to imply the same kind of abilities in materials, structures and buildings. Many of the early examples of buildings called 'intelligent' simply represented an attempt to portray and exploit the prevailing trend for incorporating increasing quantities of information technology into buildings. Early users of the term also included manufacturers defining the intelligent building in terms of their own products. The term has become a marketing label which is assured of bestowing a project with instant credibility, and as such has been liberally applied.

The intelligent building

A building designed by Skidmore Owings and Merrill (Chicago) in Hartford, Connecticut in the USA is widely heralded as 'the world's first intelligent building'.[3] There will probably be as much dispute over this as there has been over the meaning.

The 38-storey office tower, City Place, was completed in 1984 containing a totally integrated services system linked by a 'data highway' of fibre optic cables. The network provided a link for both building systems controls, and tenant word and data processing. The building was described as providing the 'nervous system' to link together the previously separated functions of 'breathing' (air conditioning), 'circulation' (lifts) and the 'senses' (safety system). On further examination, the building is simply 'well-wired', with few aspirations towards true artificial intelligence. It will be noted that some of the case studies included in this book pre-date the City Place project, and strive much closer towards a level of true building intelligence.

▲ Skidmore Owings and Merrill's office building of 1983 in Hartford, Connecticut, USA was widely heralded as the world's first intelligent building. Here the word 'intelligent' relates to electronic controls. This sort of intelligence is only one paradigm, however. The building is like a powerful brain trapped in a suit of armour. The comparison between this building and the Commerzbank (see Case Study 3) shows how much architecture and the concept of intelligence has evolved, and how quickly.

Research for this book found over 30 separate definitions of intelligence in relation to buildings.[4] However, very few seem to acknowledge the true origins from which the term was derived, namely artificial intelligence. As has already been said in the introduction to this chapter, the intelligence aspect is described as relating more to the automation of building technology, rather than any pseudo-intellectual faculties. As the term is most often applied to commercial buildings, it also seems to imply a building's adaptability and responsiveness to satisfying an organization's business objectives over time. Some definitions even go as far to suggest that an intelligent building is one that is fully let, or even better, lets itself!

In practice, building intelligence is often used to relate to buildings that may incorporate sophisticated cable management, flexible and adaptable planning layouts, or complex computer control systems. Professor Walter Kroner of Rensselaer Polytechnic Institute claims that many so-called intelligent buildings are merely 'electronically enhanced' architectural forms.[5]

One widely quoted definition resulted from a study conducted by DEGW and Technibank in 1992. The study described an intelligent building as 'any building which provides a responsive, effective and supportive environment within which the organization can achieve its business objectives.'[6]

The intelligent building is defined by the European Intelligent Building Group as one that 'incorporates the best available concepts, materials, systems and technologies. These elements are integrated together to achieve a building which meets or exceeds performance requirements of the building stakeholders. These stakeholders include the building's owners, managers and users as well as the local and global community.' [7]

These broad definitions depict the use of the technical wizardry, gadgetry and sophistication that has become almost synonymous with the term intelligent building. The aspects of the intelligent building so described can be seen as desirable by those who like automatic and responsive systems controlling the working tasks of a building, such as the operation of its fittings and equipment. They may even be seen as 'intellectual' in that they apply reason. However, conventionally the definition does not extend into the domain of the autonomic 'health' of the building, and maintenance of its optimum environmental conditions, by means of instinctive automated changes to the building fabric.

Buildings which 'know': cognitive science

In Brian Atkin's book, *Intelligent Buildings*, reference is made to the three attributes that an intelligent building ought to possess (after Bennett *et al.*):[8]

- Buildings should 'know' what is happening inside and immediately outside.
- Buildings should 'decide' the most efficient way of providing a convenient, comfortable and productive environment for the occupants.
- Buildings should 'respond' quickly to occupants requests.

These key attributes of knowledge, decision and response begin to imply a closer affinity with cognition, the act or process of knowing. Cognitive science also includes the study of other human attributes such as attention, perception, memory, reasoning, judgement, imagining, thinking, and speech, all of which may in time become more relevant to the evolving intelligent building.

What all of these definitions, and many others like them, fail to acknowledge is that intelligence relates to faculties found in living beings, and as such it could include a kinship with life-preserving autonomic 'natural intelligence' by adopting some of the naturally adaptive and responsive systems seen in nature. True building intelligence should be more closely related to the realms of both artificial and natural intelligence, with the ability to respond and react to external stimuli in a predictable manner.

The efficiency of life and environmental responsibility

If buildings were animals considered over evolutionary time scales, the species which survived would be those which lived in the environment of the planet with the least effort, and the least expenditure of energy to maintain life. This extension of the biological metaphor may seem unnecessary, but the idea of economy of means lies at the root of many aspects of design (such as engineering). What is potentially equally important is the fact that the use of large amounts of energy to maintain the metabolism of a building also creates depletion of limited resources of fossil fuels, and the use of such fuels creates pollution and climate change as outlined in Chapter 2. The idea of the intelligent building addressed in this programme, and this book, attempts to integrate the notions of adaptation to environment as seen in evolution, with its connotation 'least energy', with the idea of environmental responsibility: the striving for optimal performance and increased comfort, all with the minimum consumption

▲ Animals and plants survive in the world because they have evolved to create a metabolism that is consistent with their environment. Food and waste balance each other. The sun provides the energy. Artificial supplies and waste removal are not necessary, and the naturally occurring waste is recycled. In many, if not most, climates this balance is achieved with buildings. Coats moult, leaves drop, and season and behaviour correspond.

of energy. The biological metaphor is evident with the idea that living beings which survive best are those which live in the contextual environment with least effort. This is partly related to 'passive' notions of adaptation, and partly to the efficiency of their metabolisms. It is possible to imagine hominids, for example, which survive and adapt, but which have to work so hard in terms of their circulatory system that their life is short and precarious. Such a species would die out. The question arises in this context whether the modes of reaction should be energy importing systems, or building fabric adjustments systems. This is a question that must be answered in relation to capital and running costs, environmental effectiveness and flexibility.

The intelligent building redefined

A redefinition of the term 'intelligent building' is described in this book as having a closer kinship with both 'natural intelligence' and the science of artificial intelligence. As such, it is defined as a building with the ability to know its configuration, anticipate the optimum dynamic response to prevailing environmental stimuli, and actuate the appropriate physical reaction in a predictable manner. It is expected that the system will strive to exploit the use of natural forces and minimize the need to import energy from non-renewable sources. The truly 'intelligent building' should therefore be endowed with some of the human characteristics that give it the ability to learn, adjust and respond instinctively to its immediate environment in order to provide comfortable internal conditions and use energy more efficiently.

The intelligent façade

The 'intelligent façade' is an intrinsic part of the newly defined intelligent building, referring to that element which performs the function of enveloping the inhabited interior. Accepting the biological metaphors, it seems more appropriate to describe this element as the 'intelligent skin', emphasizing its affinity with the human epidermis.

The intelligent skin

The intelligent skin incorporates the notion that the fabric of the building may not be inert, but may itself change dynamically, in order to reduce the energy requirements of the building. Early versions of such buildings tended to be concerned with changes achieved manually. The idea of manual change to the otherwise inert nature of the building, equivalent to what has been discussed as somatic response, has been around for centuries. The simplest components which reflect this are the shutter, the venetian blind and the opening window. The ability for manual change has now advanced into the capacity for automatic, mechanical and motorized change, and even more 'instinctive' autonomic adjustments.

The intelligent skin is therefore defined in this book as a composition of construction elements confined to the outer, weather-protecting zone of a building, which perform functions that can be individually or cumulatively adjusted to respond predictably to environmental variations, to maintain comfort with the least use of energy. In such a skin, the adaptability of the façade elements is actuated instinctively through self-regulated adjustments to their configuration. Energy flows through the building fabric (in both directions) are autonomically controlled for maximum gain, and minimal reliance on imported energy. The skin forms part of a building system, and is connected to other parts

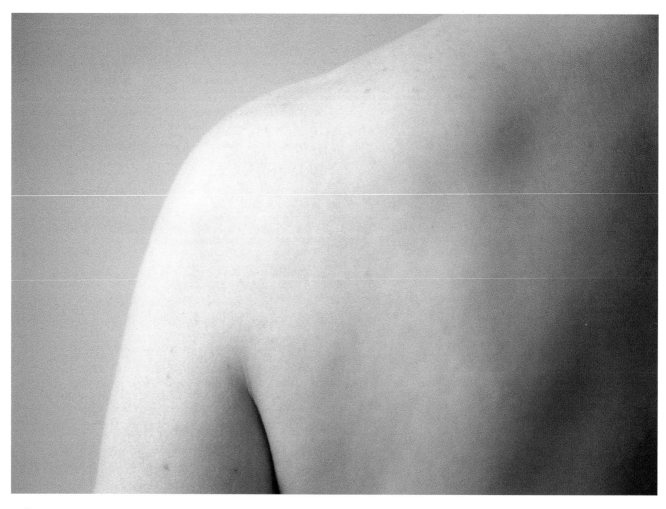

▲ The challenge: to create a building which emulates some of the capabilities of the human skin.

of the building outside of the enveloping zone, such as sensors and actuators linked together by command wires, all controlled by a central building management system – the brain.

Intelligent design

Before moving on to a consideration of this new type of building skin in more detail it is important to put the whole issue of the intelligent skin in the context of a very different, but not unrelated idea: the notion of 'intelligent design', where human designers produce an architecture which is itself intelligent, rather than just an assembly of intelligent components. The idea presented by Walter Kroner[9] is about restoring the basic priorities of 'bioclimatic design' by working in alliance with environmental engineers to achieve interior comfort through responsive climatic design.

The concept is demonstrated by the analogy of the igloo, and other indigenous inert architectures, which exhibit a great deal of intelligence in design, often without the incorporation of any intelligent technologies: Walter Kroner speaks of the occupant's ability to change the performance of the igloo by putting a knife through the wall to let in daylight. It should be assumed that the truly intelligent building has been intelligently designed as a prerequisite. Perfectly adapted creatures existing as a result of evolution are shaped and constructed in such a way as to minimize the effort required to run metabolisms. This is consistent with Darwinian principles, which involve the evolution of configurations that reduce the need for large energy use in the process of survival.

What the intelligent building provides is building morphologies which, both by the shaping of form, and the application of ingenuity to its fabric reduce the need for importing energy for heating, cooling, lighting or ventilation.

As Walter Kroner has said 'intelligent design means striving to have our buildings in harmony with nature, to protect its qualities, and to recognize its dynamic (and unpredictable) qualities, whether assets or liabilities.'[10]

References

1 Schaur, E. ed., What do we mean by intelligence?, *Building with Intelligence: Aspects of a Different Building Culture*, IL41, Institute for Lightweight Structures, University of Stuttgart.
2 Bhatnager, K., Gupta, A. and Bhattacharjee, B., Neural Networks as Decision Support Systems for Energy Efficient Building Design, *Architectural Science Review*, Vol. 40, June, pp. 53–59, 1997.
3 *Architects Journal*, 23 November, Vol. 178, No. 47, pp. 114–130, 1983
4 Definitions are listed at the end of the book.
5 Kroner, W.M., An intelligent and responsive architecture, *Automation in Construction*, 200, 1997.
6 DEGW and Technibank, *The Intelligent Building in Europe*.
7 European Intelligent Building Group (www.sonnet.co.uk/intesys/eibg).
8 Atkin, B. ed., *Intelligent Buildings: Applications of IT and Building Automation to High Technology Construction Projects*, Kogan Page, 1988.
9 Kroner, W.M., An intelligent and responsive architecture, *Automation in Construction*, 200, 1997.
10 Intelligent architecture through intelligent design, *Futures*, August, pp. 319–333, 1989.

▲ The human body comprises different intelligence systems, which enable it to operate in an unconscious and conscious way. 'Thinking' operates to permit argument and strategic planning. The athlete performs somatically: the strategic thought 'to run' is converted into innumerable complex actions involving instruction from the brain. Concepts of action are broken down and made into coordinated instructions, much too fast for 'thinking'. The heart beats, and breathing happens, autonomically: 'thinking' is not necessary. the 'intelligent' building incorporates aspects of all these, sometimes decentralized.

26   The intelligent skin: the deepening metaphor

Seen in the context of the ideas of intelligence set out in the previous chapter, the intelligent skin is defined as a responsive and active controller of the interchanges occurring between the external and internal environment, with the ability to provide optimum comfort, by adjusting itself autonomously, with self-regulated amendments to its own building fabric. It is assumed that, as an objective, this is achieved with the minimum use of energy, and minimal reliance on the importing of energy. The intelligent fabric of the building envelope becomes a flexible, adaptive and dynamic membrane, rather than a statically inert envelope. Information to assist responsiveness and control is gathered through different sensors, and fabric configuration, and thus behaviour is modified in response, to produce predictable actions.

Before embarking on a discussion of the potential sophistication of the intelligent skin, it should be remembered that, as a starting point, however complex or simple it may be, a building skin is the enveloping outer fabric of a building, forming a weather-protecting enclosure which keeps water out, protects us from inclement temperatures, and allows air and light in. It is the threshold between inside and outside, providing security and privacy, access and views and modulating the flows of energy in the form of light, heat, sound and air.

In the context of the building skin as part of an overall building system, it is important to consider its spatial and technical boundaries. The term 'skin' emphasizes the close comparisons with the human epidermis, the largest organ in the human body; it also highlights the intrinsic and integrated quality of the whole building fabric, rather than the veneer characteristic associated with the 'chocolate wrapper' approach to building design so common in commercial architecture. The skin operates as part of a holistic building metabolism and morphology, and will often be connected to other parts of the building, including sensors, actuators and command wires from the building management system.

It has long been understood that the building skin may be made up of many layers, with multiple functions and integrated control[1]. In the last few decades both multiple and conventional building skins have been complemented by developments in passive solar design, and other manifestations of technical sophistication, including building management systems, originally conceived to optimize and reduce energy use. These were generally introduced on the premise of enhanced use of building services, essential resource and energy conservation, and user benefit, all relying on the advantages offered by computers and control systems. The evolution of the intelligent skin has derived from an integration of the complex multiple skin, and the building management systems developed concurrently with them.

The human skin

The term 'skin' has been too easily and simplistically transferred and adopted by building designers. The source of the skin metaphor, the human skin, is a protective organ that guards against the action of physical, chemical, and bacterial threats to the internal organs. Consideration of this contains clues to

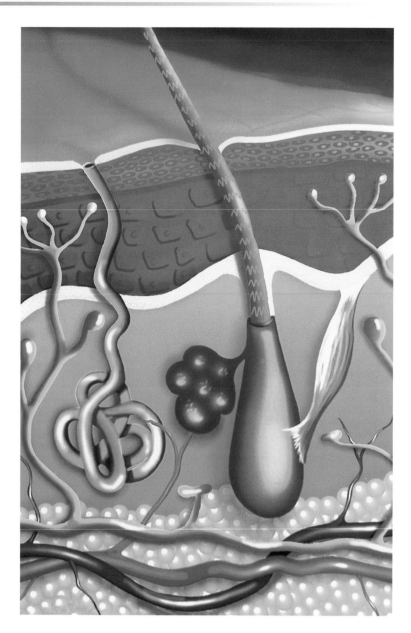

▶ The human skin is a good model for how we would like the building skin to behave. It adapts to temperature and humidity, can feel a breeze or the slightest touch, and can repair itself. It is waterproof and yet permeable to moisture. This artwork shows the principal functioning elements of the human skin, the protective layer that keeps the inner organs of the body free from infection, and (in many climatic conditions) comfortable. It is made up of several layers. The uppermost is the epidermis (red, upper centre) which is tough, and covered in a dead layer of skin cells. Below that is the dermis (orange), which contains the sebaceous glands (blue, centre left) which release sweat, and hair follicles (grey, lower right) from which hairs grow. Below the dermis is the subcutaneous tissue, containing fat cells (yellow), nerve cells which reach to the epidermis and give the sense of touch, and capillaries (red, purple, bottom) which provide the skin with blood.

how the intelligent building skin might develop. The human skin consists of two distinct layers, the 'epidermis', which forms an outer layer, and the inner layer known as the 'dermis'.[2] Architecture has been described by Ted Kruger as 'our collective epidermis'.[3] The thickness of the skin varies from 0.5mm on the eyelids, up to 4mm on the palms of the hand and soles of the feet.[4] The epidermis contains pigments, pores, and ducts, and is only a few cells thick. It is mainly composed of dead cells, whereas the inner layer (dermis) consists of a network of protein collagen, blood vessels, nerve endings (sense receptors), fat tissues, and the bases of hair follicles and sweat glands. The cells of the dermis are continually multiplying to replace those cells that are shed from the outer surface.

Kruger describes the building as our 'second skin', but this is actually provided by the clothes we wear, which provide a significant level of thermal and protective control. This makes the building skin perform the function of a 'third skin'.

If the human skin is to act as the basis for metaphor, the full implications of its actions should be considered. The thermal action provides a good example. As part of the human skin's role of regulating the body temperature at 36.8°C, the sweat glands can cool the body by secreting moisture, which evaporates, and cools the body surface. The blood vessels in the dermis can supplement temperature regulation by contracting to reduce blood flow, and thus reduce radiant heat loss through the skin. The opposite effect is used to dissipate body heat. A fall in body temperature results in a reduced rate of metabolism, and if the temperature rises too high the functions of the cells may become impaired. These 'autonomic' processes, and many other similar ones, are controlled involuntarily by the brain, the various distinctive operations of which deserve a separate mention.

Natural analogies

The human nervous system has already been described as providing involuntary actions *autonomically*, and the voluntary and intentional control of skeletal muscles *somatically*. Many of the controlling functions within the human body are autonomic, and do not require conscious control, for example the actions of the iris of the eye, and the beating of the heart. The intelligent skin as described in this book possesses similar pseudo-autonomic abilities.

Nature is full of many similar 'smart' examples, which can sense and react to their environment. The chameleon is able to change its body colour when it is frightened and in response to light, temperature, and other environmental changes: the colour change is activated by hormones that affect special pigment-bearing cells in its skin.[5]

All such examples in nature share the characteristics of a response to a varying environment, resulting in a change in shape or material as well as a modification of energy flow. An imitation of such 'natural intelligence' provides the building skin with additional functionality, redefining its previous limits of acting only as an energy flow system and envelope.

The brain

Both autonomic and somatic actions depend on the brain, and the use of the anthropocentric metaphor can be extended to the human reasoning system. A building's 'brain' is manifested in the intelligent building as a computerized building management system, which with current levels of technology can be accommodated in a standard desktop PC.

Applying this concept to previous natural analogies, the building management system can be regarded as analogous to the human brain, and in particular the 'hypothalamus'. This organ, located at the centre of the base of the brain, serves as a link between the autonomic nervous system and the body's endocrine system (hormone-releasing glands). The function of the hypothalamus is to integrate and ensure appropriate response to internal and external stimuli. It plays an important role in the regulation of most of the involuntary mechanisms of the body, including body temperature, sexual drive, and the menstrual cycle.[6]

The dependence of humans on the functioning of the hypothalamus for sustained life highlights the vulnerability of reliance on a single control system. The hypothalamus of the intelligent building, the sophisticated building management system of the future, needs to be robust, well protected, healthy, and well maintained. This aspect of the intelligent building is referred to at the end of this chapter.

▲ The human eye is a wonderful example of supreme adaptability. It has a lens that is self-adjusting (intelligent auto-focus), responding to signals from the brain telling it what to look at. A shutter stops up and down to deal with changes in light level. Automatic lubrication keeps it moist and clean. An eyelid made of skin provides a form of 'black out' and shuts when we need to sleep, to remove stimuli. The eyelid is so protective it closes in a fraction of a second if danger is sensed. The messages sent to the brain behind it provide the principal information needed by all humans, whether athletes or less active members of the race.

Variability

Unlike living beings, buildings are essentially static, inanimate objects (although there are examples of buildings that actually move in response to the position of the sun, as can be seen in Case Study 13). The concept of a building skin with variable characteristics was first suggested by Michael Davies in 1981.[7] He presented the idea of a multifunctional skin that could act as a nanometric absorber, radiator, reflector, filter, and transfer device. Following this speculative, but well-informed, proposition, the intelligent skin has now evolved conceptually into an envelope with the ability to change its thermophysical properties (thermal resistance, transmittance, absorptance, permeability), switch between transparent and opaque, modify its colour, and vary its optical properties. This can either be performed by physical elements attached to the intelligent skin, or at the nanometric level by materials with inherent variable properties, such as chromogenic glasses.

The need for variability has already been demonstrated. Many buildings are unoccupied for at least half of the time. As a general rule, residential buildings remain at least partially unoccupied during many days and other buildings are uninhabited at night; these two time periods have very different climatic and environmental characteristics. The seasons also bring different climatic environments, as does the regional distribution of buildings in different climatic zones. While buildings and their occupants can benefit from a degree of variability in response to the vagaries of the weather, we require them only to vary within comfortable limits.

The other major variation imposed on buildings comes from within, in the form of 'churn', which is an American term used to describe an organization's constantly changing accommodation strategies. User habits vary, and the way that they interact with the building envelope is a constant source for variation.

The idea of introducing variability into the fabric of a building to respond to these changes, rather than relying on building services, offers tremendous advantages. This is known from the venetian blind and the curtain. To propose an intelligent skin, able to provide a 'responsive' system that can physically react to improve building energy performance and internal comfort, with dynamic abilities to provide an optimal response to external variations, simply extends ideas and principles already well established in building, and accords with the propositions of Darwin, who held that the capacity to survive depends on the ability to adapt to a changing environment.

This notion is neither new, nor necessarily complex. The idea of building intelligence is simply an extension of the idea of the central heating thermostat.

While thermostats conventionally act on building heating or cooling systems, they, or other devices related to other environmental characteristics, can activate changes to the variable fabric of the building. These can be made effectively autonomic, by actions within the fabric of the building, because it has learned how to cope with what has happened to it, what is happening to it now, and what will happen in the near future.

One of the strongest examples of the potential benefit of variability, particularly if it is autonomic, relates to the interaction between light and heat. In building design, the openings for views and light have long been regarded as weak points in thermal terms. Despite five-fold increases in glazing performance, this problem remains. Short-wave solar radiation passes through glass, and is not always welcome. Glazing is also comparatively permeable to thermal transmittance, the heat flow resulting from conduction and convection. The U-value of a construction element is to a large degree

▲ The use of variation in the building skin is well established: the venetian blind and curtains are two of the oldest examples. They give protection from light and heat, and provide privacy. Considered as a glare-reduction device the venetian blind's role is simple, but it is now a potential heat collector. The multi-functional nature of such a device poses problems of contradiction. The wishes of the user at 2pm may contradict the needs of the building for the next 24 hours. This one of the challenges for the intelligent skin.

characterized by the path of least thermal resistance, and in glazing the thermal resistance is minimal. What variability offers is the opportunity to control such properties, and vary performance. This is exemplified by recent developments in advanced glazings, which can inherently alter their properties physically (e.g. thermochromics), or change them electrically at the 'flick of a switch' using chromogenic devices such as electrochromic glazings. The moving into position of an insulating shutter (a thermal 'eyelid') can affect the thermal transmittance of a glazed opening significantly. With the intelligent skin such changes, in relation both to radiation and transmittance, could be activated automatically or autonomically.

The need for such thinking in architecture was enunciated at a conference in Berlin in 1996. 'The permeability of the skin of a building towards light, heat and air, and its transparency must be controllable and capable of modification, so that it can react to changing local climatic conditions'.[8]

Learning abilities

In parallel with being able to achieve variability, the skin needs to 'know' when to act, and why. Over time, the intelligent skin, with some of the characteristics of human intelligence, should develop an ability to learn, an ability to adjust and adapt, to cope with new situations, and an ability to anticipate the future.[9] Advances in cognitive science mean that the intelligent skin can actually develop abilities to learn usage patterns and the optimum response to specific climatic conditions. This is part of the evolution of the intelligent building.

Users

Of course, the building skin is not the envelope of a single living being: it accommodates many people, each with a different set of requirements, varying from time to time, and each in a different location.

The idea that individual and personal comfort control is a desirable objective is already established with all building designers, and in government thinking. A paper published in 1995 stated: 'The Occupant expectation of a comfortable and healthy environment must not be underestimated since this will inextricably be linked with productivity, although this is almost impossible to show quantitatively'.[10]

It is well established that building occupants should be offered maximum personal control over their immediate environment. Although the variable building fabric can still be effective with manual control, this places unsustainable demands on the predictive capability of occupants, and requires their continuous or very frequent presence. The intelligent building resolves this difficulty, because it looks after itself, and it can also facilitate and guide user control.

Users have increased their demands and thresholds for comfort in line with the technology to meet them. The low cost of energy and the resourcefulness of technology have made this an easy transition. There is an increasing desire for individual control of the inhabited environment, enfranchising the building occupant. Involving building users in the decision making associated with their environmental comfort provides a sense of participation as well as an ability to control and vary the local environment. It is probably essential from a psychological point of view that users at least feel that they are in control.

Having said this, there may be occasions when unchecked occupant control will compromise energy reduction strategies, and this imposes a further set of criteria for the designer of the intelligent skin. In these instances, an automatic response may need to prevail in order to achieve the most efficient performance. Users will need to be more explicitly informed about how the building system works, so that they have more confidence that the computer might know best. A system of central control may prevail, but it is important to provide the facility for local fine-tuning, equivalent to the ability to undo one's top button.

With individual local personal control now an objective, we are faced with problems of expertise, and the counterintuitive nature of some of the control actions. Buildings are beginning to challenge the competency of human intelligence. An intelligent building may even have better instincts than occupants in some regards, for example in its (pre-programmed) instincts for energy-efficiency. It will be necessary to create some additional intelligent features to cope with this.

A user might happily leave a window open in winter while heat is being provided to the space. The building's intelligence would compensate for this user decision by automatically reducing the heat to that zone; instead of compensating for inappropriate human action, by pumping heat to the 'affected area', the building could respond with a discomfort warning, analogous to the human pain reaction, but in a mild form. A combined strategy for user control and computerized monitoring ensures that energy consumption is minimized and building occupants are kept in the manner to which they are increasingly accustomed.

Having considered the way the intelligent skin might behave, and the varieties of internal environmental characteristics it might have to provide, some of the environmental considerations and generators should themselves be briefly considered, in particular the prime source of the energy and climate, the sun, and the resource and energy considerations which generate our performance criteria.

The sun

In many cases the renewable resource of the sun can be a principal contributor of energy to a building, both passively and actively. In the past, buildings have been largely 'passive' in their exploitation of this resource. Intelligent systems can be used to control and modify and exploit this ultimate renewable resource 'actively'.

The sun offers great potential in terms of passive and active gains for heat and electricity. However it can also be detrimental to internal comfort conditions, and as such it is often necessary to mitigate against its harmful effects, which include glare and radiant overheating. Intelligent control systems provide 'passive' buildings with the ability to react physically to the variable characteristics of the sun at different times of the day and year, and the resultant variation in intensity. In particular, the flow of solar energy can be actively harvested to improve user comfort, exploit natural daylight and reduce the need for artificial (i.e. mechanically driven) comfort control.

It is also possible that the passage of this energy can be utilized further for the generation of electricity with photovoltaics. This is briefly referred to below.

Low-energy buildings

There is growing evidence to suggest that many of the purported benefits of passive low-energy design are not actually being achieved in practice.[11] A building with a responsive skin system can make a significant contribution to the reduction of energy use in buildings, and assist in maintaining and improving

▲ The House for the Future at the Museum of Welsh Life by Jestico + Whiles exploits the benefits of the sun both passively and actively. On the roof is an array of photovoltaic panels (800W) and a solar water heating collector. Internally the space is partly heated by the large areas of glazing to the south facing wall and one-third of the roof.

internal comfort levels.[12] In the absence of the user, even for short periods, the intelligent skin is able to operate the building fabric automatically for maximum efficiency, even when it is unoccupied. The brain of the intelligent building can be programmed to learn how to do this.

Zero-energy operation

A European charter published in 1996 proclaimed the feasibility of significant reductions in energy use by intelligently designed 'passive' buildings. The charter stated: 'It should be possible to meet comfort requirements largely through the design of the building by incorporating passive measures with a direct effect. The remaining energy needs in terms of heating, cooling, electricity, ventilation and lighting should be met by ecologically sustainable forms of energy'.[13] The intelligent building offers the possibility of reducing the energy used for comfort still further, potentially to zero in many climates.

Research work has been in progress for at least 10 years which shows that the imported energy used to maintain comfort can be reduced to zero for many building types in the European climate, provided that the fabric of the building can be varied to suit the availability of free solar energy, and can change its performance to suit the varying external environmental conditions, diurnally and seasonally. An intelligent skin, in an intelligent building, can dispense with the energy load associated with mechanically conditioned internal environments, by the use of intelligent control systems. The concept of zero operational energy buildings is brought closer to reality with intelligent controls to optimize the use of the numerous energy flows passing through the building façade, all of which are ripe for exploitation. Intelligence should negate the requirement to import energy for cooling, heating, lighting to virtually zero and may be able to deliver surplus energy for sale or exploitation elsewhere.

Electrical autonomy

One of the aspects of so-called 'zero energy buildings' is that the only energy imported is electricity, to provide lighting outside daylight hours, and to provide necessary power. However, it is becoming more common for buildings to strive for electrical autonomy through self-generation. This extends the concept of buildings with living capabilities. In the same way that animals and humans require food for energy, buildings are able to harness their energy from renewable sources. Buildings may also share some of the in-built efficiencies of the human body, using every available resource and conserving and recycling as much as possible. As is shown in some of the case study buildings, this is already being done, by collecting solar energy with photovoltaic cells, often integrated into the building envelope. Other autonomous techniques include the use of the wind to power turbines, and co-generating electricity with natural gas, producing both heat and electricity. Such self-sufficiency is epitomic of what the truly intelligent building ought to be.

As Stefan Behling has said: 'Ideally buildings should not use more energy to satisfy their occupants' expectations than they can harness from renewable energies surrounding them'.[14]

▲ The photovoltaics mounted on the roof of the SUVA Insurance Company in Basel provide up to 10.2kW of electricity, making a significant contribution to the building's overall power consumption. The notion that buildings can be autonomous in energy generation and consumption perfectly exemplifies what the truly intelligent building ought to be.

Maintenance

In setting out the possibilities of using intelligence to provide comfort with minimal energy use, it is right to consider the cost and life-cycle implications.

The new skins, with their moving parts, will require a different sort of care to that with which we treat the conventional buildings of today. We do not expect our bodies, or our cars, to survive without care and maintenance, and the intelligent building places the same obligation on its owner.

With high-technology, and often moving, parts, comes a greater susceptibility to breakdown, and a resultant need for increased maintenance. This will come with a cost, but may actually result in the building stock being better cared for, and might bring about improved maintenance, and hence longer life, to buildings which are currently often notoriously neglected. As the intelligent building evolves, buildings may be serviced more like cars, and perhaps even match their reliability. Buildings are bound to benefit from the annual 'MOT-style' attention and regular service that most cars enjoy, which will translate into the regular servicing of buildings using built-in diagnostic facilities.

The 'smart technology' in cars and aerospace vehicles anticipates how this might be done. Buildings have become larger and more complex, which has been partly assisted by artificial comfort control and vertical transportation, and increasing levels of technical sophistication. Computers can aid the operation of a building, performing in seconds tasks that previously consumed numerous man hours, in relation for example to automatic lighting, fault logging and maintenance scheduling. This is already extending into areas of self-diagnosis. 'Smart' technologies have made significant inroads into stress monitoring in aircraft structures. Such technologies are a main subject area in international 'smart materials' conferences. The ability of a building to examine itself regularly, and report to its owners and occupiers is easily possible in respect of many of its features, and is on the agenda for the intelligent building particularly in areas where unusual stress may occur, such as earthquake zones.

This may be essential given the complexities of intelligent buildings. Many buildings are now complex environmental filters, and the technology of control is not always simple enough to be universally understood by all users. There are those that believe that 'jet-fighter technology' means that 'pilots' will have to be employed to operate them.[15] There is no doubt that technology requires management, but the benefits described in this book seem to outweigh such scepticism about the potential benefits of technology and mechanization.

Economics

Finally, in considering the real possibility of the viability of the intelligent skin, and the intelligent building, it is important to consider the cost, in construction and use, of these new forms.

The incorporation of intelligent technologies will undoubtedly incur additional cost in the building fabric. However, this can be balanced by significant reductions in the capital cost of plant, and in the area needed for it. Furthermore, the cost of the energy needed to run an intelligent building also decreases as the fuel bill goes down. It is already being established, in parallel research being carried out in the UK, that the redeployment of capital cost from mechanical building services into a complex skin can deliver certain types of buildings at the same overall capital cost as conventional buildings.[16] Benefits accrue in terms of energy use, and in the comfort and satisfaction of occupants. The balance produced by a reduction in plant, and by reduced operating costs, is enhanced by the promise of increases in occupant productivity.

It is to be deplored that, despite the efforts of governments such as those in the UK, there is currently no costing mechanism that makes allowance for a building's reduced environmental burden. The assumption made in the intelligent building research programme is that a proportion of a building budget previously allocated to complex artificial climate control systems can be redirected into a more sophisticated and responsive fabric, with the ability to moderate and utilize energy flows through the skin. As governments learn to implement strategies which address the problems of energy management and global warming, intelligent buildings will increasingly be seen as more economic than their profligate ancestors.

The intelligent building needs real proving in terms of economics, energy, maintenance and sustainability if it is not simply to become a toy for rich clients. It is believed that the economic case can be made, and can provide a legitimate and significant contribution to the mitigation of resource depletion, pollution, and global environmental change. In the end this economic case may be seen as the real justification for the intelligent skin, and the intelligent building.

References

1 Davies, M., A wall for all seasons, *RIBA Journal*, Vol. 88, No. 2, February, 1981.
2 Funk & Wagnall's Corporation, *The Human Skin*, Microsoft *Encarta*, Microsoft Corporation, 1994.
3 Krueger, T., Like a second skin: living machines, *Architectural Design*, Vol. 66, No. 9/10, March/April, 1994.
4 Softkey BodyWorks, CD-ROM, TLC Properties Inc, CompuServe Inc, 1996.
5 Funk & Wagnall's Corporation, *Chameleon*, Microsoft *Encarta*, Microsoft Corporation, 1994.
6 Softkey BodyWorks, CD-ROM, TLC Properties Inc, CompuServe Inc, 1996.
7 Davies, M., A Wall for all Seasons, *RIBA Journal*, Vol. 88, No. 2, February, 1981.
8 READ, *European Charter for Solar Energy in Architecture and Urban Planning*, Berlin, March 1996.
9 Jankovic, L., Steps towards greater system intelligence, *Intelligent Buildings Today and in the Future*, University of Central England, 7 October 1993.
10 Energy Efficiency Best Practice Programme, *A Performance Specification for the Energy Efficient Office of the Future*, Stationery Office, 1995.
11 Nutt, B.B., The use and management of passive solar environments, *Renewable Energy*, Vol. 5, Part II, pp. 1009–1014, 1994.
12 This has been demonstrated both by Kim Jong-Jin and Jones James, *Conceptual Framework for Dynamic Control of Daylighting and Electric Lighting Systems*, IEEE Industry Applications Society, Ontario, 2–8 October 1993, and van Paassen, A.H.C. and Lute, P.J., *Energy Saving Through Controlled Ventilation Windows*, Third European Conference on Architecture, Florence, 17–21 May 1993.
13 READ, *European Charter for Solar Energy in Architecture and Urban Planning*, Berlin, March 1996.
14 Behling, S. and Behling, S., *Sol Power: The Evolution of Solar Architecture*, Prestel, 1996.
15 Bordass, W. (1997), *Measuring Energy Performance in Buildings*, TIA Workshop, Oxford Brookes University, 14 June 1997.
16 Wigginton, M. and Battle McCarthy: 'The environmental second skin'. Research carried out for the UK Department of the Environment Transport and the Regions (first published in www.battlemccarthy.demon.co.uk/research/environmentalsecondskins).

Method

The research for this study began in October 1996 as the first stage of a proposal to examine the principles and potential of the intelligent façade as it was ordinarily termed.[1] The initial stage of the research programme was to compile a case study database of built examples of façade intelligence. This book is intended to serve as a review of the current best practice in the relatively new field of intelligence in buildings. The extent of the study was confined to the embodiment of intelligence within the building façade. However, it proved necessary to consider the façade within the context of an intelligent building system, of which the intelligent skin was a constituent.

The initial search led to both published journal articles and refereed papers on the subject of intelligent buildings, as well as numerous projects that were portrayed as manifestations of building intelligence. As well as feeding a growing understanding of the subject area, this information was used to produce a database of buildings that purported aspirations to a degree of intelligence. The database of over 300 examples from across the world included both completed buildings, and unrealized proposals that often resulted from competition entries. A short description of each project described the intelligent features, and the database also included details of the location, the architect and the year of completion.

It became evident that the term 'intelligent building' had been liberally applied to a number of projects that did not necessarily warrant the title, at least in terms of the definition developed in the research programme. In the context of this study, it was decided that there needed to be an assessment of the specific role of the building envelope in manipulating the passage of energy flows in the form of light, heat, air and sound. About 30 projects were rejected on the grounds of 'false intelligence' with no demonstrable features that could be called intelligent other than raised floors for cabling and flexible partitioning systems for easy changes of use.

The study of examples of building intelligence showed that the façade was performing up to 10 different functions, which influenced the passage of energy from both the external environment to the internal environment, and the other way around. These manipulating functions were identified as:

- the enhancement of daylight (e.g. light shelves/reflectors)
- the maximization of daylight (e.g. full-height glazing/atria)
- protection from the sun (e.g. louvres/blinds)
- insulation (e.g. night-time shutters)
- ventilation (e.g. automatic dampers)
- the collection of heat (e.g. solar collectors)
- the rejection of heat (e.g. overhangs/brise soleil)
- the attenuation of sound (e.g. acoustic dampers)
- the generation of electricity (e.g. photovoltaics) and
- the exploitation of pressure differentials (e.g. ventilation chimneys).

Early attempts at defining the intelligent façade, in the context of the large number of definitions of the intelligent building, suggested that intelligence should infer dynamism in the form of an 'active' mechanism. This definitive characteristic was used to assess each project in the database on its ability to perform the above functions 'passively' (i.e. fixed), or 'actively' (i.e. moving). Each building was also assessed on whether the function could be performed by exclusive manual action, or manual action in combination with a passive or active capacity.

In January 1997, the principles of selection described above were used to produce a shortlist of 47 projects that clearly demonstrated some degree of active control of the building façade in a variety of forms. A number of historical examples were included in the list, some of which dated back to the 1960s. There were also a range of completed buildings, and a number of theoretical examples and unrealized competitions. A further literature search was conducted to find all references to these projects in order to confirm, and enhance the description of, their intelligent features.

In April 1997, the list was narrowed further by a decision to concentrate only on the completed projects, which produced a list of 37 manifestations of the intelligent façade. At this stage, each of the design teams was advised of the research project by letter, requesting further information about the building in relation to its intelligent features. After a further period of extended reading and discussions with the designers, a final shortlist was proposed to form the final group of case studies. A shortlist of 25 projects was agreed in September 1997 based on confirmation that each project demonstrated a true level of 'active' façade intelligence.

For the agreed case study projects a more intense literature survey produced a list of all references relating to each of the 25 projects. These were mainly sourced through the British Architectural Library, and were used to produce full descriptions of each of the buildings. Where possible, contact was made with at least one member of the design team to clarify particular aspects of the project. These descriptions were then used to formulate the case studies in a more condensed format, and more specifically concentrating on the intelligent features.

At the outset, it was felt important that the research programme should include visits to as many as possible of the case study buildings to produce an objective and well-informed description about each building. In all, study visits were made to 19 projects in Germany, Switzerland, the United States, and the United Kingdom. Of those buildings visited, 12 form part of the final case study that follows. The visits were not intended as measurement exercises, but familiarizing tours to understand the context of the project, a way to glean additional information and examine and photograph the intelligent features in closer detail. In most cases the visit included discussions with a member of the design team, which has informed the project descriptions.

The case studies were completed in May 1998, and drafts were sent to members of the design teams who had responded to earlier correspondence, or who had been involved in the building visits. Drafts of the case studies were sent to 58 people for information and comment, along with a list of outstanding questions. The response rate to the outstanding information was about 65%, which explains some of the gaps in the studies.

At the time of preparing this book, two additional case studies were performed to represent the period since the original research report was written in August 1998. The information for the Debis and GSW Headquarters, both in Berlin, was obtained directly from the architects and engineers.

The total number of case studies that were completed in detail as part of the research programme was 27. During publication process it was necessary to 'thin' this further to the 22 case studies that appear. Despite persistent attempts we were unable to obtain high-quality pictorial and drawn information for each of these projects suitable for publication. For reference, the projects that were taken out were the Ionica Building in Cambridge by the RH Partnership which exhibits active ventilation control using wind towers; the Learning Resource Centre at Anglia Polytechnic University in Chelmsford by ECD Architects which has automatic opening windows and daylight responsive lighting; and the Student Residences at Strathclyde University in Glasgow by the now disbanded GRM Kennedy & Partners, which uses translucent insulating material, the solar gain of which is actively controlled by motorised blinds. The other two projects that were excluded from the original research report due to a lack of information were the Solar Dairy in Mysen Norway by Per Monsen (Architektontoret GASA) and the International School in Lyon by Jourda & Perraudin.

It should be noted that the literature search deliberately concentrated on articles and books about Intelligent buildings. The research programme was not launched with the intention of disseminating knowledge into the professions, for application in practice. A conventional academic study would warrant a whole new search into the field of refereed journal papers. In a similar vein, the case studies are based on buildings that have been published in the architectural press.

The qualifying characteristic of active control of the building façade was very strictly applied. As a result, some buildings that might generally be regarded as intelligently designed, and excellent examples of low energy design, were excluded from this study of the intelligent façade. This is exemplified by the decision to exclude projects such as the RWE Building[2] in Essen by Ingenhoven Overdiek and Partners and also Bennetts Associates' Powergen Building[3] in Coventry, both of which were visited as part of the study tours and are considered exemplary in their field. These two buildings achieve their low-energy performance by relatively passive means. Whilst this is to be commended in principle, the purpose of this study was to consider those projects that provided active control of the building façade, which these projects did not satisfy.

References

1 Wigginton, M., *The Intelligent Façade: A Research Proposal*, unpublished, 1995.
2 *Architectural Review*, July 1997.
3 *Architects Journal*, 1994.

Intelligent features

The research for the case study stage of the Intelligent Façade Programme has identified a range of features which constitute built examples of the intelligent skin. It provides a depiction of what have been called the 'genetic characteristics' which might make up the intelligent skin in its fully evolved form: the genes of the intelligent façade of the future. What follows is a summarized description of some of these genes, separated into broad functional groups. These are not the same as, but act as overlays to, the manipulating functions identified in the preceding chapter.

Building management systems

Essential to the intelligent building is the 'brain', in the form of a building management system (BMS). The BMS is the central processing unit, receiving all of the information from the various sensor outstations, and determining the appropriate control response to the actuating elements. An 'intelligent' BMS is able to monitor weather changes and control and monitor the operation of both passive and active environmental systems to ensure the most efficient use of energy. One of its most vital functions is to regulate temperature by activating all of the controllable elements in the building to achieve this naturally.

Learning ability

The intelligent skin can possess an ability to learn. Some of the case study examples utilize current and anticipated weather data to calculate the optimum heating, lighting and shading levels for the building in advance. Neural networks and knowledge-based software algorithms, incorporating fuzzy logic, provide some buildings with the ability to learn their energy status and thermal characteristics, and relate historic or recent weather data, and prevailing climatic conditions, to previous operating strategies.

Environmental data

Many projects are able to collect detailed real-time information relating to environmental conditions outside and inside the building. These data are often an essential determinant in the control decisions of intelligent technologies. Typical measurements are made of wind speed and direction, outside temperature, façade and cavity temperatures, outside humidity, solar insolation, inside air and room temperatures, daylight levels and humidity.

Responsive artificial lighting

Fundamental in meeting the objective of an effective daylighting strategy is a responsive artificial lighting system, with the ability to deactivate or dim itself in response to adequate natural lighting levels. Many of the case study examples incorporate automatic lighting controls outside of the envelope zone, but very much connected to the overall performance objectives of the building skin. Intelligent lighting systems are activated by occupancy sensors and regulated (dimming from 100% to 0%) in response to sensed internal light levels. Some projects do not incorporate dimmable lighting, but enable 'sweeped' deactivation at the end of the working day, trusting users to turn lights on and off in response to ambient lighting conditions during working hours.

Daylight controllers

Given the energy consumption associated artificial light, the maximization of daylight is recognized as one of the key goals in low-energy design. The case studies display a range of active systems that respond to solar angles, providing optimum positions for motorized light-guiding, light-reflecting and light-shading devices. Light transmission can often be varied and adjusted to suit internal demand. Systems operate in response to information provided by sensors that measure outside light and solar intensity, and inside light levels and temperature.

Sun controllers

In many cases, the 'renewable' resource of the sun can be the principal contributor of energy to a building. Intelligent systems used to control and modify this valuable resource are incorporated into a number of the case studies. Computer algorithms make it easy to determine real-time solar angles by the input of time, latitude and longitude data. Such calculations are used to track the sun on its variable path throughout the day, and year.

The sun can also be detrimental to internal comfort conditions, and as such it is often necessary to mitigate against its harmful effects, including over-heating, irradiation, and glare. Computer-controlled blinds, louvres and other protective shades, all of which can intrinsically be regarded as energy absorbers, provide the most common manifestation of solar control. Many projects include venetian blinds that can be lowered, raised and tilted according to the detected presence of the sun. These are often incorporated into dual skin cavities for protection, to keep the heat out of the occupied zone, and to participate in the action of a solar flue.

Occupant control

It is widely accepted that building occupants should have maximum personal control over their immediate environment, and this can often be more realistically achieved with intelligent technologies. Most current control systems have facilities for manual override, often provided by on-screen control panels and hand-held remote control units. However, there may be occasions when unchecked occupant control will compromise general comfort and energy reduction strategies, where the BMS either reminds the user of the error or disallows continued functioning.

Electricity generators

It is now feasible for buildings to strive for electrical autonomy through self-generation. This extends the concept of buildings with living capabilities. The case studies include examples of electricity generated by photovoltaics, wind turbines, and combined heat and power systems. As the intelligent building evolves, it may develop some of the in-built efficiencies of the human body – using every available resource through maximum conservation and recycling.

Ventilation controllers

Ventilation can be automatically regulated for increased effectiveness and greater occupant control by operable elements of the building fabric, such as retractable roofs, motorized windows and pneumatic dampers. These moving elements can also be automatically closed in unfavourable conditions, such as the inclement actions of wind and rain. Intelligent control mechanisms help to overcome some of the inherent problems faced by natural ventilation, such as air and noise pollution.

Many of the case studies operate a mixed-mode approach to ventilation, and intelligent control systems are utilized to determine when to best activate mechanical ventilation. They are programmed to use mechanical ventilation only in extreme conditions, thus maximizing natural ventilation and minimizing energy usage.

One of the case studies includes examples of self-regulating vents that maintain constant airflow in changing wind speeds. The concept of occupancy dependent lighting has also been applied to ventilation, with local fan units operated only when user presence is detected. A number of the projects include air distribution systems through the building structure. Such integral airflow strategies can be compared with the human circulatory system.

Heating and temperature controllers

In many of the case study examples, intelligent technologies are employed to minimize the energy burden resulting from the highly serviced elements of heating, ventilation and cooling. Attempts are made to reduce the significant demands for space and water heating through the use of passive solar strategies, provided with more precise motorized control. Control systems ensure the optimized operation of low temperature hot water circuits. The sun is also utilized for water heating, with some examples equipped to track the sun automatically for maximum exposure.

Cooling devices

As well as employing mechanized control of established passive cooling techniques, such as earth heat exchangers, borehole water and ground water, many of the case study examples utilize a strategy for computer-controlled night-time ventilation for pre-cooling of the thermal mass. Cooled water distribution is optimized in the same way as the heating circuits (which are doubled up in a number of examples).

The double skin

The double skin is a system involving the addition of a second glazed envelope which can create opportunities for maximizing daylight and improving energy performance. There are 11 examples of such systems in the case studies, about 50% of the total. In the summer, the double façade can reduce solar gains as the heat load against the internal skin can be lessened by the ventilated cavity. A natural stack effect often develops in the solar heated cavity, as absorbed solar radiation (the glass, the structure and blinds) is re-radiated. In the winter, the double façade will act as a buffer zone between the building and the outside, minimizing heat loss, and improving U-values. Intelligent control mechanisms have been used in most examples to regulate the admittance of air into the cavity automatically, and also closing it up to create a thermal buffer.

The future

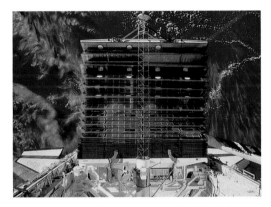

▲ Technology transfer is an important historical influence on the development of architecture. The space programme would be impossible without photovoltaic generation of electricity, and the development of photovoltaics, such as this huge folding array, is only one of the technologies emerging out of the space programme, which provide the raw material for the architecture of the future.

The research which underpins this book has confirmed the belief of its authors that the intelligent façade will be one of the principal elements in the building of the future.

The intelligent skin has been shown, both through consideration of its nature, and through the case study work, to have more affinity with some of the responsive and adaptive systems seen in nature, and as such aspires to a level of 'true' (but artificial) building intelligence, incorporating learning and autonomic response mechanisms, rather than simply motorized automatic control.

The use of the biological metaphor is not simply an attempt to legitimize the research and its subject area. It has been found to inform significantly the consideration of the intelligent skin, and the intelligent building. In consideration of neural networks and memory, for example, it is clear that we can progress more effectively by considering concepts such as a building's 'instincts'.

The basis for this consideration also contains a biological analogy, that of evolution. In this analogy we might expect buildings to strive for a state in which they were at the highest level of operational activity (what we might call 'life') with the least expenditure of energy. That is how animals have evolved, and there are good reasons for us to want buildings to evolve in the same way. This provides a conceptual, and perhaps aesthetic, basis for the intelligent building, as well as one based on efficient resource management and concerns about global warming. It may have been chance, rather than inappropriate evolution, which destroyed the dinosaurs, but the idea persists that the generation of buildings built in the last century, with their increasing need for the importing of energy, represent an unsustainable direction for the evolution of the built environment to take and also one that is deeply unsatisfactory philosophically. Evolution is not so much concerned with the survival of the fittest, but with the non-survival of the unfit. Building has been evolving in a way which undermines its legitimacy, and more advanced forms of building 'life' are essential if an expanding world population is to provide itself with comfortable buildings, with an equitable spread of technology and quality of provision. Sustainable thinking will not receive the public support which is essential to its world-wide success if developing nations are asked to accept less than the developed world has become accustomed to since the end of the nineteenth century. The energy loads, resource needs, and pollution generation, implicit in the world-wide adoption of current building practice, cannot be sustained, and it is this which creates the global imperative both for intelligent design, and for the intelligent building.

Of course, we may solve our problems in other ways. A future world population of 11 billion or more, with a significant proportion living in areas which have climates less temperate than ours (and with huge potential demand for air conditioning), may discover new means of supplying its energy needs. Nuclear energy might receive a clean bill of health. Photovoltaic or some other electro-solar technology may be developed which can serve an African continent in the twenty-second century in which the technical standard of living transcends our own now. The whole world population may, by consensus, reach a conclusion that 11 billion people cannot afford to live with the same resources and energy consumption as western Europe, Australasia, Japan, North America, Singapore and other technologically advanced countries have achieved at the end of the twentieth century, and the new world order could vote to adopt a 'green' agenda, and become 'alternative'. This all seems less likely than the continuous adoption, by larger numbers of people with higher aspirations, of the western lifestyle. The idea of buildings using 50% of the energy of a highly sophisticated world population in 100 years time is unsustainable without the wider adoption of renewable energy sources that currently seems unlikely. We must surely change the way we live, or the way we build (or both), and massive adoption of adobe may not be the answer. What is needed is a generation of buildings as close to autonomy as possible, which do not require the huge import of energy. The intelligent building as set out in this book is an answer.

The case has been presented for the applicability and feasibility of incorporating 'active' and 'intelligent' control into the building fabric. What now needs discussion, and further research and testing (in the form of real projects) is whether the purported financial, environmental and user benefits of the intelligent skin can be proved to be effective.

The intelligent building research programme, of which the study of the intelligent façade forms a part, begs many questions.

Do users feel more in control? Can they accept a degree of invisible automatic control? Are the services systems cheaper to install? Do running costs fall? Is the maintenance burden serviceable? Can designers live with the non-uniform aesthetic of variability?

Whatever the answers to these, and the many other questions which accompany consideration of building intelligence, if it can be shown that active and autonomic systems can lead to lower energy consumption and improved comfort then we should support the concept.

At the beginning of this study, we set out to research the nature of the truly intelligent building with a truly responsive, adaptive and controllable intelligent skin. It has not been found yet, but what we have called the genetic basis for evolution exists. The technology is available, and this book describes many examples, which, combined together through design evolution, might satisfy the characteristics and attributes of a truly intelligent building. The evolutionary thrust has already been given added impetus by at least one international programme that has been partly initiated by the research set out in this book. 'Glass and the Interactive Building Envelope' is the title of the research programme COST C13, funded by the European Union, which started work in 2000, and involves 16 nations to date.

The building façade should no longer be regarded as a static and inert barrier, but a dynamic environmental filter with, the energy passing through it ripe for exploitation. Such a façade can make a significant contribution to the highly evolved building of the future, designed and equipped to take advantage of the new nanometric technologies, and deliver a new aesthetic for architecture, bioclimatically devised, regionally based, technically competent, with new forms of beauty.

8   The case studies

A case study format suitable for this book was devised after a survey of other case study techniques used to present examples of low energy design and passive solar strategies (refer to the bibliography). The purpose of the case studies is to describe the range and variations of intelligent technologies employed to moderate energy flows through the building envelope. As stated previously, the emphasis is on the 'active' control of the functions that the building façade performs. The studies have been prepared by architects and are aimed primarily at design-led professionals in the building industry as a statement of the current state-of-the-art in the application of 'intelligent' technologies to the building envelope.

The intention of this study is to identify the characteristics which form part of the intelligent façade. The 22 case studies were selected on the basis of them demonstrating some of these intelligent characteristics. The study has deliberately not been limited to a particular building type, and the projects range in size from a small house to the tallest building in Europe. Although the geographical spread appears biased towards western Europe, this is more an indication of the area of primary activity, than a conscious decision to concentrate on one particular climatic zone. The studies stretch across 22° of latitude, in eight different latitudinal bands, from northern Scandinavia to the Arizona desert. There are many longitudinal variations in between. As the technology is advancing all the time, the case studies have been arranged in chronological order, with the most recent first to demonstrate the application of the most up-to-date technologies.

The case studies are presented here in a purely descriptive format. Limited qualitative assessments have been made as these would be based on the authors' subjective viewpoint. Where quantitative data have been used the source is clearly identified. The objective was not to say what is good or bad about the intelligent systems, but the variations of incorporating the technologies into buildings. Readers are left to form their own opinions on the basis of the material presented. It was not possible, or even appropriate, to enter into a full-scale monitoring and analysis programme at this stage. A more in-depth academic study would clearly warrant a greater emphasis and the finances to support such an effort. Where monitoring results are already available for projects (79%), their principal findings have been incorporated. The purpose of this study is to present in a single document, the range of intelligent façades employed in built projects from across the world.

Each case study begins with a descriptive section detailing the name of the project, the building type and the location. As well as crediting the architect, the energy consultant and client are also credited as important contributors. The dates are given from the project's inception and completion. The degree of latitude was calculated as an indicator of climate and solar geometry. The primary axis of the building's orientation is given relative to north.

The buildings are also credited with a range of intelligent features which are characteristic of intelligent systems, including a building management system with learning capabilities; if weather data are collected; whether lighting circuits are responsive to daylight levels or occupancy; if there are any sun-tracking facilities; whether occupants are able to override façade functions; self-generation systems such as CHP, PVs, and wind; whether automatic night cooling is used; and if solar water heating is employed.

The introductory section for each building describes the background to the project, and describes the key intelligent characteristics as an 'intelligence factor' – the qualifying criteria. Details of the client's briefing and programme requirements are followed by a short description of the building, the distribution of functions, the accommodating form and details of occupancy. A summary of the energy strategy describes the method used to limit energy consumption in the project. Details of the site and limited climatic data are provided to set the building in its physical and climatic context. A sunpath programme has been used to depict the sunpath for each case study building. The sun's path is shown in a continuous line for the winter extents (21 December) and in a dashed line for the summer extents (21 June). The summer and winter solar elevations at midday are also given as an indication of the peak solar altitudes.

The general description of the buildings includes details of the construction in terms of materials used and insulation thicknesses. U-values are given in W/m^2K as a quantitative measure of thermal transmission. An assessment is made by the authors of the quantity of glazing on each face of the building, including the roof, by calculating the façade transparency as a percentage. Where full-height glazing is employed transparency is assumed at 100% with no allowance for opaque construction elements. The figures are broad estimates, often rounded to the nearest 5%. An enhanced description of the glazing system is provided including U-values and light and energy transmission factors where available.

The servicing of the building is described by the three strategies employed for heating, cooling and ventilation. If the building generates its own electricity then details are provided. The other important servicing strategy relates to daylighting, where details of the overall daylight strategy are given alongside the strategies for artificial lighting and solar control. The fundamental element of the servicing strategy in respect of this study relates to the degree of control, and a full description of the controls strategy is provided. The extent of user control is also detailed. The overall servicing strategy is summarized by a description of the operating modes in winter and summer, and at night.

The degree of intelligent control is summarized in a table which assesses each project against the functions of the building envelope. The primary functions have been re-categorized as daylight adjustment (reflection/protection), glare control (blinds/louvres/fixed), artificial lighting control, heating control, heat recovery (warmth/coolth), cooling control, ventilation control, fabric control (windows/dampers/doors) and insulation (night/solar). The table charts whether these are performed passively or automatically, and whether there is any manual control option.

Each project also includes a range of data to enhance the written description. Firstly, the contract sum is given as an indicator of the project value. No attempt has been made to normalize these figures to account for currency fluctuations or time variations. The total area of the building is given in square metres, along with the depth of a typical floorplate from window-to-window or window-to-core. The number of stories is provided, and basements are noted separately. An approximate price per square metre is given in pounds sterling, again to be regarded as an indicator rather than an accurate figure for direct comparison.

As the primary objective with a large number of the schemes is to reduce energy consumption, available figures are presented for annual energy use in kilowatt hours per square metre per annum, based on delivered energy consumption. These figures are then compared against typical energy use figures for a similar building type. As a further measure of environmental performance, some projects are able to quantify their carbon dioxide output in kilograms per square metre. Again all of these figures are intended to be indicative and should be read with caution.

Energy consumption can be influenced by prevailing weather conditions (which may vary from year to year), the degree of exposure and the actual hours of occupation. There are established methods to account for these variations, by normalizing the figures, e.g. BRECSU's Normalized Performance Indices calculation. With respect to carbon dioxide emissions, it should be noted that performance in this respect is improving all the time as electricity generation moves towards cleaner generating fuels such as natural gas. It should also be highlighted that the quoted figures do not necessarily relate to treated floor areas.

The total number of sensors used in each project is given to indicate the extent of the intelligent technologies. As mentioned, 12 of the case study projects were visited as part of the study, and this is recorded. Finally, if a project has been monitored by others this is acknowledged, and the principal findings are incorporated into the description.

If the performance of the project has been monitored, the principal findings are described in the last section, including further data relating to the delivered energy consumption figures in kWh/m^2 per year. A total of 16 out of the 22 case studies have been monitored. Details of computer simulations and physical models used to support the design process are listed to describe the design and planning process.

GSW Headquarters

GSW Headquarters (tenanted upper floors)
High-rise office building
Kachstrasse 22, Charlottenstrasse
Berlin
Germany (D-10969)
Sauerbruch & Hutton *Architect*
Arup *Energy, Thermal flue, Services, Structural
   Consultant*
Arup IGH *Planning Association, detailed services and
   structural design*
Gemeinnutzige Siedlungs und
   Wohnungsbaugesellschaft (GSW) *Client*
1990–1999 *Dates*
52.27°N *Latitude*
270°N *Primary axis of orientation*

Intelligent features

Building management system	■
Learning facility	
Weather data	■
Responsive lights	■
Sun tracking facility	■
Occupant override	■
Self-generation – CHP/PV/wind	
Night cooling	■
Solar water heating	

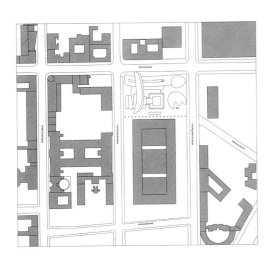

Introduction

This is the new headquarters building for Gemeinnutzige Siedlungs und Wohnungsbaugesellschaft, one of the largest providers of social housing in Berlin.
They originally occupied a complex of buildings which comprised a 17-storey
office building, together with a three-storey low block surmounted by a three-
storey drum. In 1990–91 they decided to hold a design competition to provide
themselves with additional office space. Sauerbruch Hutton won the competition, proposing a slender 22-storey tower linked to the existing tower. The building was completed in September 1999.

The intelligence factor

Two intelligent systems assist in providing comfort and energy efficiency in the
building. The building is naturally ventilated for 70% of the year, and ventilation

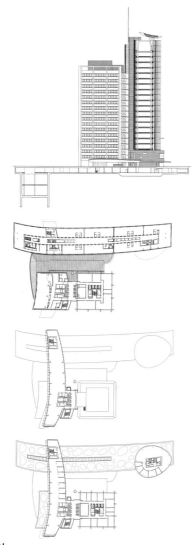

Sunpath

Latitude
52.27°

N

21 December 13° | 60° 21 June

12 pm

in low wind conditions is induced by a thermal flue formed by a single glazed skin 1m from the inner double glazed façade. Airflow into the base of the flue, and out of the top, is regulated by dampers controlled by the building management system, which also controls airflow from the building into the flue: this can be overriden by occupants. Occupant control is also possible in the other intelligent system controlling the shading system. This latter system comprises red and green lights in a control on the window transom in each office module, which recommends whether natural or mechanical ventilation should be used, with a rocker switch to open or close the blinds. The row of light fittings closest to the windows is automatically switched off by a signal sent from a solar cell when daylight illumination is sufficient. This, too, can be overriden by occupants.

Brief

The brief was to provide additional office space for the Client within a new building, to be linked to the existing buildings on the site. Following the competition, the economic climate indicated that substantial parts of the tower should be rented out, which required greater flexibility in layout and various revisions to the design concept.

Accommodation

The building comprises a gently curving arc in plan, about 65m long, 7.2m wide at the ends, increasing to a width of 11m in the centre. The floor-to-floor height was constrained by that of the existing tower, at 3.25m, which is low for a modern office building, and for any building designed for daylighting. The building is located to the west of the original 17 storey tower, thus sheltering it from the prevailing wind, and mitigating the environmental problems inherent in the original tower. The west façade of the new building incorporates the solar flue, which also provides a buffer to the wind. The original internal planning of the building incorporated a corridor down the east side of the building, serving office space to the west, but a later decision was made to use a central corridor: this led to the creation of a triple-glazed east façade with mid-pane blinds. The new tower is connected to the existing tower by a new lift and service core.

Energy strategy

A central aspect of the concept is a low energy strategy, with natural ventilation as a central constituent. A key component is the double wall on the west side, which acts both as a weather screen providing protection against heat loss, and a thermal flue, which induced ventilation in calm weather. Insulation values are high, including those of the glazing systems. The glazing system has an average U value of 1.6W/m²K, and the external walls and roof have values of 0.3 and 0.25 W/m²K, respectively. High equipment loads generate a requirement for comfort cooling, but the implementation of a 'peak lopping' system, allowing higher comfort temperatures of 27°C when the outside temperature is 32°C enable cooling to be provided without refrigeration. Thermal storage is also used, with the floors having exposed soffits.

Site and climate

The building is located in the centre of Berlin, close to the site of the Berlin Wall and Checkpoint Charlie. The climate of Berlin, as elsewhere in central Germany, is known as 'continental'. Its summers are warmer and its winters colder than in the UK or the countries in the west of the European Union. Winter temperatures can drop to −25°C and summer temperatures can rise to 35°C. Design temperatures used were −14°C and 32°C, respectively.

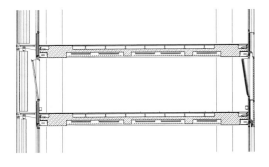

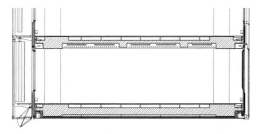

Façade transparency	
North	65%
East	58%
West	65%
South	45%

U-values	
Walls	$0.3W/m^2K$
Roof	$0.25W/m^2K$
West façade glazing (total)	$1.2W/m^2K$

Construction

The competition concept involved separating the building from the those below by using edge cantilevers, with the east side supported by a steel vierendeel and the west by a truss at third and fourth floors, all to avoid reinforced concrete beams in the low floor-to-floor height. The change to a symmetrical plan organization led to the omission of the vierendeel, and the creation of a truss at roof level with suspended columns. Economies proposed by the Contractor included the omission of the roof truss and the use of edge beams, which incorporate complex prestressing to enable the passage of ducts. Wind loads are taken by the cores, with the south core taking most of the stress. Core walls are up to 600mm thick. The basement construction required the 3m water table to be lowered during the construction.

Glazing

The glazing gives the GSW tower its character. Daylighting objectives led to the adoption of a low cill height of 600mm with the glazing extending the soffit of the floor above. Excluding the exterior single glazed system, the average U-value of the glazing is $1.6W/m^2K$. The western glazing comprises an inner double glazed system incorporating bottom-hung outward opening windows which ventilates the interior into the cavity, in which is a series of vertically pivoting and sliding panels which are 18% perforated. The opening window is the 'control point' for air flow into the flue, and model tests were made of it to ensure that its airflow/pressure loss characteristics were as modelled. The outer single skin forming the thermal flue is glazed with laminated single glazed glass. The glazing to the east side is triple glazed with mid-pane blinds, openable only for cleaning purposes. A high level hopper provides ventilation in cold weather, whilst a vertically pivoting wind protected panel allows single sided ventilation to cellular east side offices.

Heating

With high internal loads, the prime requirement is for ventilation and cooling, but winter heating is provided by the air handling system and radiators, supplied from the district heating system. Perimeter radiators are provided with individual thermostatic radiator valves, sized for a −14°C winter condition. Air extracted from the building is returned to the central plant room on the 22nd floor (below the roof) via risers, for heat recovery in the winter.

Cooling

Consistent with the environmental objectives, no refrigeration systems are used. The cooling necessary during very high summer temperatures is provided by spray coolers and dessicant thermal wheels, the latter regenerated using the district heating supply. The heat for the thermal wheels in summer is a by-product of electricity generation for the local grid, and as such adds very little carbon dioxide to the atmosphere that would not already be produced for electricity. The peak lopping principle allows internal temperatures to rise to 27°C when external temperatures are 32°C.

Ventilation

The ventilation strategy for the building is an important part of the concept, particularly given the height of the building, and the consequent need to avoid draughts and unpredictable ventilation when windows are open. The outer glazing system of the west face provides the buffer needed to protect the interior,

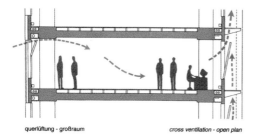

querlüftung - großraum   *cross ventilation - open plan*

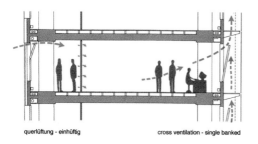

querlüftung - einhüftig   *cross ventilation - single banked*

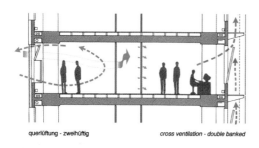

querlüftung - zweihüftig   *cross ventilation - double banked*

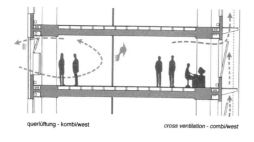

querlüftung - kombi/west   *cross ventilation - combi/west*

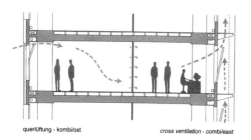

querlüftung - kombi/ost   *cross ventilation - combi/east*

and also forms the solar flue which drives the ventilation when the wind speed is low. The flue also moderates wind flow through the offices when it is windy (irrespective of wind direction). Mechanical ventilation provides air change during seasonal weather extremes, when the windows have to be closed. Air is supplied from the main plant room via the floor, using swirl diffusers recessed into a raised floor system which acts as a plenum. The floor plenum is divided into three zones, which are fed with air from local risers, allowing all floors to be mechanically or naturally ventilated, with up to three tenant zones per floor. The building's central management system determines whether to turn on the mechanical ventilation, but occupants can select individual zones within a floor in either mechanical or natural ventilation mode by a simple wall mounted zone controller.

Daylighting

The German regulations concerning daylighting accord with the environmental objectives of the Client and the design team. The low floor-to-floor height of 3.25m has led to the selection of a narrow floor plan with a maximum depth, wall to wall, of 11m. The walls are fully glazed from a low cill of 600mm to the underside of the soffit. This provides extremely good daylight to the office floors from both sides, and much reduces the need for artificial lighting even when the shading systems are closed, because good daylighting is always available from at least one side. The 18% perforations in the vertical louvres in the thermal flue provide a bright environment with spectacular views across Berlin.

Artificial lighting

The offices are predominantly daylit, but are illuminated to 300 lux by artificial lighting. The lighting in the offices consists of linear fluorescent fittings with specular 60° cut-off louvres. The light fittings are recessed into slots in the exposed concrete soffit. The lighting control system is based on the European Intrabus system (EIB), which was primarily adopted to provide flexibility and to enable room layouts to be changed without rewiring. The row of light fittings adjacent to the windows is automatically switched off by photocells within the

façade to encourage the use of daylight. The remaining lighting is manually switched in groups. Occupants can override the automated daylight-linked switching.

Solar control

The west glazing is protected by vertically pivoting and sliding panels which are 18% perforated and the east glazing by integral blinds.

Controls

The building management system (BMS) controls the key elements of the environmental system. The BMS controls airflow in the thermal flue by opening and closing the dampers at the top and bottom, and makes recommendations to the users about the selection of natural or mechanical ventilation by means of the green and red lights on the window transoms. A separate light control system switches off the perimeter lighting when daylight is sensed to be adequate for the interior. All the systems can be overriden by occupants.

User control

User control is a key feature of the building, incorporating both provision to override, and the giving of advice. Override is provided for the ventilation system, which enables the occupant to affect the airflow through the building during occupied hours. Wall mounted zone controllers allow occupants to override the BMS for mechanical or natural mode of ventilation.

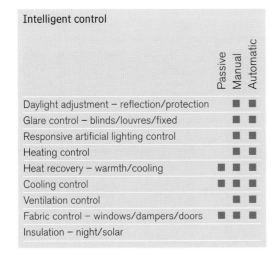

Intelligent control	Passive	Manual	Automatic
Daylight adjustment – reflection/protection		■	■
Glare control – blinds/louvres/fixed		■	■
Responsive artificial lighting control		■	■
Heating control		■	■
Heat recovery – warmth/cooling	■	■	■
Cooling control	■	■	■
Ventilation control		■	■
Fabric control – windows/dampers/doors	■	■	■
Insulation – night/solar			

Building data

Contract value	DM160m
Area	47,873m^2
Typical floorplate	800m
Number of storeys	21
Price per m^2	DM3340/m^2
Annual energy use	n/a
Typical energy use for building type	n/a
Annual CO_2 output	n/a
Number of sensors	>1000
Visited by authors	✗
Monitored by others	✔

Operating modes

The operating modes are described in the section above, and it is a characteristic of the project that modes can be switched by zone between BMS control and occupier control.

Performance

The building has only been occupied for about 1 year at the time of writing, and for much of that the BMS systems was not commissioned.

Delivered energy consumption

This has not yet been established.

Design process

The design process involved a high level of collaboration between the architects and Arup London, in the initial phases, and Arup GmbH in the implementation of the project. The necessary integration of the structural and environmental roles of the floor slabs, and the multiple functioning of the envelope required the major elements of the building to be the result of team designing.

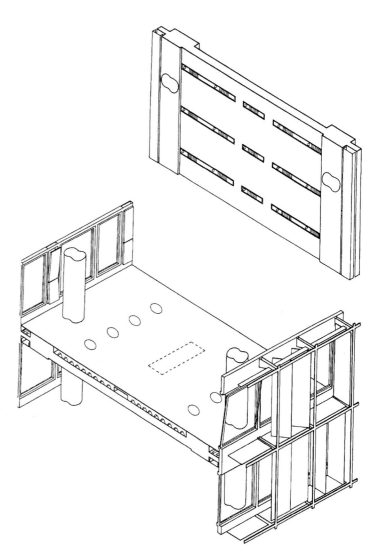

References

Sauerbruch Hutton. GSW Hauptverwaltung Berlin: Sauerbruch Hutton Architekten = GSW headquarters Berlin: Sauerbruch Hutton Architects. Baden: Lars Muller, 2000.
GSW Headquarters, Berlin, Article by Stephen Hodder, *Architecture Today,* no. 116, 2001 Mar., pp. 30–49.
GSW Headquarters, Berlin, Article by Nils Clemmetsen, and others. *Arup journal,* vol. 35, no. 2, 2000 June, pp. 8–12.
GSW Headquarters, Berlin, Article by the architects, *UME,* no. 13, 2001, pp. 24–37.
Sede centrale della GSW a Berlino. Article by Stefania Manna Industria delle costruzioni, vol. 34, no. 341, 2000 Mar., pp. 22–35.
A tale of two cities. Article by Tom Dyckhoff *Architects' Journal,* vol. 208, no. 8, 1998 Sept. 3, pp. 34–35.
Verwaltungsgebaude in Berlin [Headquarters in Berlin]. Article by Andrea Compagno and Alix Rottig *Schweizer Ingenieur & Architekt,* vol. 118, no. 3, 2000 Jan. 18, pp. 23–33.

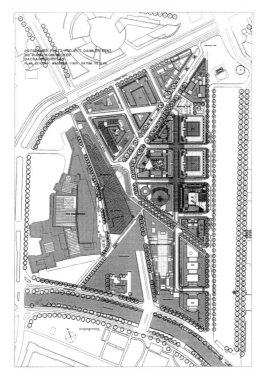

CASE STUDY 2

Debis Building

Debis Building
High-rise office building
Potsdammer Platz
Berlin
Germany
Renzo Piano Building Workshop *Architect*
Arup GmbH *Energy Consultant*
Daimler Benz Inter Services (Debis) *Client*
1992–1996 *Dates*
52.47°N *Latitude*
19°N *Primary axis of orientation*

Intelligent features

Building management system	■
Learning facility	
Weather data	■
Responsive lights	■
Sun tracking facility	
Occupant override	■
Self-generation – CHP/PV/wind	
Night cooling	■
Solar water heating	

Introduction

The Debis Building is part of the huge Potsdamer Platz project in Berlin. Potsdamer Platz had been one of the most vibrant areas of Berlin, but Post World War Two partition reduced it to a desolated area dominated by the Berlin Wall. Before the destruction of the wall, Daimler-Benz had resolved to build the headquarters of Daimler-Benz Inter Services AG (Debis) in the area, and this produced the 6.8 hectare site, stretching from Postdamer Platz to the north east to the National Library in the west. The removal of the wall in 1989 led to a masterplanning competition for the Debis site, won by Renzo Piano Building Workshop. RPBW were commissioned to design eight buildings within this masterplan, including two new corporate headquarters buildings for Debis.

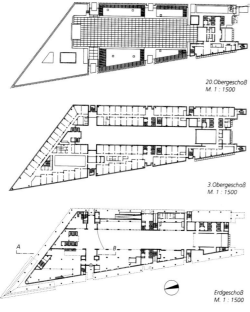

20.Obergeschoß
M. 1 : 1500

3.Obergeschoß
M. 1 : 1500

Erdgeschoß
M. 1 : 1500

Sunpath

Latitude
52.47°

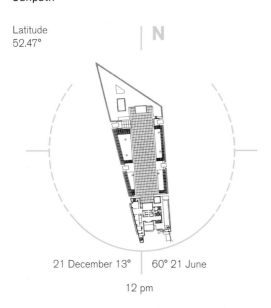

N

21 December 13° | 60° 21 June

12 pm

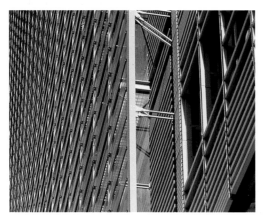

The intelligence factor

The east, south and west elevations, with the highest exposure to solar gain, incorporate a glass wall, about 700mm outside the main window wall. This outer wall comprises glass panels which can open to 70°, controlled by sensors to allow for ventilation in warm weather. In cold weather these close to create an insulating layer. The inner skin incorporates upper and lower panels of insulating glazing: the upper windows open automatically at night in warm weather, to ventilate the interior and thus remove much of the heat built up during the day.

The brief

The building was required to house the headquarters of the property, financial services, information technology, telecommunications, and media services divisions of Daimler-Benz. The status of Daimler-Benz in Germany, and their own objectives, raised the project to the status of a symbol of the Company's commitment to a united Germany, and the rebuilding of its historic capital.

Accommodation

The accommodation comprises about 45,000 square metres of office space (out of a total of 170,000 square metres of office space on the whole 6.8 hectare site, this only comprising about 50% of the whole mixed use development). The form of the building rises from a six-storey broad lower end to a narrow 21-storey narrow end. A 14m wide atrium runs 82m from north to south down the centre, providing two overlooking office wings which accord with the German regulations controlling minimum daylight levels at a workstation.

Energy strategy

Energy conservation was an important aspect of the design strategy for the building, and the project was awarded funding from the European Union Joule II research programme to help finance the design of the façades. Its Potsdamer Platz site as a whole was seen by Daimler-Benz as a place to test energy saving, and they cooperated with BEWAG, the local electricity provider, to create a new power plant which uses waste heat to drive absorption refrigeration plant. In the Debis building itself 'natural' methods keep the building comfortable for considerable parts of the year, with the double glass skin increasing the period in the year in which natural ventilation operates, and improving the office acoustic conditions both in naturally ventilating and sealed modes.

Site and climate

The buildings is located in the centre of Berlin, close to the site of the Berlin Wall and Checkpoint Charlie. The climate of Berlin, as elsewhere in central Germany, is known as 'continental'. Its summers are warmer and its winters colder than in the UK or the countries in the west of the European Union. Winter temperatures can drop to −15°C and summer temperatures rise to 32°C.

Construction

The building comprises a reinforced concrete frame, clad with two systems externally, depending on orientation and height. What the architects term an 'opaque' façade comprises a screen of terracotta units in front of a conventionally configured wall of opaque highly insulated panels providing the main weather barrier, and economical opening windows. The 'transparent' façade is used to clad the west face of the tower. The concrete floor slab is exposed at the outer edges of the floors, and acts as an absorber of solar radiation, and a temperature damper.

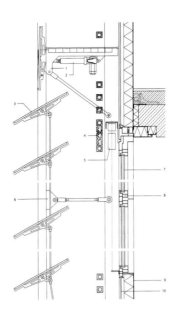

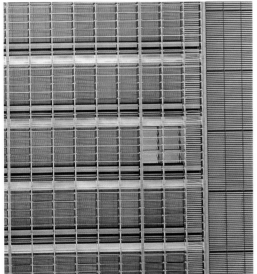

Façade transparency

North	80%
East	80%
South	80%
West	80%
Roof	90%

U-values

Walls	n/a
Slab	n/a
Roof	n/a
Windows	1.5W/m^{2}K

Glazing

The 'transparent' façade constitutes an interesting variant on the second skin principle. The outer layer of glass louvres reduces wind pressure on the main external glass wall behind, and helps keep the rain away from the inner glass envelope, where the windows can be open at all times. It also provides protection to the retractable blinds within the cavity that provide solar protection to the façade. The louvres operate in vertical banks. The inner glazing has an opening hopper in the upper part of the wall.

Heating

Heat for the building is derived from the BEWAG district heating system via heat exchangers in the basement. Perimeter finned tube heaters with thermostatic valves provide individual temperature control in offices. Thermal wheels are employed on the office ventilation system to recover heat from the exhaust air stream in winter.

Cooling

Comfort cooling is provided in the form of chilled ceilings, but is considered supplementary rather than essential. The ready access of the office occupants to an opening window, the narrow floor plates, and the external blinds mounted just outside the inner skin, provide them with sufficient control to maintain a comfortable environment.

Ventilation

Ventilation is a principal aspect of the environmental control of the building. In the summer, natural ventilation is designed to produce better conditions than mechanical ventilation as long as the ambient temperature does not rise above 30°C. At this point mechanical ventilation is activated, as is a chilled ceiling system. In the winter a similar system operates, when outside temperatures are below 5°C, at which point mechanical ventilation and heating come on. As a result of this strategy for each season, it is predicted that natural ventilation will be adequate for 40% of the year at the top of the building, and for 55% in the lower parts of the building. This will reduce the energy loads of the building by 40% if fully exploited by occupants. The ventilation operates in winter by using

Intelligent control

	Passive	Manual	Automatic
Daylight adjustment – reflection/protection	■		
Glare control – blinds/louvres/fixed	■		
Responsive artificial lighting control		■	■
Heating control		■	■
Heat recovery – warmth/cooling			■
Cooling control		■	■
Ventilation control		■	■
Fabric control – windows/dampers/doors			■
Insulation – night/solar			■

Building data

Area	45,000m²
Typical floorplate	180m lower floor; 35m tower
Number of storeys	6–21
Annual energy use	n/a
Typical energy use for building type	100kWh/m²
Annual CO₂ output	n/a
Number of sensors	n/a

References

Renzo Piano Building Workshop: Volume 4: Peter Buchanan, Phaidon Press, 2000, pp 169–181
Architectural Record, October 1998, pp 124–35
Deutsche Bauzeitschrift, June 1998, pp 39–46
A+U, June 1998 (extra edition), pp 104–108
Architectural Review, January 1998, pp 40–42
L'Architettura Cronache e Storia, November/December 1998, pp 626–41

the louvres in closed mode to trap air as an insulating 'blanket', and in summer as a flue, driving the ventilation, and drawing in cool fresh air.

Daylighting

Daylight levels are generous throughout the offices and always comfortably achieve the German standard of a 2% daylight factor. Offices on the western side, with the double skin façade, enjoy daylight factors of nearly 5%, and electric lighting is needed for less than 40% of the working year. The atrium is flooded with controlled light which permeates through large glass panels, fritted to provide solar shading, to prevent direct views of the sky, and to reflect artificial light at night.

Artificial lighting

For the offices artificial lighting is conventional, with significant contributions from recessed downlighting. In the atrium the fritted glazing provides a reflecting ceiling at night, complemented by powerful downlighters.

Solar control

Solar shading is provided by blinds located in the cavity of the 'transparent' glass wall. These blinds have a shading factor of 0.3.

Controls

The building management system for the building controls and monitors all central plant (heating, cooling, transformers etc), and the mechanical ventilation systems which serve the offices. The BMS also, on the basis of 'reading' the external light, temperature, and radiation conditions and wind speeds, adjusts the setting of the glazed louvres in the external façade and the positions of the cavity blinds. A separate lighting control system automatically switches off perimeter lighting when daylight levels are adequate.

User control

Users have control of many aspects of their environment: they can control the electric lighting in their own rooms, the heating from the perimeter finned tube system, and the position of the cavity blind, and can adjust the ventilation of their rooms using the operable windows. Users can also modify the set point for the comfort provided by the chilled ceilings.

Performance

The building was only occupied for a short time at assessment, and no records were available.

Delivered energy consumption

No in-use monitoring statistics are available. However, extensive modelling was conducted as part of the Joule II study, and total energy consumption of between 80 and 100kWh/m² were forecast.

Design process

The development of the environmental systems for the building resulted from close collaboration between Renzo Piano Building Workshop, the engineers Ove Arup and Partners, and the project managers Drees and Sommer.

Commerzbank Headquarters

Commerzbank Headquarters
High-rise office building
Grosse Gallusstrasse/Kirchnerstrasse
Frankfurt-am-Main
Germany (D-60005)
Foster & Partners *Architect*
Roger Preston & Partners *Energy Consultant*
NERVUS Generalübernehmer *Client*
1991–1997 *Dates*
50.11°N *Latitude*
–7°N *Primary axis of orientation*

Intelligent features

Building management system	■
Learning facility	
Weather data	■
Responsive lights	■
Sun tracking facility	
Occupant override	■
Self-generation – CHP/PV/wind	
Night cooling	■
Solar water heating	

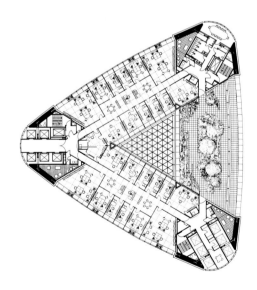

Introduction

An international architectural competition was launched early in 1991 to design a new office headquarters for Commerzbank on the centrally located Kaiserplatz site, adjacent to its existing 27-storey tower built in the 1970s. The closed competition invited entries from 12 practices from Germany, the USA and the UK. First prize was awarded to Foster Associates, who were asked to develop their ideas further alongside the second placed entry by Christoph Ingenhoven. Construction of Foster's scheme began in May 1994 and the 40m high antenna was erected in October 1996, making it Europe's tallest building at just under 300m.

The intelligence factor

The inner skin of the external windows and the atrium are equipped with motor-driven sashes that are controlled by the central building management system (BMS), or by the occupants using wall-mounted switches. The windows can be closed by the BMS in unfavourable conditions, and air conditioning automatically activated. Lighting in the office areas is controlled automatically according to daylight penetration and occupancy. Night cooling can be instigated through the motorized opening of windows on summer nights.

Brief

The client's brief insisted on the need to create a building capable of expressing current values, with particular emphasis on the bank's ecological policy, where 'the environmental friendliness of the design shall be as important as functional worth'. The criteria used for evaluating the competition entries included design, ecological awareness/energy efficiency, and functionality as an office building in the years ahead. It also had to be economic and buildable. The city of Frankfurt was

Grundriss Erdgeschoss
Ground Floor Plan SNFP

Sunpath

Latitude
50.11°

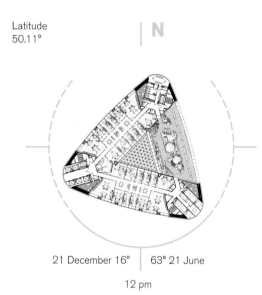

N

21 December 16° | 63° 21 June

12 pm

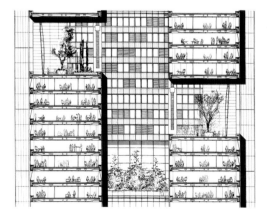

keen to see the new tower create a strong symbol for the banking district. The new headquarters brought together the various head-office departments, previously situated in 34 different locations within Frankfurt.

Accommodation

The plan of the tower is triangular in form, with 60m long sides that are curved to maximize space efficiency. The lift and staircase cores were originally designed as a separate triangular 'fishtail', but were eventually located on each corner of the triangle as a result of the value engineering exercise. In the competition entry, Foster returned to the idea of 'gardens in the sky' first proposed for the Hong Kong and Shanghai Bank, utilizing them for a system of natural air conditioning that would have been inconceivable in Hong Kong. Gardens spiral up the 48-storey tower to become the climatic, visual and social focus for four-storey clusters of offices located on the remaining two sides of the triangular plan. The gardens are linked to a 200m high atrium which has been divided into 12-storey 'villages', with a glass floor at each village boundary, which provides fire separation and defines internal ventilation and smoke ventilation zones. The employees can use the sky gardens for relaxation, lunch breaks and meetings. They each contain trees of different vegetation zones, depending on their orientation (Mediterranean, Asian and North American). There are nine gardens in all, three on each side of the triangle, and a tenth garden at level 43, at a height of approximately 160m. This garden is completely exposed to the elements from above and protected only by a 2m high glass wall. Roof vegetation is also planned for the lower level perimeter buildings, which include a banking hall, auditorium, shops, apartments and a covered plaza.

It is normal in Germany for most office space to be cellularized, but the new tower incorporates a proposal for 'combination' offices, which is new to Germany, where individual offices are combined with open-plan team areas. The building now houses 2400 Commerzbank employees, relocated from offices around Frankfurt. Each 'petal' of the triangular plan accommodates a working group of about 40 people, with approximately 650 people sharing each sky garden.

Energy strategy

The building has been designed to utilize natural ventilation for a large proportion of the operating cycle, using mechanically assisted air conditioning only under extreme conditions. Natural ventilation and lighting are achieved through openable perimeter windows that are optimally controlled by a central computer.

Site and climate

The building rises from a low-level context of four- to seven-storey buildings that are maintained around the perimeter of the 80m square city block, achieving an overall plot ratio of 13.5:1. A public thoroughfare has been preserved across the site between Kaiserplatz and Grosse Gallusstrasse. The climate of Frankfurt is described as 'Continental', with warmer summers and colder winters than the UK. Daytime temperatures can peak as high as 35°C in the height of summer.

Construction

The opaque elements of the steel-framed building are clad with prefabricated spandrel panels, incorporating black enamelled glass and 80mm of mineral wool insulation. Elsewhere triple glazed window assemblies provide openings for

Façade transparency

North	58%
East	58%
West	58%
Roof	12%

U-values

Walls	n/a
Slab	n/a
Roof	n/a
Windows	1.10 W/m²K

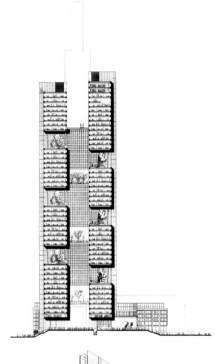

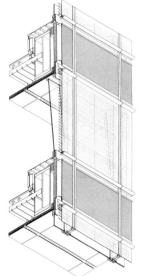

lighting and ventilation. The reinforced concrete basements sit on a 4.5m transfer slab and 111 bored piles up to 45m deep. It was necessary to use radar-attenuated glazing on the airport side of the building. The tower structure is supported by pairs of vertical steel masts at the corners of each core, which in turn support eight-storey vierendeel beams. Secondary beams span from the vierendeels to a perimeter beam at the atrium edge.

Glazing

The windows facing the atrium consist of insulating glass, and windows that are side hung for maintenance, and bottom hung for motorized ventilation. On the outer face, the windows are double glazed (low-e coating) with a third protective pane providing a ventilated cavity. The outer windows are side/bottom hung motor-driven sashes, located 252mm behind a protective outer pane (8mm laminated safety glass). The cavity is ventilated at the top and bottom through 125mm continuous slots. The inner pane is insulated 'Ipasol' glazing, with a light transparency of 66%, and an energy transmission value of only 34%.

Heating

In a building with high internal loads and good levels of insulation, heat will rarely be a requirement, even when it is 0°C outside. Static heating convectors are provided along the external and atrium façades to provide heating during cold spells, which is predicted not to exceed 17% of the operating cycle. It is anticipated that there will be a degree of passive solar build-up between the outer single glazed screen and the double-glazed opening light. This will provide some preheating of ventilation air, and radiant warming of the room. When the air conditioning is operational (estimated to be 40% of the time) heat from the return air is recycled to preheat incoming fresh air.

The gardens act both as solar collectors and thermal buffers. They are kept at minimum temperatures of 5°C, warmed with exhaust air from the offices and underfloor heating locally to the serving bars. The structure to the glazed garden walls also contains a water heating system to offset cold downdraughts.

Cooling

Cooling is the more predominant load in this building. The computerized BMS is programmed to facilitate night cooling of the concrete floor slabs through the opening of motorized perimeter windows. Local cooling can be provided during the day in office areas by means of a water-based chilled ceiling system. Chilled water is produced by absorption chilling plant at 17°C without the use of CFCs. The chillers are supplied with steam from the city utility network. The design team predicted that active cooling would be required for just over one-quarter of the time.

Ventilation

Natural ventilation is achieved across the 16.5m floorplates by computer-controlled perimeter windows. The 14m high garden façades can also be opened in good weather to ventilate the atrium space (connected to two other gardens) and indirectly provide fresh air to the offices facing the atrium. Outward-facing offices are ventilated directly from outside by means of a motorized inner window which is situated behind an outer protective pane. This creates a 200mm ventilated cavity, which also contains a motorized blind. All of the offices have these motorized bottom-hinged windows which can be controlled both by the occupants and the BMS.

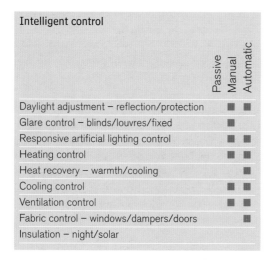

Intelligent control	Passive	Manual	Automatic
Daylight adjustment – reflection/protection		■	■
Glare control – blinds/louvres/fixed		■	
Responsive artificial lighting control		■	■
Heating control		■	■
Heat recovery – warmth/cooling			■
Cooling control		■	■
Ventilation control		■	■
Fabric control – windows/dampers/doors			■
Insulation – night/solar			

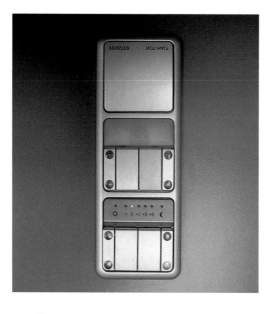

The air change in the cavity increases with rising solar insolation on the façade. The sun heats the glass, the frame and the blinds, and the surrounding air is warmed by these surfaces and experiences uplift. The warmer the façade elements get compared to the surrounding air, the stronger the uplift effect, and the stronger the air circulation in the cavity. Consequently more heat is extracted from the surface of the blinds and the sun shading effect of the façade improves with increasing solar insolation.

The design team envisaged that the motorized windows would provide effective means of ventilation for nearly 60% of the total hours of usage. In periods of bad weather, or excessive heat or cold, each 12-storey village is provided with its own back-up air-handling unit to supply fresh air mechanically. These comprise supply and extract fans, thermal wheels, filters, cooling coils, heating coils, a humidifier, and fresh air/recirculation dampers. A mechanical air supply and exhaust system serves the central corridor zones of each storey at all times.

Daylighting

German regulations stipulate that occupants should be no more than 7m away from a window. This has been achieved in the Commerzbank with 16.5m floorplates, which can be naturally lit and ventilated. Daylight is provided directly to the outside offices through the windows, and indirectly to offices facing the gardens that are lit both from the side and above (the atrium is also lit from the side).

Artificial lighting

High-efficiency lighting can be dimmed in response to variations in daylight levels on both the external and atrium façades. Lights in corridors and offices are activated automatically by movement sensors.

Solar control

Each window incorporates a motorized blind for solar shading, permitting individual control of solar admittance. The blinds, protected from the elements by the outer glass pane, can be operated safely up to wind speeds of 20m/s.

Controls

The BMS monitors numerous sensors and has full control over the internal climate system. It is operated according to the number of people in the building, the usage of the system and the outdoor climate. It can reduce the quantities of supply and exhaust air, and completely deactivate the air conditioning for parts of the building not being used. The computer determines the optimum position of the external sunshading and the motorized windows, in conjunction with the operation of the chilled ceilings, air conditioning and perimeter heating. The BMS is zoned into the 12-storey 'village' units and is informed by weather stations at four levels. The system monitors nine sensors in each of the internal gardens, adjusting temperatures and activating underfloor heating in these areas during cold weather.

User control

The control network also facilitates full occupant override when the external climate is appropriate, which is decided by the BMS in consultation with data describing the external weather conditions. User intervention to vary heat, air and light permeability is provided by an enhanced 'light switch panel', with facilities for controlling not only the lights, but also temperature, window openings and blind positions. The individual room control units are linked over a bus network.

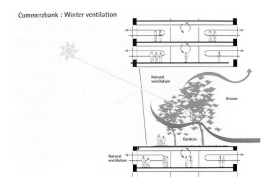

Commerzbank : Winter ventilation

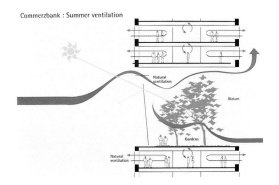

Commerzbank : Summer ventilation

Operating modes

There are two principal building management options which vary throughout the day as well as throughout the seasons, i.e. even on a summer's day natural ventilation may be feasible until after lunch. The first operation mode is the artificial control of the building's climate, with windows controlled shut, air conditioning fully operational and cooling provided by chilled ceilings. The low-energy option of natural ventilation involves the motorized opening of windows, and the deactivation of the air conditioning. Artificial heating and cooling is prevented in the low-energy mode.

Building data

Contract value	DM530m
Area	85,503m^2
Typical floorplate	16.5m
Number of storeys	48 + 2B
Price per m^2	~£2064/m^2
Annual energy use	n/a
Typical energy use for building type	n/a
Annual CO$_2$ output	n/a
Number of sensors	n/a
Visited by authors	✔
Monitored by others	✔

Credits

Client: NERVUS Generalübernehmer (which includes the bank)
Architect: Foster & Partners (Partner in charge: Spencer de Grey)
M/E Engineer: J Roger Preston & Partners with Pettersson und Ahrens
Electrical Engineer: Schad & Hölzel
Environmental Services (competition): HL Technik (JRP subsequently appointed as lead environmental engineers)
Structural Planning, Traffic and Fire Engineering: Ove Arup & Partners (Chris Wise) with Krebs und Kiefer
Façade Engineer: Ingenieurbüro Schalm
Façade: Josef Gartner & Co, Gundelfingen
Glass: VEGLA GmbH, Aachen; Interpane mbH & Co, Plattling
Landscaping: Sommeriad
QS: Davis Langdon & Everest
General Contractor: HOCHITEF Niederlassung
Site Engineer: Ingenieursozietät Professional Dr Ing Katzenbach und Dipl Ing Quick
Site Supervision: BGS Ingenieursozietät/HPP Gessellschaft für Projektmanagement

References

A&V Monografias, 38 (1992), Norman Foster, 'Gardens in the Air'
Architects Journal, 20 February 1997
Architects Journal, 27 March 1997
Architectural Monographs, No 20, 'Foster Associates: Recent Works', Academy Editions/St Martins Press, 1992
Architectural Review, May 1992, Vol CXC No 1143
Architectural Review, July 1997
The Arup Journal, 2/1997, Vol 32, No2, Peter Bailey, Harry Bridges, Paul Cross, Gabriele Del Mese, Chris Smith, Sean Walsh, Chris Wise, 'Enlargement of Commerzbank's Headquarters in the Banking District, Frankfurt am Main'
Building, Vol 259, No 2825, 7 January 1994
Building, Supplement December 1996, Vol 26, Issue 7969, 6 December 1996
Casabella, Vol 59 No 626, September 1995
Commerzbank, Commerzbank Information Pack
Concepts in Practice: Energy, Peter Smith and Adrian C Pitts. Batsford, 1997
D'Architectures, No 59, October 1995, 'Foster en Banque a Francfort', p45
Fassade/Façade, 4/96, pp 47–56, Dr Winfried Heusler/Johann Ernst, Translation supplied by Foster & Partners
l'ARCA, The International Magazine of Architecture, Design and Visual Communication, March 1992, No 58
Solar Energy in Architecture and Urban Planning, 'Commerzbank: The Winning Project', pp 24–31, Thomas Herzog, Prestel, p 108
Sven Ollman/Jo Olsen/Stefan Behling, Foster & Partners

Performance

The whole building will be extensively monitored while in use. The building was completed in May 1997.

Delivered energy consumption

It is predicted that this 'ecological skyscraper' will consume approximately 25–30% less energy than a comparable conventional building. The following computer simulated energy consumption figures were calculated during the design phase (assuming 60% natural ventilation):

Ventilation motors	18kWh/m^2/year
Cooling at 0.7 heat rate per absorber	115kWh/m^2/year
Heating including 10% heat loss	36kWh/m^2/year

Design process

A number of different façade concepts were physically modelled and tested during the design process. Computer modelling suggested that natural ventilation would be effective for up to 60% of the year.

Office design temperatures were set at 20°C (max. 40% RH) minimum in winter and 27°C (max 60% RH) maximum in summer. There is an installed heating load of 4.5MW and an installed cooling load of 5MW.

Stadttor (City Gate)

Stadttor (City Gate)
Speculative office development
Düsseldorf
Germany
Petzinka Pink und Partner *Architect*
DS-Plan *Energy Consultant*
Engel (developer) *Client*
1991–1997 *Dates*
51.29° *Latitude*
99°N *Primary axis of orientation*

Intelligent features

Building management system	■
Learning facility	
Weather data	■
Responsive lights	
Sun tracking facility	
Occupant override	■
Self-generation – CHP/PV/wind	
Night cooling	■
Solar water heating	

Introduction

A competition was launched in 1991 to explore the possibility of designing a high-rise building above the new road tunnel that brings traffic into the centre of Düsseldorf. The competition was won by Ingenhoven Overdiek Petzinka und Partner and built by the re-formed practice of Petzinka Pink und Partner. The new building was to be part of a new 'creative' mile that was proposed for the old harbour with offices, studios, media and advertising developments.

The intelligence factor

The building is controlled by a building management system (BMS), which determines natural ventilation or mechanical ventilation modes automatically. Natural ventilation is achieved through computer control of ventilation flaps within the depth of the building envelope. Venetian blinds within the cavity are lowered and raised automatically according to light and insolation levels, and the need for nighttime insulation.

Brief

The Stadttor project is an office building that is designed to give a good quality of light, individual spaces and an attractive working environment. It was speculatively developed.

Accommodation

The building is composed of two separate rhomboid towers, connected at the top with three bridging levels, defining the top of a huge atrium void, 50m high. The top three office floors have their own inner atrium that is lit from a roof light. These were the first floors to be let. The 20-storey building is supported by two vertical triangular trusses, which are connected by the top three floors of office accommodation, forming a structural bridge. The whole building is supported on the subterranean tunnel. A double skin cavity up to 1.4m in depth provides

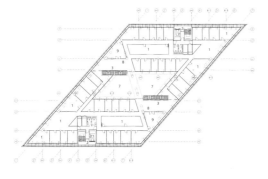

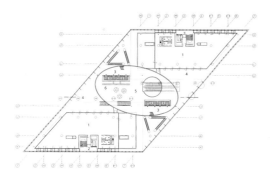

Sunpath

Latitude
51.29°

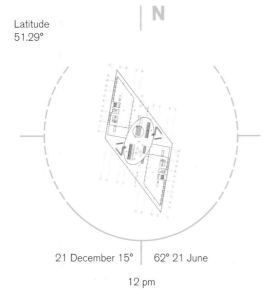

21 December 15° | 62° 21 June

12 pm

an enclosed balcony for all offices. The office floors are to speculatively let to multiple tenants.

Energy strategy

The building is predominantly naturally ventilated through computer-controlled ventilation flaps, which run in horizontal bands at each floor level. The BMS has sensors for wind, temperature, rain and sun to exercise optimum control strategies for heating, cooling and fresh air supply. The ventilated double skin limits the required cooling loads, by ventilating away the solar heat build up in the cavity.

Site and climate

The tower occupies a rhomboidal site and is split into two parallel towers with an atrium space between, which affords maximum views of the city and the Rhine, which is close to the Stadttor. The site is very exposed, and experiences strong wind speeds.

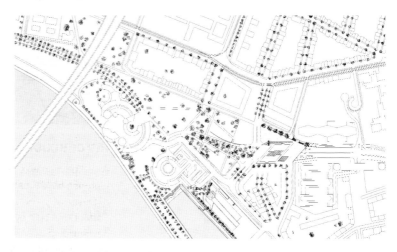

Construction

The structural frame consists of steel columns filled with reinforced concrete, and composite floors. The outer face of the building is entirely clad with planar glazing panels between horizontal bands of aluminium ventilation boxes.

Glazing

A double skin cavity envelops the three sides of the office floors, creating a ventilated perimeter zone, varying between 1.4 and 0.9m in depth. The outer face of the double skin is 15mm toughened planar glazing. It is a low-iron 'opti-white' glass for maximum transparency. The inner skin is made from vertically pivoted high performance timber windows. The full-height double glazing has a low-e coating. The overall energy transmission equates to 50%, without the blinds, and 10% with the blinds lowered. Light transmission through the envelope is 68%. The vertical atrium walls are single glazed with planar glass.

Heating

Heating is provided by a low-temperature hot water system (LTHW), which is fed by a district heating system that uses waste heat from a power station, and is supplied to the building at 100–120°C in winter and 70°C in summer. LTHW is distributed at about 40°C to radiant ceiling panels (metal ceiling tiles with coils

Façade transparency

North	100%
East	100%
South	100%
West	100%
Roof	22%

U-values

Double skin (vents open)	1.2 W/m^{2}K
Double skin (vents closed)	1.0 W/m^{2}K
Slab	0.4 W/m^{2}K
Roof	0.1 W/m^{2}K

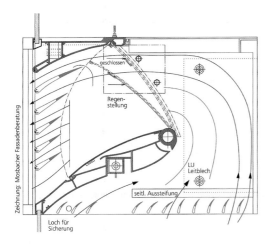

Intelligent control

	Passive	Manual	Automatic
Daylight adjustment – reflection/protection			
Glare control – blinds/louvres/fixed		■	■
Responsive artificial lighting control		■	
Heating control		■	■
Heat recovery – warmth/cooling			■
Cooling control		■	■
Ventilation control		■	■
Fabric control – windows/dampers/doors			■
Insulation – night/solar			■

behind) and underfloor heating in some areas. The atrium is not heated except for localized underfloor heating in occupied areas.

If the mechanical ventilation is operational (approximately 25% of the time in heating mode), the supply air is pre-heated by a heater battery in the air handling units, which is also fed by the district heating system.

Domestic hot water is heated electrically at point of use.

Cooling

Cool water is supplied from groundwater sources at 8–10°C, which is heat exchanged, stored and filtered in eight tanks in the basement. The water is distributed to radiant ceiling panels at about 17°C.

If the mechanical ventilation is in operation (approximately 5% of the time in cooling mode), the air can be pre-cooled by 'sorptive cooling'. This involves cooling the air with the heat supplied by the district heating network, which would otherwise be waste heat in the summer. Outgoing air is deliberately humidified and heated to condition the incoming air by heat and humidity exchange. Incoming air gives up its heat by heat exchange to the humidification process. There is no active cooling in the form of chillers, condensers or towers.

The regulation of building temperature and humidity levels is assisted through the use of automatically controlled blinds in the double skin cavity.

A nighttime cooling facility is available if required. The ventilation flaps are automatically opened and the users leave the inner windows open.

Ventilation

It has been predicted that natural ventilation will be achievable for 70% of the year, when temperatures should be between 5°C and 22°C. For 25% of the year, temperatures are likely to be below 5°C, and pre-heated mechanical ventilation will be used. For the remaining 5%, temperatures are likely to be above 22°C, and pre-cooled mechanical ventilation is needed. Mechanically distributed air is supplied pre-conditioned as described above through ceiling diffuser slots. It is also extracted through the ceiling.

Ventilation boxes at each floor level are integrated into the depth of the façade, with an automatically controlled damper. Alternate boxes act as inlet and outlet vents, with grilles into the cavity from the top and bottom of the box respectively. The flaps can be completely closed or completely open. If it is raining or wind speeds are high, then the flaps are only opened by 10%. After closure, the flaps first open by 10%, and then by the full 100%. In all, there are 3.3 linear kilometres of ventilation boxes in the façade of this building.

For natural ventilation, it is necessary for the users to open their inner windows manually. The ventilation flaps in the outer façade, which admit air into the cavity, are automatically controlled. Outer offices are side ventilated from the double skin cavity, and inner offices secondarily from the atrium.

A red light on the room 'switching' panel notifies users when the mechanical ventilation is in operation, and good practice would result in them closing the inner windows (may need education).

The atrium is naturally ventilated. Four areas of glass louvres provide 40m^2 of openings in the two end walls. One bank of louvres is situated at the bottom of the glazed wall, and the other at the top. Various control strategies can provide 25%, 75%, and 100% opening. The glass louvres are controlled according to wind speed and direction. In windy conditions, one side can be closed to avoid wind travelling through the building.

Corridors, toilets and conference rooms in the centre of the plan are mechanically ventilated in line with German regulations.

Daylighting

Full-height glazing ensures maximum exposure to daylight, and views over the city. Inner offices are secondarily lit from the atrium, which has fully glazed walls at each end. The top three office floors have their own central atrium, lit from above.

Artificial lighting

The artificial lighting is not responsive to daylight conditions. Users are responsible for turning lights off when daylight is sufficient. However, there is automatic provision for sweeped shut-down at the end of the working day. A highly efficient light fitting was specially developed, utilizing fluorescent tubes to provide both uplighting and downlighting.

Solar control

Ventetian blinds are situated 200mm behind the outer face of the building, within the double skin cavity. The blinds are automatically lowered in response to photocell detectors on each façade, which indicate if the sun is shining on a particular building face. Once they are lowered, a second impulse adjusts their tilt to 45°, which still allows daylight into the building, but reduces glare. If the sun is not directly shining on a particular façade, then the blinds are raised. The blinds have three tilting positions, which can be adjusted by the user's light 'switch': completely closed, 45° tilt, and horizontal for the reflection of high summer sun. Users also have the facility to override whether the blinds are up or down through the same switch.

The 1.4m depth of the cavity also provides a degree of solar protection in ensuring that most (high angle) direct sunlight is prevented from entering the inhabited zone.

Controls

A BMS controls the atrium vents, the ventilation flaps, the blinds, lights, mechanical ventilation, heating and cooling, fire and security. A European installations bus connects the control system for the lighting and blinds. A separate bus system is used to control the heating, cooling and ventilating plant.

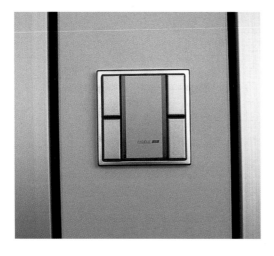

There are sensors for wind speed and direction, outside temperature, cavity temperatures, outside humidity, global insolation and photocells outside light levels.

The ventilation boxes are controlled according to pressure differentials across the office floors. Pressure difference is limited to 50Pa, so that doors are not difficult to open. Air tubes from the façade and atrium connect to a special mon-

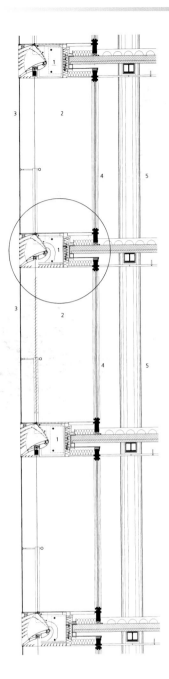

itoring facility on the fifteenth floor. The differential pressure is measured for each side of the building, and the ventilation flaps adjusted accordingly.

User control

Users have a special 'switch' panel by the door, which enables them to turn lights on and off, and adjust the cavity blinds. Room temperature can be varied by ±4°C by a separate turntable dial. A 'How to …' booklet provides users with information about the building's operating strategy.

Operating modes

In winter, mechanical ventilation will operate when temperatures fall below 5°C. The flaps in the ventilation boxes are closed when the mechanical ventilation is in operation. The atrium will be opened periodically to avoid condensation, automatically activated by humidity levels. The atrium vents are only opened at the top, to avoid cold downdraughts. The radiant heating panels will be charged between 6 and 9am, with heating provided by occupancy gains during the remainder of the day. The cavity blinds will operate automatically according to insolation.

At night in the winter, all ventilation flaps are closed, and the cavity blinds can be lowered for additional insulation.

On a normal day, all ventilation flaps are opened unless wind speeds exceed 9m/s. If this threshold is reached, the flaps are damped to the 10% position. If the pressure differential exceeds 50Pa, the flaps are closed. Inner windows are opened according to user desires. If the ventilation flaps are closed a red indicator light notifies users that mechanical ventilation is in operation, and that inner windows should be closed. There is unlikely to be any demand for heating, which will be satisfied by incident gains.

If the outside temperature exceeds 22°C, pre-cooled mechanical ventilation takes over from the natural ventilation. However, the ventilation flaps are kept open to prevent the blinds in the cavity from overheating.
On summer nights, all ventilation flaps are opened for nighttime cooling of the building structure. Users are asked to leave the inner windows open overnight.

Performance

Monitoring has been performed by DS-Plan. In particular, the performance of the façade is being closely monitored. Tests have shown that air leaving the cavity is 6°C hotter than incoming air, suggesting that it is performing a useful cooling effect on the blinds. Air coming into the offices is only 1 or 2°C hotter than outside air.

Delivered energy consumption

Delivered energy consumption figures are not yet available, as the building is not fully occupied. During the design phase, heating was simulated at 30kWh/m^2 per year.

Design process

There were many simulations performed during the design stage, particularly on the ventilation boxes. Thermal simulations were done using 'DS-therm' and computational fluid dynamic simulations were made of the ventilation boxes and the double skin cavities.

Building data

Contract value	DM150m
Area	40,000m^2
Typical floorplate	16.5m
Number of storeys	20 + B
Price per m^2	~£1250/m^2
Annual energy use	n/a
Typical energy use for building type	n/a
Annual CO_2 output	n/a
Number of sensors	40+
Visited by authors	✔
Monitored by others	✔

Tests were also conducted in the wind tunnel. A test cell was constructed by Gartner as a mock-up of the façade. They also performed acoustic tests on the ventilation boxes.

Credits

Architect: Petzinka in Overdiek, Petzinka & Partner, Ingenhoven Overdiek Petzinka & Partner, and now Petzinka Pink und Partner
Energy Consultants , Building Physiscists and Energy Monitoring: DS-Plan
Service Engineer: Jaeger, Mornhinweg Partner
Structural Engineer: Ove Arup – Lavis Stahlbau, Drees & Sommer AG
Façade: Josef Gartner & Co, Steiner Infratec
Project Manager: Dress & Sommer
Controls Installer: Johnson Controls International

References

Architectural Design, Vol 66 No 7/8, July/August 1996, 'Architecture on the Horizon', pp 36–39
l'ARCA, The International Magazine of Architecture, Design and Visual Communication, June 1993, No 72, 'A Tunnel High Rise', pp 40-45, Paolo Righetti
AIT Spezial: Intelligente Architektur 12, February 1998
Prof Dipl Ing Karl-Heinz Petzinka/Thomas Pink/Karl-Martin Selz, Petzinka Pink und Partner
Mr Rolf Lieb, DS-Plan Ingenieurgessellschaft für ganzheitliche Bauberatung-u Planung mbH

GlaxoWellcome House West

GlaxoWellcome House West
Headquarters building
Greenford
West London
United Kingdom
RMJM *Architect*
RMJM *Energy Consultant*
GlaxoWellcome plc *Client*
1995–1997 *Dates*
51.73°N *Latitude*
18°N *Primary axis of orientation*

Intelligent features

Building management system ■
Learning facility
Weather data
Responsive lights ■
Sun tracking facility
Occupant override ■
Self-generation – CHP/PV/wind
Night cooling
Solar water heating

Introduction

A new building was required on the Greenford campus of Glaxo Wellcome to consolidate operations, and serve as a headquarters building for the newly merged company. The architects were commissioned in August 1995, with a start on site in March 1996, and occupation in December 1997.

The intelligence factor

Occupant glare is reduced by automatic roller blinds that are activated by daylight sensors. Motorized dampers, which open and close automatically according to weather conditions and the desired thermal effect, moderate temperatures in the ventilated double skin.

Brief

The brief called for openness and transparency in the style of working within the building, and this had to be reflected in the design. A precisely controlled and comfortable environment was also required, to remain unchanged throughout the year.

Accommodation

The new building provides three major office levels above a semi-basement area incorporating a staff and visitors cafeteria. The simple rectangular plan is 72m long and 32m wide. It runs approximately north–south, with a full-height atrium at the centre, and enclosed service cores on the north and south ends. The long elevation, open to the east and west, is clad with a fully glazed double-skin façade above ground floor level. The building will accommodate up to 180 people.

Sunpath

Latitude
51.57°

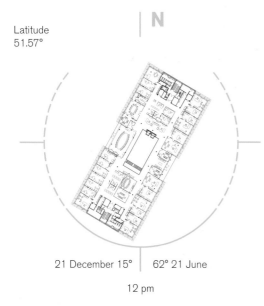

21 December 15° | 62° 21 June

12 pm

Façade transparency

North	40%
East	100%
South	40%
West	100%
Roof	0%

U-values

Double skin	1.20W/m^{2}K
Slab	n/a
Roof	n/a
G/F glazing	1.70W/m^{2}K

Energy strategy

The thermal flue on the east and west elevations was designed to intercept solar gain with horizontal timber louvre blades that shade against direct sun, protecting the conditioned office space from direct solar insolation. The second skin not only protects the solar control devices, but can also be used to temper the internal environment. Internal cooling loads are reduced in the summer by natural ventilation of solar gain in the glazed cavity, and in the winter heating demand is reduced by the closure of the cavity, creating a thermal blanket around the conditioned interior.

Site and climate

The building is located within a large established site, which largely dictated its orientation. Weather data were based on that available for Kew.

Construction

The reinforced concrete frame is largely clad with full-height glazing, which is a double skin above ground floor level. The north and south cores are covered with terracotta tiles. The structural frame was cast *in situ* with flat slabs and a steel-frame roof.

Glazing

The double skin wall on the east and west façades consists of an inner double glazed unit of 12mm laminated low-e glass, a 12mm cavity, and an outer sheet of 15mm clear float annealed. The glazed cavity contains automatically controlled roller blinds and fixed timber louvres.

Heating

The relatively deep floorplates are fully air conditioned. Some solar heat gain is predicted from the dual skin, which can be closed in winter to act as a thermal buffer, reducing the heat loss through the façade. Centralized direct gas-fired heaters provide the hot water. Heat recovery is provided by recirculation within the variable air volume (VAV) air handling plant.

Cooling

The offices are artificially cooled with a full air-conditioning system. The 1100mm glazed cavity can be opened up in summer to increase air flow, and extract heat at high level. Louvres and maintenance walkways in the glazed cavity act as heat absorbing elements, creating convective air currents, and drawing cool air from low level trap doors to be released through similar trap doors at roof level. This allows solar heat to escape from the thermal flue, and thus reduce the cooling load.

Ventilation

The building is fully air conditioned, utilizing a VAV system comprising three air handling units. The inner windows of the double skin are only openable for maintenance access. The thermal flue is naturally ventilated with control dampers to release dissipated solar gain.

Daylighting

The central atrium has large rooflights, which provide top light and vent the smoke in the event of a fire.

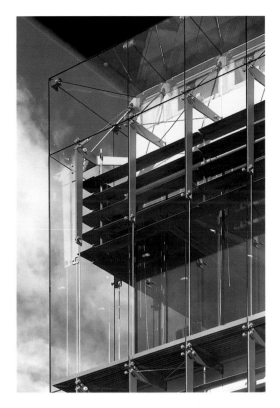

Artificial lighting

The lighting scheme is designed to maintain an illuminance level of 400 lux within cellular and open plan offices. This is achieved with high frequency dimmable downlighters, spaced horizontally at 2.4m. Individual task lighting is also provided to every desk, allowing personal control over local light levels. Presence detectors are used to activate lighting in core areas and corridor zones. Within the open plan areas, lighting is linked to photosensitive cells, which will allow the illuminance to be constantly maintained under varying daylight conditions. The executive cellular offices are provided with wall switches to enable local on/off/dimming control. The remaining office and common areas are under automatic control.

Solar control

The space inside the outer skin contains large horizontal sun control louvres, glare control blinds and slatted timber maintenance walkways. There are five 400mm wide louvres, made from western red cedar, set horizontally above standing eye level to keep out the high summer sun, while minimizing loss of views. The louvres are pivoted so they can be moved for maintenance access. Automatically controlled glare reduction blinds, activated by daylight sensors and heat sensors on three faces, drop automatically to prevent the penetration of low-angle winter sun. The blinds are made of a dark open-weave vinyl coated glass fibre, which cuts out 90% of incident light, providing additional protection for VDU users. The views out of the building remain largely unaltered.

Controls

A PC-based building management system (BMS) with a distributed intelligence structure controls the air conditioning. It supports outstations for the main plant control and outstations in the risers for the VAV terminal units. An historical data logging facility provides logging graphs with a two-week historical view. Heat and light sensors are used to determine whether to activate the fabric roller blinds. There are four zones covering each elevation, all controlled from a master panel. Each floor can be switched on or off at the BMS supervisor for maintenance and window cleaning.

User control

Local control of the blinds is also provided in specific areas where automatic control may be distracting, such as conference rooms and the second floor executive offices.

Operating modes

In the winter, the sun is low and the heat produced, if any, is beneficial. The dampers at the top and bottom of the double skin are kept closed and the cavity acts as a warm 'blanket' to the building for increased thermal insulation. The cloak of warm air also reduces heat loss at nighttime.

In the summer, air is let into the double skin cavity at the bottom, and out at the top, through motorized dampers that ventilate the cavity and keep temperatures down. The summertime effect creates a cavity that intercepts solar gain and protects office spaces from direct insolation. It encloses and protects additional shading devices, louvres and walkways. These fixed elements absorb heat from solar gain, creating air currents, which draw in cool air from low level. Cool air is warmed as it extracts heat from the louvres and walkways and heat gains through insolation are expelled from the cavity at high level.

The air-conditioning system is shut down at night in both summer and winter.

Intelligent control

	Passive	Manual	Automatic
Daylight adjustment – reflection/protection	■		
Glare control – blinds/louvres/fixed		■	■
Responsive artificial lighting control			■
Heating control			■
Heat recovery – warmth/cooling			■
Cooling control			■
Ventilation control			■
Fabric control – windows/dampers/doors			■
Insulation – night/solar			■

Building data

Contract value	£17.84m
Area	8350m²
Typical floorplate	30m
Number of storeys	4
Price per m²	£2135/m²
Annual energy use	~300kWh/m²*
Typical energy use for building type	568kWh/m²†
Annual CO_2 output	~119kg/m²‡
Number of sensors	183§
Visited by authors	✗
Monitored by others	✔

*Estimated during design phase.
†BRE figures.
‡Assuming a 1/3:2/3 split between gas and electricity and CO_2
  outputs of 0.19 kg and 0.50 kg respectively [BRE].
§VAV box temperature sensors.

Performance

The building was monitored during its first year of operation. A facilities management contractor performs energy monitoring on behalf of the client by pulse modulation metering.

Delivered energy consumption

Early calculations in the design phase suggested an estimated energy consumption of approximately 300kWh/m².

Design process

Arup Façade Engineering thermally modelled the flue to calculate air temperatures and velocities under different conditions, and to size the top and bottom dampers. Other computer simulations were performed to calculate sun shading effects, and the exact angles at which protection would be required.

The following figures were calculated for the double skin.

Mean solar gain factor (proportion of sun's heat transmitted into room)	0.08–0.12 (0.26 norm)
Summer U-value:	1.2W/m²K (1.8W/m²K norm)
Winter U-value:	1.5W/m²K (2.4W/m²K norm)
Cavity temperature (peak summer)	28.6–35.8°C
Roomside glass temperature (peak summer)	24.5–29.8°C (45.3°C norm)
Sound insulation	30dB(A) (24dB(A) norm)

Credits

Client: GlaxoWellcome Plc
Architect: RMJM London Ltd
Structural Engineer/Building Services/Landscape Architect:
  RMJM London Ltd
QS: Yeoman & Edwards
Façade Engineer: Arup Façade Engineering
Construction Manager: Mace

References

Architects Journal, 'Glass Act', 12 June 1997
Lighting Control Strategy, anon
Ventilated Façade Solar Control and Glare Study, RMJM, London
  Ltd, February 1996
Shane Lincoln/Jack Lubinski, RMJM
Andrew Hall, Arup Façade Engineering

The Environmental Building

The Environmental Building
B1 office building
Building Research Establishment (BRE)
Garston, Hertfordshire
United Kingdom
Feilden Clegg Architects *Architect*
Max Fordham & Partners *Energy Consultant*
BRE *Client*
1994–1996 *Dates*
51.73°N *Latitude*
–7°N *Primary axis of orientation*

Intelligent features

Building management system	■
Learning facility	
Weather data	■
Responsive lights	■
Sun tracking facility	■
Occupant override	■
Self-generation – CHP/PV/wind	■
Night cooling	■
Solar water heating	

Introduction

The BRE initiated the design of new offices for the Fire Research Station, which was to be relocated to its Garston site in April 1994. The architects were selected by competition from over 80 architect-led teams. The new building is a landmark building, intended to be a replicable example of cutting-edge environmental design. The project was to be based on the new performance specification, Energy Efficient Office of the Future, devised by BRECSU in collaboration with a group of key companies and other interested organizations. It was also decided to adopt a new method of procurement, in the form of the New Engineering Contract. As a result, all consultants were involved from the earliest stages of design, and were joined by the main contractor during the production information stage to assist with value engineering and advising on buildability. The completed building has since been heralded by the government as a 'key exemplar of leading edge British creativity' [BD 1319] and was nominated as a 'Millennium Product'.

The intelligence factor

This building is naturally ventilated with the assistance of automatically controlled windows at high level. Users are equipped with infrared remote control devices to individually determine ventilation levels (windows), shading (glass louvres) and lighting. In addition, daylight sensors automatically regulate the lighting according to daylight levels. The building is night cooled by automatically controlled ventilation of the concrete structure. As well as co-ordinating the user requirements, a sophisticated building management system (BMS) controls the heating, ventilation and cooling systems for optimum comfort.

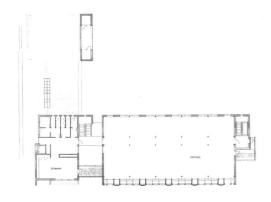

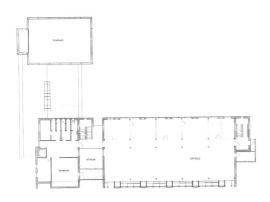

Sunpath

Latitude
51.73°

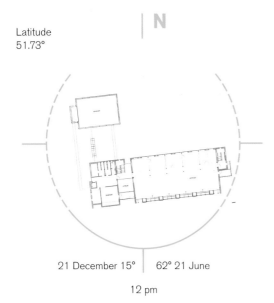

21 December 15° | 62° 21 June

12 pm

Brief

The initial brief simply called for a flexible and functional office for 100 people, suitable for a mix of open-plan and cellular spaces. The stringent requirements of the performance specification set consumption levels at 30% better than BRECSU's best-practice targets. This equated to 47kWh/m^2/year for gas, 36kWh/m^2/year for electricity and a fabric leakage rate of no more than 5m^3/m^2 of envelope at an internal pressure of 25Pa. For comfort, internal temperatures were not to drop below 18°C, and in summer the temperature (dry resultant) was targeted not to rise above 28°C for more than 1% of the working hours, and no higher than 25°C for 5% of annual hours of operation. Seminar facilities for the whole BRE site were also added to the brief, but these did not have to meet the same stringent performance criteria.

Accommodation

The resultant building is an L-shaped plan with a three-storey office wing (30m by 13.5m), fronting a landscaped area to the south and a new parking area for 70 cars to the north. The offices (1350m^2) are on a long axis running roughly east-west, with a southern zone for open plan spaces 7.5m deep, a 1.5m circulation route and a 4.5m zone to the north to accommodate cellular offices. The seminar facilities and exhibition space are located adjacent to the entrance atrium, with the main seminar room (100) on the northern side of the building, and two smaller seminar rooms on the first and second floors (2 × 20) on the south side. The building has been designed to accommodate 100 staff, and offers seminar facilities for up to 140 people.

Energy strategy

As well as benefiting from some passive solar gain, the building is heated by a low-pressure hot water system supplying an underfloor heating circuit and perimeter radiators. The building is naturally ventilated as the main method of controlling summertime temperatures, using the slab to absorb heat during the day and be cooled down by ventilation at night. The underfloor heating circuit can also be used for summertime active cooling, fed by borehole water at 10–12°C. Cross-ventilation is the predominant mode of ventilation, with single-sided ventilation for the cellular offices, and some stack effect ventilation on the south side via the chimneys. Building integrated photovoltaics on the south-facing wall contribute up to 1.5kW to the building's electricity supply.

Site and climate

The BRE campus is located on the outskirts of Watford in southern England, adjacent to the M1 motorway. It consists of a large number of buildings surrounded by countryside. The site for the new Building 16 is at the heart of the campus, and had previously been occupied by workshop buildings that were destroyed by fire. Average temperatures are in the region of 10.7°C (1994) over the year, and solar radiation averages 144W/m^2 (1994).

Construction

Steel columns on a 6m grid support precast concrete shells with an *in situ* filling. The walls are faced with second-hand stock bricks, with 100mm of cavity insulation, and an inner leaf of 150mm blockwork, finished with dense plaster. The seminar room on the north side is clad with cedar boarding. Aluminium cladding on the roof covers 150mm of insulation, with 75mm timber or 150mm concrete (north) panels on the inside soffits for thermal mass. Internally, the

Façade transparency

North	45%
East	5%
South	45%
West	5%
Roof	10%

U-values

Walls	$0.32W/m^2K$
Slab	$0.33W/m^2K$
Roof	$0.24W/m^2K$
Windows	$2.00W/m^2K$

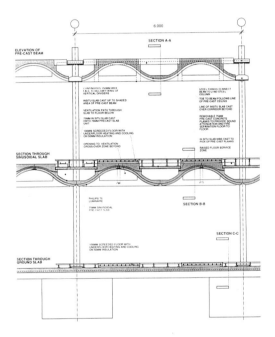

soffits to the sinusoidal concrete slabs are left exposed. Recycled mahogany is used for parquet flooring, and carpet is laid on screed (gypsum) in the offices.

Glazing

The main windows are composite, with lacquered softwood frames internally and white powder-coated aluminium outside. The double glazing has a low-emissivity coating and an argon gas filling between the panes, giving a U-value of $2.0W/m^2K$. The windows can be opened manually at low level, or automatically by the BMS at high level.

Heating

Two low-NO_x natural gas-fired boilers feed a low-pressure hot water heating loop with a total capacity of 240kW. The lead boiler is a condensing boiler (110kW). The three heating circuits supply the underfloor heating, the perimeter radiator circuit for the offices, and the underfloor heating coil and perimeter heating coil for the main seminar room. Pipes for the underfloor heating run in bands in the floor screed, covering 38% of the office floor area. The response of the underfloor circuit is slow and perimeter radiators (fitted with TRVs) were provided to give a faster response, and to give occupants some sense of control over their thermal environment. The heating system has standard optimizing software, with a self-learning facility to adopt the most efficient operation.

The fresh air inlet into the seminar space is also fitted with a heater battery to maintain a minimum supply air temperature. In winter, any fresh air that is required in the offices is partly pre-heated by the slab as it is admitted through high level windows via designated concrete ducts.

Hot water is supplied from a central calorifier in the first floor plant room. To reduce distribution losses the office kitchens have storage electric water heaters.

Cooling

Natural ventilation is used to control summertime temperatures, and can be supplemented by active cooling, where cold water is pumped through the underfloor heating circuit. Windows have lower side-hung casements, which can be manually opened, and upper motorized hopper windows with translucent glass. The upper windows connect alternately via holes in the edge beam to the upper side of the sinusoidal concrete slab and on via a precast concrete duct to the corridor zone. The exposed slab soffit is the main exposed thermal mass, helping to limit peak temperatures and provide the thermal inertia required to shift the highest temperatures until later in the day. It also allows some heat transfer between air and concrete in the form of 'coolth' which has been stored in the slab from the previous night. The top floor's pitched roof is framed in glulam beams with 75mm thick timber boarding providing some additional thermal mass. At this level, automatically controlled clerestorey windows promote cross ventilation. The upper windows throughout the building can be opened by the BMS at night to induce cooling of the thermal mass.

Cool water can be drawn from a 70m deep borehole, which can be pumped into the plantroom at around 1.5 litres/second, maintaining all-year round temperatures of between 10 and 12°C. In the plantroom, two stainless steel heat exchangers connect the borehole water to the underfloor circuit for the offices and seminar room. It is estimated that the active cooling should reduce peak temperatures by 1–2°C.

Ventilation

Cross-ventilation is the predominant mode of air transfer, with single-sided ventilation for the cellular offices. There are both high-level hopper windows under BMS control and low-level openable windows for user control. The building is 'purged' at night with cool air drawn through the floor slabs to cool the structure for the next day. During the day, ventilation is controlled on temperature sensors in the main office areas and by CO_2 levels in the main seminar room. The ground floor toilets are ventilated by a mechanical system, whereas opening windows ventilate the kitchen and smaller toilets on the upper floors.

The south façade has five ventilation towers which are fronted with etched glass blocks, offering the opportunity for BRE to investigate whether there is a useful solar contribution to the stack effect here. The ventilation stacks are openable at their backs on the ground and first floor to provide additional (solar preheated) air inlets, so improving passive fresh-air ventilation and night cooling when needed. It is hoped that there will be a degree of stack-driven airflow from the ground and first floors, assisted by small propeller fans in extreme conditions, with a 'siphon effect' drawing fresh air in through the windows on the north façade.

The second floor, which rises to 5m at its apex, is different in that it is not connected to the stacks, but instead has a split-pitch roof with automatically controlled north-facing clerestorey windows. They provide additional daylight and a route for air to leave by natural buoyancy or wind forces.

In the main seminar space, air is drawn through a heating/cooling battery in an undercroft below the stage, and then through ducts within the raised seating. Extract air is released at high level, with automatically openable doors to control the flow.

Electricity generation

The south-facing wall of the seminar rooms is clad with a $47m^2$ array of photovoltaic (PV) cells, producing a peak output of 1.5kW. The installation was funded by the DTI late on in the design process. Electricity is generated as DC current, and fed directly into the main electrical switchroom, where two inverters convert the power to 240V AC. The PV cells are thin film amorphous silicon, and have generated over 1500kWh during the first year of operation [BRE]. Averaged over the year, output is estimated to provide approximately the same electrical power as the anticipated artificial lighting load for the building. BRE will be evaluating the effectiveness of photovoltaics mounted on a vertical face, with improved exposure to low winter sun, which coincidentally is when electricity is needed more and when lower ambient temperatures should lead to increased operational efficiency.

Daylighting

Daylight is maximized with large areas of glazing on the north and south façades, giving daylight factors of over 2% across the 13.5m floorplate. Penetration is assisted by 3.7m ceiling heights, which are also painted white, and glass louvres on the south side which double as lightshelves in their horizontal position (50% reflectance). As well as the main windows, etched-glass hoppers to the rear of the glass block ventilation stacks provide some additional daylight.

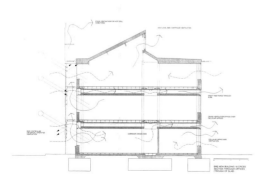

Artificial lighting

A fully integrated lighting system has been installed that automatically compensates for daylight levels and occupancy, controlling each light fitting separately. Highly efficient fluorescent tubes (Phillips T5) provide 300 lux on the working plane. Integral sensors measure internal light levels and movement, dimming the lamps (100% to 0%) if there is sufficient daylighting, or switching them off if a room is unoccupied. The sensors also have an infrared receiver, which allows users to control light levels by means of a hand-held controller.

Solar control

The south façade is protected both by an external steel framework providing access walkways, and rotating glass louvres designed to cut out all direct sun to the interior, whilst still letting in considerable diffuse skylight. The translucent glass louvres span in bays between the ventilation towers, and are programmed to intercept the sun during the hours it can penetrate the south façade. When it is dull, they park above horizontal, becoming lightshelves. The translucent glass louvres (40% light transmission) are 400mm deep and made of 10mm toughened clear float glass, with a screen-printed white ceramic coating on their underside. The motorized louvres are adjusted by the BMS every 15 minutes. Occupants can override the automatic setting of the louvres to reduce glare if they wish (BMS resets them to optimum position at the end of the day). The protruding ventilation stacks are also conceived as providing some shading against low angle oblique sun from the east and west. Internally, blue fabric roller blinds are provided for additional occupant-controlled glare reduction.

The Environmental Building **79**

Intelligent control	Passive	Manual	Automatic
Daylight adjustment – reflection/protection		■	■
Glare control – blinds/louvres/fixed	■	■	■
Responsive artificial lighting control		■	■
Heating control		■	■
Heat recovery – warmth/cooling	■		
Cooling control			■
Ventilation control		■	■
Fabric control – windows/dampers/doors			■
Insulation – night/solar	■		

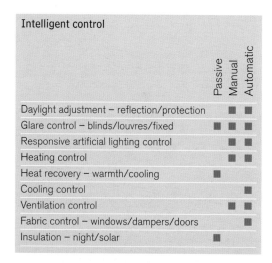

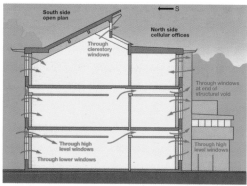

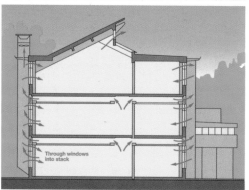

Controls

The BMS was developed jointly by Trend and Phillips (Trend Echelon Lon-Works™) to control ventilation systems, heating, window shading and lights. All the controls for the BMS go through a common network provided by a LON network. The computer algorithm used to control the degree, and period of automatic window opening, relies on the sensing of internal temperature. The control algorithm for the louvres is determined by the calculated sun angle, with a provision for occupant override from the hand-held controllers. The whole system provides for 5-minute data logging over an extended period, and was linked to Max Fordham's offices for fine tuning during the first year and commissioning.

Each bank of luminaires is fitted with two sensors that act as occupancy sensors, light-level sensors and infrared receivers for a hand-held controller, which will be used by occupants to call for more ventilation, lighting, or solar shading. On receiving a signal, a message 'packet' is sent on the LON network to be picked up by the BMS and translated as a command to move the relevant window, switch the lights, or adjust the bank of glass louvres. The BMS also collects weather data from a rooftop station that measures wind and outside air temperature. Other standard energy-saving techniques are also employed by the BMS.

User control

Every control system is planned to be capable of being overridden manually, with sensor-based automatic reset after a set time limit. An infrared controller allows users to control lights and override the programmed settings of nearby windows and louvres. Users can also open low-level windows for local ventilation and lower roller blinds for additional glare control. Each heating zone is provided with a local thermostat offering temperature control via a 'plus or minus' dial.

Operating modes

Winter day – the windows into the ventilation ducts in the slabs in the offices will open to provide minimum fresh air, allowing the slab to pre-heat the air. Manually operated trickle vents in the windows provide fresh air to the top floor offices. The radiators and the underfloor heating will run to maintain minimum temperatures. The system will favour the underfloor heating coils over the radiators, as this form of heating is slightly more efficient.

Winter night – provide no ventilation to the building and only heat to prevent frost within the building.

Summer day – provide minimum ventilation to the building unless the building is above its summer temperature set point. In this case, the automatic windows will open to cool the building and the borehole cooling will run if required. If the outside air is hotter than the internal air, then the windows will remain in their minimum position. If it is windy and raining, then the travel of the windows will be limited to 25% open. If it is raining, the stack windows will close, as these are top-opening hopper type windows. If the temperature in the offices exceeds a second set point, then the stack fans (48W) will be activated to increase ventilation.

Summer night – the upper windows will open to remove the excess heat that has built up in the building over the previous day, but only if it is cooler outside than inside. This free cooling is given a chance to lower the internal temperature. If it is not cooling the building fast enough, then the borehole pump will run, and additional cooling will be delivered to the underfloor coils.

The main seminar room operates in a very similar way to the offices, except that CO_2 sensors control the fresh air ventilation. In the winter, the air will be pre-heated to maintain a minimum supply air temperature.

Performance

Research and monitoring criteria were developed at the planning stage, and performance assessment, which has run from the outset, is continuing after occupation. The building is to be extensively monitored, and the results disseminated by BRECSU as part of the DETR-funded Energy Efficiency Best Practice Programme. The University of Westminster is also involved in the monitoring and analysis of the 'novel features' of the project as part of a THERMIE-funded grant. The post-occupancy monitoring will cover energy consumption, quality and comfort of the internal environment, daylighting levels, performance of the glass louvres, airflow in the stacks and floors, air change rates, open plan space utilization, stresses in the superstructure from construction and occupancy loads, and photovoltaics.

Delivered energy consumption

Energy consumption is set to remain within the target of $83kWh/m^2$ per year. Monitoring began in the summer of 1997. The building received a record BREEAM rating on completion, with 39 out of a possible 42 credits, making it the highest number of credits which any building has been awarded.

Building data

Contract value	£2.65m
Area	2050m^2
Typical floorplate	13.5m
Number of storeys	3
Price per m^2	£1293/m^2
Annual energy use	83kWh/m^2
Typical energy use for building type	120kWh/m^2
Annual CO_2 output	34kg/m^2
Number of sensors	300
Visited by authors	✔
Monitored by others	✔

Design process

CFD modelling was used to predict temperatures and airflow (Colt Virtual Reality Ltd). Other computer simulations indicated that the lighting control system would reduce peak temperatures by around 1°C due to the reduced power consumption caused by more efficient control of the lamps. A TAS simulation was performed by EDSL.

In addition, physical modelling was performed by Cambridge Environmental Research Consultants with a salt-water model of the natural ventilation strategy for the building. The following design loads were used: solar – 3.6W/m^2, occupancy – 8.2W/m^2, lighting load – 8.5W/m^2 and equipment – 10W/m^2. The external glass louvres were tested by Colt International (EOF member) and the University of Westminster.

Credits

Client: BRE (DoE/BRECSU/EOF Group) – Mike Clift
Architects: Feilden Clegg Architects
Service Engineer: Max Fordham & Partners
Structural Engineer: Buro Happold
Landscape Architect: Nicholas Pearson Associates, Bath
QS: Turner & Townsend, Bristol
Project Manager: Bernard Williams Associates (BWA Project Services), Bromley
Contractor: John Sisk & Son (NEC Contract)
M/E Contractor: Norstead
Controls Installer: Palcon Systems
CDM Planning Supervisor: Symonds Travers Morgan
EOF Members: Arup R&D, British Gas Plc, BRE, BRECSU, Caradon Trend Ltd, Colt International Ltd, Eastern Electricity, Electricity Association, Hepworth Building Products Ltd, Laing Technology Group, Philips Lighting Ltd, Pilkington United Kingdom Ltd and Stanhope Properties Ltd.

References

A Performance Specification for the Energy Efficient Office of the Future, Energy Efficiency Best Practice Programme, Crown Copyright December 1995
AIT, Spezial: Intelligente Architektur, 11, December 1997
Architects Journal, 23 May 1996, Vol 203, No 20, pp 51–53
Building, 22 November 1996
Building Design, No 1192, 30 September 1994, pp5
Building Design, No 1319, 5 September 1997, pp1
Building Services Journal, May 1995, Vol 17, No 5
Building Services Journal, March 1997, Vol 19, No 3, pp 18–23
Description of the Mechanical and Electrical Services in the New Low Energy Office and Seminar Facility for the Building Research Establishment, Max Fordham & Partners, August 1997
RIBA Profile, April 1997, pp 18–25
The Environmental Building: A Model for the 21st Century, *BRE promotional literature*
The New Environmental Office: BRE, Watford, Energy Matters Conference, 2 December 1997
Bill Gething/Peter Clegg, Feilden Clegg Architects
Matt Grace/Mike Clift, Building Research Establishment
Bart Stevens, Max Fordham & Partners

Helicon

Helicon
Speculative office and retail development
One South Place
City of London
United Kingdom
Sheppard Robson *Architect*
Ove Arup & Partners *Energy Consultant*
London and Manchester Property Asset
  Management *Client*
1992–1996 *Dates*
51.50°N *Latitude*
17°N *Primary axis of orientation*

Intelligent features

Building management system	■
Learning facility	
Weather data	■
Responsive lights	■
Sun tracking facility	
Occupant override	■
Self-generation – CHP/PV/wind	
Night cooling	
Solar water heating	

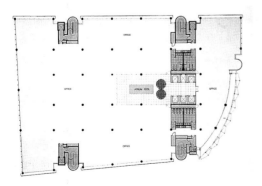

Introduction

This project was realized despite the recession of the early 1990s largely because of a pre-let for a flagship Marks & Spencer retail store for five of the 11 floors. This was combined with a new bank which resulted in a development comprising 43% of pre-let retail space. The remaining six floors provided 11,500m^2 of offices arranged around a raised atrium, which were to be let on a speculative basis. It was desired by the architects to provide maximum transparency for the building, whilst realizing the requirement for adequate solar control without resorting to tinted and reflective glasses.

The intelligence factor

The void of the double skin glazing can be naturally ventilated with automatic openings, which induce a stack effect to dispel unwanted solar gain. Blinds in the cavity can be lowered and tilted automatically in response to outside light and solar intensity, and inside light levels and inside temperature. Timed sweeps, occupancy detectors, and photocell sensors automatically control the lighting.

Sunpath

Latitude
51.50°

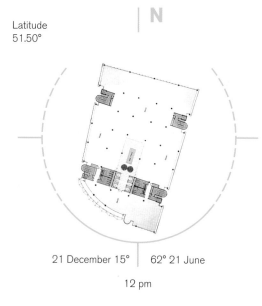

21 December 15° | 62° 21 June

12 pm

Façade transparency

North	15%
East	100%
South	70%
West	100%
Roof	10%

U-values

Walls	0.40W/m²K
Slab	n/a
Roof	n/a
Windows	1.10W/m²K

Brief

The main aim of the brief was to design a building with an improved comfort and energy agenda over previous generations of speculative office developments.

Accommodation

The six office floors, which start on the third storey, are arranged around an atrium with setbacks inside and out to provide terraces and accessible outside spaces. The first three levels and two basements provide 9000m² of shop floor, storage and delivery access for the retail units.

Energy strategy

The energy strategy relies on the control of solar energy through the façade to minimize the importing of energy to maintain internal comfort. This is provided by a displacement ventilation system with chilled ceilings, and relies on minimum fresh air provision, with heating and cooling provided within the space.

Site and climate

The building occupies an island site in the City of London, bound by roads on all four sides: Finsbury Pavement, South Place, Dominion Street and Lackington Street.

Construction

Opaque elements are clad with a silver-grey powder coated aluminium panel system. The glazing on the east and west façades consists of a triple glazed façade, creating an 885mm cavity that contains solar control blinds and the support structure.

Glazing

The double skin consists of an outer pane of frameless single glazing (12mm toughened) and inner double-glazed panels. It is designed to act as a thermal flue with automatically controlled vents and tilting blinds for solar control. Bombproof 44.5mm laminated double-glazing protects the retail frontages. Large hanging vertical steel trusses suspended from roof level support a structural glazing assembly on the southwest façade. The atrium roof is glazed with 50% reflective glass.

Heating

Heating in winter is provided partly by a perimeter heating system with finned tubes laid in trenches, and partly through a tempered air supply. Standard non-condensing boilers in the basement plantroom provide hot water for the ventilation air handling units, perimeter heating and domestic hot water. A third small capacity boiler can provide DHW only for summertime operation.

The double skin system on the east and west façades can be kept closed to act as a thermal buffer, reducing wintertime heat loss.

Cooling

A chilled ceiling system makes internal conditions feel more comfortable than space temperatures would indicate, with a radiant cooling effect. Chilled ceiling panels integrated into the perforated metal ceiling tiles account for around 36% of the ceiling area, with almost complete coverage in the outer 4.5m

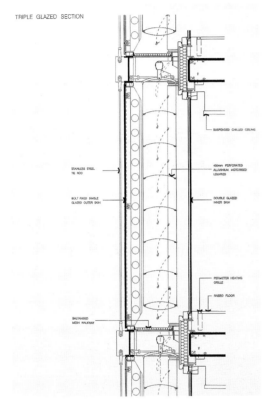

TRIPLE GLAZED SECTION

SUSPENDED CHILLED CEILING

STAINLESS STEEL
TIE ROD

450mm PERFORATED
ALUMINIUM MOTORISED
LOUVRES

BOLT FIXED SINGLE
GLAZED OUTER SKIN

DOUBLE GLAZED
INNER SKIN

PERIMETER HEATING
GRILLE

RAISED FLOOR

GALVANISED
MESH WALKWAY

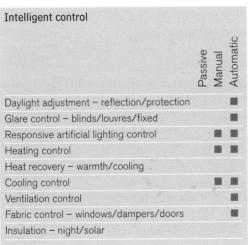

Intelligent control

	Passive	Manual	Automatic
Daylight adjustment – reflection/protection			■
Glare control – blinds/louvres/fixed			■
Responsive artificial lighting control		■	■
Heating control		■	■
Heat recovery – warmth/cooling			
Cooling control		■	■
Ventilation control			■
Fabric control – windows/dampers/doors			■
Insulation – night/solar			

perimeter zone (to offset solar gain). A two-port valve connected to an adjustable room thermostat is responsible for the control of each cooling zone (13.5m^2). Chilled water is distributed to local on-floor heat exchangers at 8°C flow, with water leaving the heat exchangers at 15°C. It is supplied by two dual-compressor centrifugal chillers, which use the ozone-friendly refrigerant R134a. The system can be run directly from the cooling towers for part of the year (estimated at 16%), when wet bulb temperatures should be low enough to meet the 15°C supply without the need to run the chillers.

The double skin system on the east and west façades can be automatically opened with low- and high-level openings, which produce a stack effect to take away unwanted solar build-up in the cavity, before it gets into the building. Aluminium blinds in the cavity are raised, lowered and tilted in response to external solar gains, lighting levels and temperatures.

Ventilation

The five-storey double skin system allowed the internal environment to be designed without the VAV systems usual in speculative office developments. It was estimated that despite the 15% increase in the cost, that less plant space (premium space location) would be required, and that operating costs should be 16% lower.

Air is fed into a pressurized floor plenum supplied from four risers that connect to the air handling plant. It is supplied into the space through floor-mounted circular grilles at 18°C, providing approximately three air changes per hour (2.5litres/s/m^2). As the inlet air is warmed by contact with warmer bodies, such as people and computers, it rises to meet the water-chilled ceiling panels (flow temperatures of 15°C). Extract is via a similar plenum at high level, with air passing through the luminaires on exhaust. It is then expelled at high level in the atrium.

Daylighting

Full-height glazing provides daylight to the relatively deep floor plates of the retail areas. Higher up the building, daylight into the office areas is maximized by stepping back the office floorplates to increase daylight levels at the base of the atrium (three storeys up).

Artificial lighting

Office lighting is provided by fluorescent luminaires recessed into the metal ceiling. The lighting is automatically controlled by timed sweeps, passive infra-red detectors and photocells. All of the lights can be locally overridden. The control strategy relates to banks of luminaires parallel to the outer façade.

Solar control

Maintenance walkways within the double skin void provide a degree of solar protection at each floor level. Dynamic solar control is provided by aluminium louvre blades, which can be automatically adjusted to control solar gain and glare. The large horizontal louvres are made from curved aluminium sheet 450mm wide, 3m long and with a vertical spacing of 425mm. Each blade is 14% perforated, giving a maximum solar absorptivity of 0.3 and a minimum solar reflectivity of 0.7. The louvres, which are provided between floors two and six, can be tilted (up to 70°) according to solar conditions. They should not be down simultaneously on east and west façades. Studies suggested that the blinds

Building data

Contract value	£27.85m
Area	27,000m^2
Typical floorplate	~10–16m
Number of storeys	9 + 2B
Price per m^2	£1030/m^2
Annual energy use	177kWh/m^2
Typical energy use for building type	348kWh/m^2
Annual CO_2 output	n/a
Number of sensors	n/a
Visited by authors	✔
Monitored by others	✗

Credits

Developer: London and Manchester Assurance
Client: London and Manchester Property Asset Management
Structural: John Savage Associates
Space-frame wall: Ove Arup & Partners
Service Engineer: Ove Arup & Partners
QS: Silk & Frazier
Main Conractor: Laing London
Cladding: Scheldebouw bv (De Schelde)
Louvres: Technical Blinds

References

Architects Journal, 13 July 1994, Vol 200, No 2
Architecture Today, AT 73, November 1996
Building, 3 November 1995, Vol CCLX No 7915, Issue 44
Building Design, No 1174, 27 May 1994
Building Services, September 1996, Vol 18 No 7
Alistair Guthrie, Ove Arup & Partners
Graham Francis/Graham Anthony, Sheppard Robson
London and Manchester Property Asset Management

would be lowered for 20–30% of the year (assuming an occupancy of 07:00–19:00), and up to 45% of the time in summer. Fixed external shading at high level provides solar shading to recessed upper levels.

Controls

As well as providing the traditional functions of controlling lifts, fire services, security and HVAC, the building management system (BMS) also controls the opening of the ventilated double skin cavities. A temperature sensor mounted in the cavity is linked to the BMS, which will open the louvres to ventilate away excess solar gain if void temperatures exceed 28°C. It is also programmed to remain closed in winter to provide a thermal buffer of warmed air.

For ease of installation and commissioning, a separate control system was provided for the solar control louvres in the dual skin cavity. The blinds can be lowered to the shading position in response to either a solarimeter mounted on the roof, or an external light level detector in the cavity. The blinds are lowered automatically on a floor-by-floor basis when the solar radiation on the façade exceeds 150W/m^2. The angle of tilt is primarily controlled by a photocell detecting the internal light levels, but a zone temperature thermostat can also close the blinds in a given zone to minimize solar gain. When the space temperatures subsequently fall, zone control will revert to maximizing daylight and the tilt angle of the louvres will be reduced. Overall there are two control zones per façade (floors 2, 3 and 4, and floors 5 and 6). A time delay of 30 minutes on the blind response ensures that the blinds are not constantly adjusting to variable conditions.

User control

Users have control over the chilled ceilings and perimeter heating system through local thermostats.

Operating modes

In winter, the double skin void is kept closed to provide a thermal barrier on the outside of the building, and reduce heat loss from the offices.

In summer, the void can be opened to provide a stack effect which takes away unwanted solar gain from the cavity and the heated louvres before it gets into the building.

Performance

The predicted energy consumption for the building was 177kWh/m^2 per annum. The building has only been fully occupied for a short period and more accurate results are not yet available.

Design process

A computational fluid dynamics (CFD) study was performed during the design phase to analyse the displacement ventilation and chilled ceiling strategy. The performance of the façade was tested on the OASYS room programme.

A physical mock-up of the blind system was constructed as part of the design process.

Calculations were based on predicted internal cooling loads of 45W/m^2 (occupants – 10W, lighting – 15W, small power – 20W).

Tax Office Extension

Tax Office Extension
Government office building
Enschede
The Netherlands
Ruurd Roorda, Government Building Agency *Architect*
W/E Consultants and Esbensen Consulting Engineers
  Energy Consultant
Rijksgebouwendienst *Client*
1994–1996 *Dates*
51.57°N *Latitude*
135°N *Primary axis of orientation*

Intelligent features

Building management system	■
Learning facility	
Weather data	
Responsive lights	■
Sun tracking facility	
Occupant override	■
Self-generation – CHP/PV/wind	
Night cooling	■
Solar water heating	

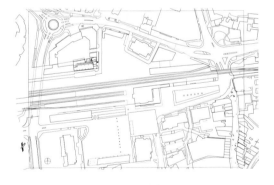

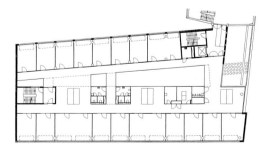

Introduction

An extension was made to the existing tax office building in Enschede by an in-house team of the Dutch Government Building Agency, which began the design process in March 1994. The project was partly funded by the Energy Comfort 2000 scheme through the European Commission's THERMIE programme. EC2000 funded the design and development of eight non-domestic buildings to demonstrate that environmentally friendly design and construction is possible. This project was completed in November 1996, and occupied in December of that year.

The intelligence factor

Intelligent vents that adjust the degree of opening based on pressure differences control the admittance of fresh air into the building, thus maintaining a

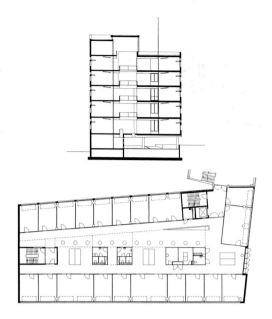

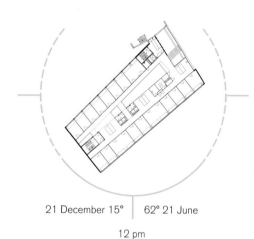

Sunpath

Latitude
51.57°

21 December 15° | 62° 21 June

12 pm

Façade transparency	
North	35%
East	25%
South	35%
West	5%
Roof	10%

U-values	
Walls	n/a
Slab	n/a
Roof	n/a
North windows	1.30W/m²K
South windows	1.60W/m²K

constant airflow in all conditions. The occupants are responsible for determining whether a vent is open or not. Vents can be left open overnight for night-time cooling, assisted by ventilation exhaust fans. The lighting can be automatically dimmed down to 30% depending on available daylight. The external sunblinds are operated partly automatically and partly manually. The building management system (BMS) controls the temperature of the heating system and manages the night ventilation system.

Brief

The EC2000 targets aim to reduce energy consumption by 50%, and CO_2 emissions by 50–70%. This is to be achieved by minimizing the energy use of air conditioning, or avoiding its use altogether, and by allowing individual control of lighting, heating and cooling where possible. The building was therefore designed to be an example of a 'passive' building with natural ventilation and optimal use of daylight and maximum control by the occupants with the intention of stimulating environmentally friendly design and construction.

Accommodation

The new extension provides two strips of 5m deep cellular offices around the support accommodation and a full-height atrium, whch is lit by a clerestorey at high level. The south facing wing has offices on the perimeter and a corridor in the middle between the toilets and computer rooms that face into the atrium. On the north side, the floor depth is narrower, with a circulation route between the atrium and the perimeter offices. A semi-basement area providing parking spaces for bicycles and cars, is also lit from the atrium above through glazed lights set into the floor. A connection with the existing building has been maintained on four of the five storeys. The extension is designed around a grid that assumes two people per office zone, which is 3.6m wide, 5.1m deep and 3m high.

Energy strategy

The energy strategy relies on natural ventilation and the use of daylight-dependent lighting to reduce energy consumption. A BMS controls the temperature of the heating system, and manages the night ventilation exhaust fans.

Site and climate

The tax office is close to the station in the centre of Enschede, with the railway alongside the main façade on the south-eastern side.

Construction

The walls are clad with a slate grey recyclable ceramic tile on the south and east sides. A pale blue render is used on the north wall. The structure is a concrete frame, with flat slabs and mushroom capped columns. The concrete ceilings are painted white internally.

Glazing

Each storey has a double row of horizontal strip windows with a lower 'vision' window for views, and an upper 'daylight' window for natural daylighting. The south-facing 'daylight' windows have a special glass that reflects solar energy whilst maintaining adequate daylight transmission (65%). Recycled aluminium window frames are used on the outer walls and softwood frames in the atrium. Manually controlled external blinds provide solar protection to the lower

vision windows. The daylight windows have a glass light transmission of 65%, and a total energy transmission of 38%. The vision windows admit up to 77% daylight, and have a total energy transmission of 65%.

Heating

Heating is provided by a perimeter radiator system, which is fed by a gas-fired high-efficiency boiler. The concrete slab is left exposed so that heat is collected and stored in the building mass.

Cooling

In line with the aims of the EC2000 project, mechanical cooling was avoided. This has been achieved by using a combination of glazing with low solar transmission (Ipasol) on the south façade, passive ventilation driven by the wind and stack effect, and exposed thermal mass. In the summer, the building can be ventilated at night at four times the daily air change rate to cool the thermal mass.

Ventilation

The building is naturally ventilated through the 23m high atrium. Fresh air enters the offices by means of 'intelligent' ventilation grilles located at high level within the wall, adjacent to the workstations on the outer façades. The vents are located above the daylight windows, at ceiling level so that the incoming air remains close to the ceiling, thus eliminating the risk of draughts. Each workstation has two vents that can be opened or closed manually. Normally one vent provides sufficient ventilation, but an extra vent is used during the summer for night cooling. The air is drawn from the office space to the atrium by means of a duct located in the space above the suspended ceiling in the corridor in order to bypass the inner areas. Acoustic attenuators in the duct avoid noise being transferred between the rooms and the corridor. In most instances, the stale air will rise up through the atrium by the stack effect. At the top of the atrium, six large ventilation outlets expel the air, assisted by a negative wind-pressure coefficient. These are controlled in response to windspeeds and internal and external temperatures. Mechanical ventilators can extract air from the atrium in exceptional conditions, for example when there is no wind, or when extra night ventilation is necessary. Individual windows can also be opened during the day to provide additional fresh air ventilation.

Air enters the rooms through self-adjusting 'intelligent' vents positioned just beneath the ceiling which adjust the amount of incoming air based on pressure difference. These 'Heycop' vents maintain a constant flow rate across the ceiling, even though the wind pressure on the façade may vary. The occupants are responsible for controlling whether a vent is open or not. The original idea was that a message on the computer screen of each occupant would advise on the optimum position for the vent. The lower 'vision' windows can also be opened manually for additional ventilation but there are acoustic problems associated with the proximity of the railway line.

Daylighting

The aim of the daylight strategy was to maintain outside views, maximize daylight, minimize the need for artificial light and avoid glare. The windows on the outer façade are split into two separate strips. A lower continuous strip of windows is intended to provide a view, whilst above, pairs of 'daylight windows' are used solely to allow extra daylight to enter the space. Aluminium lightshelves about 0.9m deep are mounted on the inside of the south-facing windows, between the two window strips. These are designed to prevent glare, and reflect part of the daylight deep into the room via the suspended ceiling units. All glazing was specified to maintain high light transmission values.

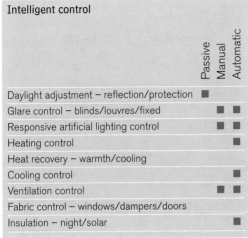

Intelligent control	Passive	Manual	Automatic
Daylight adjustment – reflection/protection	■		
Glare control – blinds/louvres/fixed		■	■
Responsive artificial lighting control		■	■
Heating control			■
Heat recovery – warmth/cooling			
Cooling control			■
Ventilation control		■	■
Fabric control – windows/dampers/doors			
Insulation – night/solar			■

Artificial lighting

High-frequency gas discharge lamps are incorporated into the lightshelves, and into suspended islands at ceiling level which also provide an acoustic absorber. Artificial light can be automatically dimmed down to 30% in response to available daylight levels. All lights are automatically switched off at the end of the working day. Local wall switches provide manual override. Monitoring has shown that the strategy produces an even distribution of daylight across the plan, with daylight factors of between 1% and 2%, and very low energy consumption for lighting of 2.5kWh/m^2.

Solar control

Venetian blinds have been mounted on the outside of the lower vision windows. The blinds are operated partly automatically, and partly by hand. A central computer control system closes the blinds in the morning as soon as necessary. During the day their operation is then left to the individual users. Internal blinds are provided for additional user-controlled glare protection. The south-facing daylight windows are not physically shaded, relying on the low transmission glazing (Ipasol).

Controls

The BMS controls the temperature of the heating system and manages the night ventilation exhaust fans. These fans can also be instructed to take over the natural ventilation ducts under certain weather conditions and in response to high internal room temperatures. The BMS also controls the external shading devices, adjusting them before the occupants arrive each morning, and again at night.

At the end of every day, a computer message informs the user of the required position of the vents. During nighttime in winter it may be necessary to close both vents, but in summer both vents must be opened to cool down the thermal mass of the building. At the very end of the day technical staff make a round through the building to ensure vents are in the correct position.

User control

Occupants have full control over the high-level vents, the windows, lighting and the sun blinds during the day. All occupants have been informed in special group sessions, through newsletters and through permanent written information on their desk about the ventilation strategy.

Operating modes

The passive ventilation strategy will run effectively in all but extreme summer conditions, such as high outside temperatures and no wind. Additional nighttime cooling and mechanical fans to assist the stack effect in the atrium will offset this effect.

Performance

The project was monitored as part of the EC2000 scheme between November 1996 and March 1998. However, the building was only 65% occupied during this period and figures should be adjusted accordingly. In general, users were found to be highly satisfied with the new extension (60% response rate). Most highly rated by the occupants were the control possibilities for heating ventilation, sun shading, artificial lighting, and glare protection.

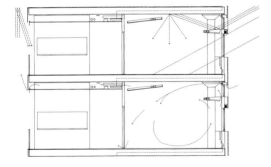

Building data

Contract value	n/a
Area	4300m^2
Typical floorplate	6.5–10m
Number of storeys	5 + B
Price per m^2	n/a
Annual energy use	141kWh/m^2*
Typical energy use for building type	342kWh/m^2
Annual CO$_2$ output	117kg/m^2
Number of sensors	n/a
Visited by authors	✗
Monitored by others	✔

*Temperature corrected figure.

Delivered energy consumption

Energy consumption was anticipated during the design phase at 165kWh/m^2, and was measured at 141kWh/m^2, which has been temperature corrected.

Design process

The proposed ventilation strategy was simulated using W/E's multi-zone ventilation model MVRM 5.0 (similar to BREEZE). Esbensen used the Radiance programme to perform a series of daylight calculations. Thermal simulations were conducted with tsbi-3, which was also used to analyse different cooling strategies.

A typical office space was also tested in a climate chamber by Peutz & Associes. All calculations for the passive cooling strategy assumed that internal loads would not exceed 37W/m^2, including occupants.

Credits

Client: Rijksgebouwendienst, Directie Oost, Arnhem (Dutch Government Building Agency, East Directorate, Arnhem)
Architects: Ruurd Roorda, Rijksgebouwendienst, (now Drexhage, Kingma en Roorda Architecten BNA, Rotterdam)
Energy Consultants: W/E Consultants (Woon Energi Adviseurs Duurzaam Bouwen), Gouda and Esbensen Consulting Engineers, Copenhagen
Building Physics: Peutz & Associes BV, Mook, NL
Structural Engineer: Rijksgebouwendienst, Directie Ontwerp en Techniek, den Haag
Contractor: Van Wijnen, Eibergen

References

Building Services, 'Future Buildings', March 1996
de Architect, The Architect (The Hague), December 1996, Vol 27 No12
New Wing Tax Office, Anon
Space for Architecture in Passive Office Building, Chiel Boonstra and Rik Vollebregt
Tax Office Extension, Enschede, The Netherlands, Partial Final Report, Energy Comfort 2000, W/E Consultants and ECD Energy and Environment
Windows – the Key to Low Energy Design, *Information Dossier No 5, March 1998*, Esbensen Consulting Engineers for EC2000
Ruurd Roorda, Drexhage, Kingma en Roorda Architecten BNA
Chiel Boonstra, W/E Consultants
Rachel Waggett, ECD Energy and Environment

Headquarters of Götz

Headquarters of Götz
Owner-occupied office building
Würzburg
Germany (D-71612)
Webler + Geissler *Architect*
Loren Butt and Marcus Püttmer *Energy Consultant*
Götz GmbH *Client*
1993–1995 *Dates*
49.71°N *Latitude*
0°N *Primary axis of orientation*

Intelligent features

Building management system	■
Learning facility	■
Weather data	■
Responsive lights	■
Sun tracking facility	■
Occupant override	■
Self-generation – CHP/PV/wind	■
Night cooling	■
Solar water heating	■

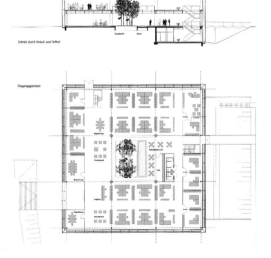

Introduction

The Götz cladding company have used this prize-winning building as a prototypical application of their range of cladding products, incorporating a sophisticated system of controls for energy conservation. The new building houses the company's sales, administrative and design departments in a light and open two-storey glass and steel pavilion.

The intelligence factor

A double skin with a 600mm cavity encloses the fully glazed building. Automatically controlled inlet and outlet flaps are used to vary the thermal performance of the glazing. Corner fans provide lateral equalization of solar gain on the north and south faces. Workplace occupancy detectors activate the artificial lighting. Tracking solar collectors feed an absorption heat pump, which provides both heating and cooling. Additional cooling can be provided by the night ventilation strategy, activated by the ventilation flaps in the double skin, sliding inner windows and a retractable roof. The BMS is programmed with neural network knowledge-based software incorporating fuzzy logic, providing the system with the ability to 'learn' the energy status of the building. Users are provided with on-screen control panels for local environmental control.

Brief

Each worker has approximately 20m² of open-plan office space, with some glazed cellular offices and meeting rooms located in the corner of the plan on the ground floor.

Accommodation

The building is simply constructed with a steel frame that spans 12m, giving 12m wide office floorplates and a central, full-height atrium measuring 12m by 12m. The atrium is lit from above by a retractable glass roof, and contains a landscaped pond and an adjacent refreshment area. Accommodation is provided for 100 people.

Energy strategy

The building is enclosed on all façades by a glazed double skin with a 600 mm cavity containing reversible venetian blinds. The lower louvres are dark coated on one side for increased absorption, and reflective on the other. The cavity collects and moderates all incident energy falling on the building face for lighting, heating and ventilation. An absorption heat pump is fed with heat from co-generating plant and active solar collectors to provide both hot and cold water.

Site and climate

The Götz office and factory are located on the industrial outskirts of the small town of Würzburg, surrounded by open countryside. The climate is described as 'continental'.

Construction

The building is constructed with a very simple steel frame spanning the full 12m bays. The floor slabs are composite construction of steel and concrete. Internally, glazed partitions are used to separate the few cellular spaces. Floors are granite for added thermal mass and fabric ceiling panels, which allow thermal contact to be maintained with the slab, hide the concrete soffit.

Glazing

The double skin which envelops the whole building consists of an outer skin of full-height double glazing, a venetian blind in the 600mm cavity, and an inner skin of double glazing with a low-e coating and sliding doors. The elevatable and sliding glass roof is triple glazed.

Heating

The building was designed to maintain a minimum internal temperature of 20°C, utilizing passive solar energy and incident heat gains from people and equipment. In low temperature conditions the double skin can be closed to allow air in the cavity to be warmed directly by the sun, or indirectly by the absorption

Façade transparency	
North	100%
East	100%
South	100%
West	100%
Roof	10%

U-values	
Double skin	1.50W/m^{2}K
Slab	1.90W/m^{2}K
Roof	0.30W/m^{2}K

louvres. The lower set of louvres are black on one side and reflective on the other, and can be rotated to absorb solar radiation, or reflect it according to internal requirements. Solar heated air can be distributed laterally around the building by ventilators to equalize the thermal load on all sides of the building.

Additional heating can be provided through the underfloor heating circuit (granite floors) which can either be supplied by solar water heating panels that track the position of the sun, or a combined heat and power unit fuelled by natural gas. The solar water heating system consists of $200m^2$ of flat-plate collectors, and is located remotely from the main building. The array is mounted on a steel framework, which is programmed to rotate according to the position of the sun, and can be turned away from the sun if heating is not required. In periods of low solar insolation the thermal energy can be boosted to a usable temperature of 28–30°C by means of an absorption heat pump. As the underfloor heating is slow to respond, the heating can be augmented by using the ceiling cooling units, which have a quicker response time (less mass). Extract air can be passed through an air-to-water heat exchanger to provide further heat input for the absorption heat pump.

The domestic hot water is provided by the tracking solar panels in the summer, and the co-generating plant in the winter.

Cooling

An absorption heat pump located in the basement facilitates the conversion of low-grade heat into either hotter water or cooler water, depending on the absorption cycle. For cool water, the heat pump is either fed by hot water from the active solar system, or from the combined heat and power unit. Cooling is then provided to the space through the underfloor heating circuit and the ceiling coil units fed by cold water from the absorption heat pump at between 4°C and 20°C. The ceiling-mounted coil units are positioned adjacent to the atrium and at the building periphery, behind open grid ceiling panels. Elsewhere, fabric ceiling panels allow contact to be maintained between the space and the mass of the floor slabs. The time of maximum output from the solar panels coincides with the period of maximum demand for cooling. The ventilated double skin is able to reduce cooling loads by reflecting and expelling incident solar energy by natural ventilation.

The building can be further cooled at night in the summer by allowing cool outside air into the building through the ventilation flaps in the outer skin and the sliding doors of the inner skin. The roof can also be opened to increase the throughput of air, as can the operation of the mechanical extract system. 'Coolth' is then stored in the heavyweight slabs ready for the next day. On warm days, outside air is prevented from entering the space, and the cavity is fully opened to maximize air movement and hence reduce unwanted solar build-up. In the atrium intensive planting and a water feature help to humidify and purify the air.

Ventilation

The building can be naturally ventilated through the glazed double skin. Ventilation flaps at the base of the outer skin control the entry of fresh air, and manually controlled sliding doors in the internal skin allow fresh outside air into the space. A mechanical extract system in the toilets, kitchen and cellular offices expels waste air, recycling any heat through a heat exchanger. In summer, the retractable glass roof provides an additional ventilation outlet, increasing natural ventilation. Fresh air can also be supplied by electrically driven windows at high level, which are automatically operated for summer night cooling.

Electricity generation

A gas-fired co-generation plant in the basement provides combined heat and power for the building. During the first 2 years the machine generated 24,000kWh of electricity to 48,000kWh of thermal energy. It has not been possible to sell excess electricity back to the grid.

Daylighting

As the building is fully glazed on all sides, daylight is exploited to the maximum. The upper band of glazing is shielded by a separate set of louvres that can be adjusted to reflect light onto the ceiling, and reduce glare.

Artificial lighting

If required, workplace occupancy detectors activate electric lighting, and also register and optimize light intensity. Each luminaire is centrally mounted in a ceiling panel (fabric or open grid) 2400mm by 2400mm with three double-bend compact fluorescent tubes. They are progressively activated and deactivated according to the principle of 'more light' or 'less light', rather than a simple 'on/off' switch.

Solar control

Glare is controlled by the aluminium venetian blinds in the cavity, which can either be controlled by the computer, or the occupants. The lower bands of louvres are perforated to maintain external views. The mitigation of glare through the atrium roof was to be provided by externally mounted reflecting louvre blades, which could rotate according to the position of the sun.

Controls

The building management system (BMS) for this building uses fuzzy logic and neural networks. This new technology allows the computer to be programmed with information about what is good, and it can learn optimum responses, ie teaching it how to 'learn'. Based on its constantly updated knowledge of the building, the neural network is able to predict how the building will react to external influences and to the measures taken to deal with those influences. The computer 'learns' the energy status of the building and finds the optimum combination of solutions to apply in response to changing atmospheric conditions. The knowledge-based software incorporating fuzzy logic enables the definition of the parameters of such a complex system in a more flexible, even imprecise and, in extreme cases, contradictory way. In combination with the neural network's ability to think for itself, the BMS is able to accomplish its task more efficiently.

The system is fed with information by a 'nervous system' that consists of two cable networks through which a range of sensors can communicate with the BMS, and each other. In this building there is a local operating network (LON) and a European Installations Bus (EIB). Over 250 sensors provide the BMS with information such as wind direction and speed, rainfall, outside air temperature and humidity, workplace occupancy, lighting intensity and internal air temper-

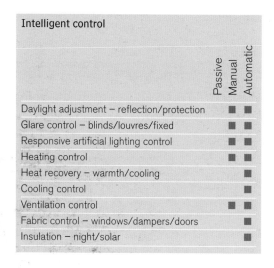

Intelligent control	Passive	Manual	Automatic
Daylight adjustment – reflection/protection		■	■
Glare control – blinds/louvres/fixed		■	■
Responsive artificial lighting control		■	■
Heating control		■	■
Heat recovery – warmth/cooling			■
Cooling control			■
Ventilation control		■	■
Fabric control – windows/dampers/doors			■
Insulation – night/solar			■

ature and humidity. In response to this information the BMS communicates with over 1000 operators, via the 'Bus', to control the solar collectors, the co-generating plant, the heating and cooling systems, the louvre and ventilation settings and artificial lighting. The upper louvres and the tracking solar array are programmed to respond to the position of the sun according to an algorithmic calculation.

User control

Users are provided with an on-screen control panel across the ordinary computer network. From each workstation, occupants can control heating and cooling according to designated zones. Lights can be controlled through the computer with a facility to call for 'more light' or 'less light'. The blinds in the cavity can be tilt adjusted, lowered, or raised according to individual preferences for each bay. The underfloor heating system is separated into occupancy zones, which can be locally controlled. However, it is slow to respond, and the ceiling-mounted coils provide a faster response.

Operating modes

On a winter's day, the low winter sun is reflected deep into the plan by the upper band of reflective venetian blinds. Hot air from the extract system is recycled to provide heat input to the absorption heat pump, which can also be fed by the solar panels and the co-generating plant, and distributed at between 30°C and 80°C. The ceiling coils can supplement the underfloor heating if necessary. The glazed cavity is kept closed to minimize the thermal loss from the building, acting as a warm air buffer between inside and out. The cavity fans are operated to transfer warm air around façade. The computer adjusts the venetian blinds into absorption mode (black surface up).

Building data

Contract value	n/a
Area	3,400m^2
Typical floorplate	12m
Number of storeys	2 + B
Price per m^2	n/a
Annual energy use	35kWh/m^{2*}
Typical energy use for building type	n/a
Annual CO$_2$ output	n/a
Number of sensors	250+
Visited by authors	✔
Monitored by others	✔

*Excludes electricity consumption, which can be largely self-generated.

On a summer's day, the sun is reflected away by the venetian blinds set in reflective mode. Recycled heat from the extract air and the solar panels provides warm water for the absorption heat pump, which is then cooled to between 4°C and 20°C. The cooled water is distributed through the underfloor and ceiling circuits. The double skin cavity is fully opened for maximum ventilation to reduce solar gain. The roof can be raised for increased stack effect ventilation.

At night, the cavity vents are opened to admit outside air through the sliding doors. The roof can be retracted for increased stack effect ventilation. The fans can also be operated to transfer cool air around the building perimeter.

Performance

Marcus Püttmer of Götz is monitoring the building as part of a Doctorate study.

Delivered energy consumption

During the design phase it was estimated that a primary energy saving of 60% would be achieved when compared to conventional energy saving buildings. The combined heat and power plant has not proved economic to operate because the electricity company offered such a low price for any surplus. Marcus Püttmer's monitoring of the energy consumption has recorded heating energy at 32kWh/m^2/a and cooling energy at 3kWh/m^2/a. Electricity consumption can be offset by the building's co-generation plant.

Design process

Computer simulations were performed using the TRNSYS programme.

Credits

Client: Götz GmbH
Architects: Webler + Geissler Architekten BDA
Energy Concept Consultant: Loren Butt
Energy Management Systems: Marcus Püttmer
Structural Engineer: Ing Buro Rudi Wolff
Contractor: Götz

References

Architecture + Urbanism, 97:05, No 320, May 1997, Special Feature: Sustainable Architecture Sustainable Environment
Architectural Review, Vol 200, No 1197, November 1996
A Low Energy Intelligent Building: Götz Headquarters, Würzburg, M Webler, G Geissler, Solar Energy in Architecture and Urban Planning, 4th European Conference on Architecture, March 1996
Baumeister, 2/1996
Marcus Püttmer, Götz GmbH
Martin Webler/Valerie Lark-Webler, Webler + Geissler

Phoenix Central Library

Phoenix Central Library
Public library
Central Avenue
Phoenix, Arizona
United States of America
Bruder/DWL Architects *Architect*
Ove Arup & Partners, LA *Energy Consultant*
1990–1995 *Dates*
33.57°N *Latitude*
0°N *Primary axis of orientation*

Intelligent features

Building management system	■
Learning facility	
Weather data	
Responsive lights	
Sun tracking facility	■
Occupant override	
Self-generation – CHP/PV/wind	
Night cooling	
Solar water heating	

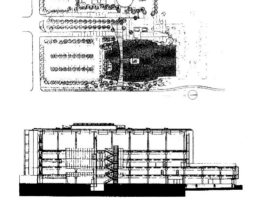

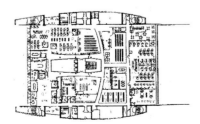

Introduction

Phoenix's new library is part of a conscious effort to make a cultural infra-structure commensurate to the city's growth into one of the ten largest urban areas in the United States. It is seen as an anchor for the southern portion of the proposed arts district, which will include a new art museum, history museum, and public art programme along the many highways.

The intelligence factor

The building has fully glazed elevations to the north and south, and opaque flank walls to the east and west. Electronically operated external louvres protect the glazing on the south façade, and fixed shade sails protect the north-facing glass wall. At the top of the atrium, nine computer driven, tracking skylights with mirrored louvres reflect sunlight into the depths of the building.

Brief

The ground floor functions as an information forum, with a large auditorium, a children's library, and a 'mediatheque'. The first floor contains general reference, periodicals and the interlibrary research department, and the second floor is used for staff areas and storage. The rare book collections are on the third floor, which also has space for seminars and lectures. At the top a grand reading room lit from above contains the entire non-fiction collection.

Accommodation

The five-storey building has been described as a 'warehouse of books'; with huge floorplates measuring 90m by 60m. The floors are punctured only by a

Sunpath

Latitude
33.57°

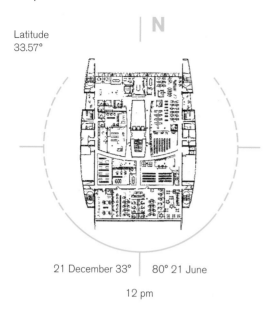

21 December 33°   80° 21 June

12 pm

Façade transparency	
North	100%
East	0%
South	100%
West	0%
Roof	5%

U-values	
Walls	n/a
Slab	n/a
Roof	n/a
Windows	n/a

small light slot, which also accommodates the vertical circulation. The atrium, labelled as the 'crystal canyon' by the architect, has the main entrance lobby at its base. To the east and west of the rectangular floorplates are narrow service zones that have outer walls curved in plan and which project beyond the plane of the north wall to help shade its glass face. These 'saddlebags' contain fixed services such as stairs, toilets and mechanical and electrical equipment. To the south, a fully glazed wall is equipped with a sophisticated array of computer controlled louvres that adjust according to the position of the sun. The north wall is further protected by vertical sails of teflon-coated acrylic fabric whose profiles have been calculated to offer shading in spring and autumn without obscuring the views of the mountains beyond.

Energy strategy

Despite the tough environmental conditions, characterized by a desert climate, light and heat have been kept under control and utilized both to make the interior layout more dramatic and to enhance the building from a functional and environmental point of view. A complex system of computer-controlled louvres intercept and reflect the rays of the sun to limit the harmful glare and heating effects of the sun.

Site and climate

The new library is located in the centre of the city, alongside the intersection of Central Avenue and the east-west transit freeway. It fronts a park created by a submerged freeway that lies beneath a landscaped slab. The environmental conditions are very tough, characteristic of the arid desert climate which gives it the name 'Valley of the Sun'.

The Arizona winters are mild, with daytime temperatures in the range of 15–21°C. Night temperatures drop dramatically with the clear sky to just above freezing. Summer temperatures can reach as high as 48°C in the day, and night temperatures remain in the range of 26–32°C. Humidity is low, generally in the 20% range, except for the monsoon season which occurs in August and September, with humidity levels in the upper 50% range. Annual rainfall averages 200–230mm. The air generally contains a lot of dust particles due to the vast amounts of exposed soil, and limited natural vegetation in the region.

Construction

The east and west walls are clad with a perforated copper. The structural frame is made from precast reinforced concrete columns and beams and floor units. A steel structure supports the 'saddlebags' on the east and west walls. An innovative 'tensegrity' structure supports the roof of the reading room.

Glazing

The glazed façade to the north is protected by fixed teflon sails, and electronically operated external louvres protect the south-facing glazing. Glazed rooflights provide natural lighting to the reading room on the top floor.

Heating

When heating is required, batteries in the ventilation system warm the humidified and filtered air to comfortable temperatures. The loadbearing concrete flank

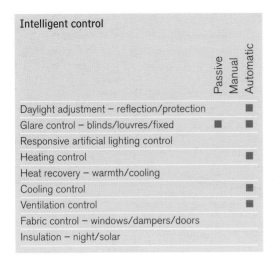

Intelligent control

	Passive	Manual	Automatic
Daylight adjustment – reflection/protection			■
Glare control – blinds/louvres/fixed		■	■
Responsive artificial lighting control			
Heating control			■
Heat recovery – warmth/cooling			
Cooling control			■
Ventilation control			■
Fabric control – windows/dampers/doors			
Insulation – night/solar			

walls (300mm) on the east and west sides of the library can act as a thermal flywheel, absorbing heat during the day, and emitting it during the colder nights.

Cooling

Cooling seems inevitable in the Phoenix climate, but also for the preservation of books and other library materials. A cooling coil in the air conditioning system ensures cooled air is delivered to the space. Chilled water is provided by compressors, pumps, and cooling towers. The central atrium originates at its base with a black-bottomed pool of water, which acts as a natural cooling feature as the warm air passes over the water. Surrounding the pool of water, aluminium benches absorb the cooler temperatures. The high altitude sun is prevented from entering the space by the opaque flank walls and the sophisticated shading systems on the north and south façades.

Ventilation

The library utilizes eight air handling units per floor, and two air handlers per zone, to provide adequate ventilation which is heated and cooled according to need. Tempered air is supplied through circular vents in a raised floor in the reading room. On the lower four floors of the library, air is supplied through grilles in the ceiling. Along the east-west perimeter walls perforated aluminium panels conceal huge supply and return air ducts and other services, all feeding from the 'saddlebags'. Services are distributed laterally suspended beneath the floor slabs with aluminium panels to conceal the ducts and cables and enclose the space around light fittings.

Daylighting

A small central atrium known as the 'Crystal Canyon' measuring 8.5m by 14.5m provides some daylight in the depth of the floorplates. Light is reflected down the void by nine computer-driven mirrored louvres set in stainless steel rotundas, which reflect sunlight down into the space below.

The great public reading room at the top of the building incorporates circular rooflights above the tensegrity roof structure. The 2m diameter lights that sit above each column on the upper level are glazed with blue laminated glass in the middle of which is a 400mm diameter hole that is clear to admit zenithal beams of sunlight. A slot of rooflights against the sidewall stresses the hovering of the lightweight roof, and washes the concrete flank walls with light.

Artificial lighting

The library uses fluorescent lighting predominantly, while restricting incandescent illumination for special effects. Some areas of the lower floors need electric light even in the summer.

Solar control

The glazed southern elevation is protected with automated solar tracking devices that minimize heat gain and glare. The computer-controlled louvres are intended to follow the angle of the sun, providing maximum solar protection and reducing the load on the mechanical cooling system. On the north wall, a system of 28 'shade sails' cover the entire glazed surface, eliminating the harsh glare of the summer sun, while optimizing views out over the low rise city, and the mountains beyond. The atrium skylights are protected by a second set of solid steel louvres, sus-

Building data

Contract value	$28m
Area	26,000m^2
Typical floorplate	~20m
Number of storeys	5
Price per m^2	~£670/m^2
Annual energy use	n/a
Typical energy use for building type	n/a
Annual CO$_2$ output	n/a
Number of sensors	n/a
Visited by authors	✗
Monitored by others	✗

pended below the mirrored blades. These block the overhead midday sun from penetrating between the mirrored louvres.

Controls

The control system manages the control of the mirrored louvres above the 'Crystal Canyon' and the adjustable aluminium louvres on the southern elevation. A row of six sensors mounted on the library's roof measure sky conditions for brightness. Computers also track the sun's position in the sky. These data are fed to computers that determine the optimum angle of the mirrored reflectors, and rotate the aluminium louvres during the course of the day to follow the path of the sunlight.

Performance

The library has received the maximum credit rebate offered by Arizona Public Service for energy efficiency in a commercial building, and an additional credit for use of sunlight for illumination.

Credits

Architects: William P Bruder and DWL Architects & Planners (joint venture)
Acoustics, Structural and General Engineering: Ove Arup & Partners California
Building Systems: Bates/Valentino Associates
Structural Engineer: Michael Ishler (tensegrity)
Civil Engineering: Hook Engineering
Landscape Architect: Martino & Tatasciore
Cost Consultants: Construction Consultants Southwest
Project Manager: Carleton van Deman (DWL)
General Contractor: Sundt Corp
Structural fabrics: FTL/Happold
Daylight regulation systems: Tait Solar Company

References

Archis, Architectur Stedebouw Beeldende Kunst (Architecture Urbanism and Visual Arts), 7.96 July, Netherlands Architecture Institute in association with Misset Publishers, Doetinchem
Architectural Review, March 1996, Vol CXCIX, No 1189, pp 48
Architecture, April 1995, Vol 84, No 4
Architecture, August 1991, Vol 80, No 8
Architecture, October 1995, Vol 84, No 10
l'Architecture d'Aujourd Hui, 307, October 1996, p74
Architecture Interieure Cree, No 271, June/July 1996, pp 104–109
Blueprint, September 1995, No 120
GA Document, No 46, 1996
l'ARCA, The International Magazine of Architecture, Design and Visual Communication, April 1996, No 103
l'ARCA, The International Magazine of Architecture, Design and Visual Communication, September 1996, No 107
Progressive Architecture, February 1994, Vol 75, No 2
Web site: www.public.asu.edu/~bah24/c-index.htm – student case study of phoenix central library
Carleton van Deman, DWL Architects + Planners Inc
Tim Christ/William P Bruder, William P Bruder Architect Ltd

The Brundtland Centre

The Brundtland Centre
Exhibition and conference centre
Brundtlandparken 2
Toftlund Sønerjylland
Denmark
KHR Architects *Architect*
Esbensen Consulting Engineers *Energy Consultant*
Brundtland Center Danmark *Client*
1992–1994 *Dates*
55.11°N *Latitude*
45°N *Primary axis of orientation*

Intelligent features

Building management system	■
Learning facility	
Weather data	
Responsive lights	■
Sun tracking facility	
Occupant override	■
Self-generation – CHP/PV/wind	
Night cooling	■
Solar water heating	

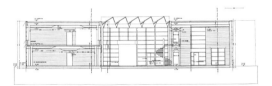

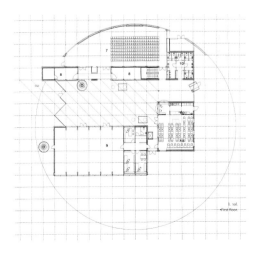

Introduction

In 1992 Toftlund was declared a 'Brundtland Town' with the aim of realizing the recommendations made in the UN Commission's Brundtland Report, *Our Common Future*. The town in southern Jutland is attempting to reduce energy consumption by between 30% and 50%, thereby reducing environmental pollution caused by energy use. These were the levels of reductions that Brundtland's Report claimed would need to be applied across all industrialized countries in the next 30–50 years. The Brundtland Centre was designed as an exhibition, promotion and administrative centre for the Brundtland Town, and its strategies for energy reduction and care for the environment. It has become a centre for exhibition and educational activities in energy-related topics with dissemination papers, conferences and courses, and many forward-looking energy and environmental ideas and products. The building itself serves as a demonstration of energy-efficiency in buildings.

The intelligence factor

The daylight windows are fitted with reflective interpane blinds that are automatically tilted to maximize daylight penetration and reduce glare. The artificial lighting is automatically controlled in response to daylight levels. Ventilation fans in offices are activated only by movement sensors, which confirm occupation. The central atrium is used to pre-heat ventilation air, and can be naturally ventilated through openings in the roof. Photovoltaics on the atrium roof generate electricity.

Brief

The design was developed from the winning entry of an EC architectural ideas competition, 'Working in the City', won by KHR and Esbensen with ISLEF as

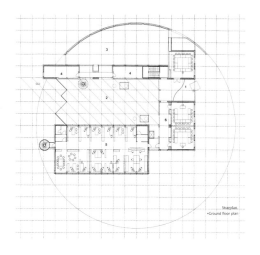

Staarplan.
·Ground floor plan

Sunpath

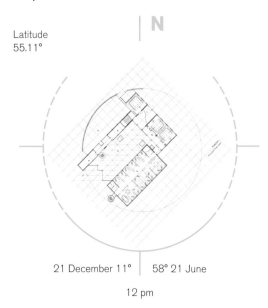

Latitude
55.11°

N

21 December 11° | 58° 21 June

12 pm

developers. The scope of the project was to demonstrate a 50% reduction in energy consumption in line with the recommendations of the Bruntland Report.

Accommodation

The building is set into a circular plateau, recessed into the south-facing slope. Within the circle, the accommodation is arranged as three separate, two-storey elements around an atrium, with views over the surrounding farmland. The various functions were positioned according to the points of the compass, according to their internal gains and whether passive solar gain could make a useful heating contribution. The conference facilities and classrooms occupy the northern and western sides of the building because of their high occupancy gains, and the main exhibition space and offices take advantage of passive gain on the southern side of the building. The cafeteria wing with additional classrooms above is situated on the north-east side. The atrium serves as an entrance court and supplementary area for the surrounding primary functions. The building is run by a staff of five people and has many visitors each day.

Energy strategy

The Brundtland Centre was designed to take maximum advantage of passive and active solar energy. High levels of daylighting are provided and the artificial lighting is automatically responsive to daylight. Natural ventilation strategies were employed as far as possible with a minimal amount of ductwork and mechanical ventilation. Active cooling was completely avoided. The overall goal of the project is to demonstrate how energy consumption in non-domestic buildings can be reduced to around half of the normal energy consumption of buildings designed in line with current building codes.

Site and climate

The new building is situated on the southern outskirts of the town of Toftlund on a high and very visible site. The climate is described as 'northern coastal' with 1922 sunshine hours per year (direct radiation $>120W/m^2$). The minimum average temperature is $-1.1°C$ in February and the maximum average temperature is $16.7°C$ in July. The minimum global radiation on a horizontal surface is $384Wh/m^2$ per day in December and the maximum global radiation on a horizontal is $6188Wh/m^2$ per day in June. There are 3014 heating degree days (base 17°C).

Construction

Reinforced concrete columns support concrete slabs and loadbearing brickwork. The clay brickwork is insulated with 150mm of insulation, and is faced internally with a smooth yellow brick. Finishes include wooden floors and exposed concrete ceilings with acoustic islands.

Glazing

A lightweight aluminium curtain wall provides the frontage to the entrance atrium. The office and exhibition wing has windows divided into three parts. The upper area is equipped with daylighting windows with reflecting blinds (U-value 0.9-$1.8W/m^2K$; transmission – 0.20–0.70), the middle band has windows for views out (U-value 1.1-$1.8W/m^2K$; transmission – 0.10–0.67), and the lower part of the façades has special elements with built-in solar collectors and photovoltaic panels. The atrium roof is arranged as a 'sawtooth', with photovoltaic cells

Façade transparency

North	40%
East	0%
South	80%
West	40%
Roof	20%

U-values

Walls	0.30W/m²K
Slab	n/a
Roof	0.20W/m²K
Atrium roof glazing	1.60W/m²K
Daylight windows	0.90–1.80W/m²K
Vision windows	1.10–1.80W/m²K
Atrium glazing (SW)	1.40W/m²K

integrated into the southern incline of the low-e double glazed roof pitches pitches, allowing 20% daylight to enter between the cells. The other pitch provides glare-free northlight.

Heating

The heating load is reduced because of the passive solar gain strategy, which collects solar energy via the windows and the atrium. The heavyweight concrete mass stores incidental heat from the sun, people and equipment. The suspended ceiling panels are made from perforated aluminium plates, and also support an acoustic dampening material. They are suspended to maintain air movement around the slab. The central atrium accumulates solar heat and as well as reducing heat loss from the surrounding accommodation, preheats incoming ventilation air. When the window louvres are closed in their vertical position at night, the U-value is said to improve by 25%.

The office spaces on the south-east side of the building are heated and ventilated by decentralized heat exchangers (60% efficiency), with integral fans. Movement sensors activate these units so that they are only operational if an office is occupied. Elsewhere a low temperature hot water distribution circuit, fed by a condensing natural gas boiler, provides supplementary heating. Radiators on the first floor are the first on the hot water distribution route from the boiler, followed by underfloor heating on the ground floor. This means that the return hot water from the radiator circuit is passed through the underfloor heating circuit before its return to the boiler, thereby resulting in a very low return temperature as the boiler's condensing set point. The radiators are controlled centrally in response to air temperature in the room and movement sensors.

Cooling

Active cooling was deliberately avoided as it is only permitted in the Danish Building Code for special buildings. The need for cooling is reduced by the building's thermal mass and a semi-passive night ventilation system. The atrium roof

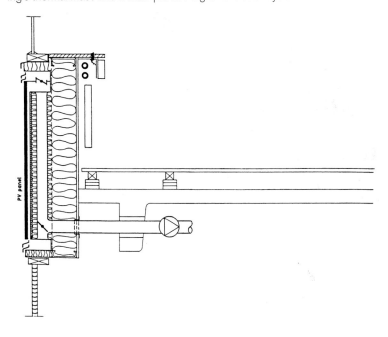

can be opened for nighttime ventilation and the exhaust air system can be used to pull the cool air through the adjacent spaces.

Ventilation

Incoming air enters the building via two ventilation columns in the atrium. As well as passing through a heat exchanger, the fresh air in the atrium volume can be preheated by solar gain during much of the year (fully glazed south-west wall and glazed roof). Air is supplied to the surrounding accommodation by means of a pressure differential, induced by an exhaust air system. Preheated air from the atrium passes into the individual rooms through an opening spandrel, which has a radiator for additional heating when required. Exhaust air from all rooms is ducted to the two central heat exchangers (in the atrium) to preheat incoming fresh air. Operable sections in the glazed roof can also be used to ventilate the atrium. The use of electricity for fans is minimized due to the demand-controlled ventilation strategy, which is only activated by occupancy sensors.

The south-east facing offices are ventilated with decentralized units incorporating local fans and heat exchangers. The double fans are controlled by movement detectors so that only occupied offices are ventilated. The lower band of windows can be opened for additional ventilation. It was originally intended that incoming air would be preheated by waste heat from photovoltaic cells, but this proved unfeasible. In the double-height lecture space, a displacement ventilation system is used.

Electricity generation

The 'sawtooth' atrium roof that incorporates photovoltaic cells on its southern incline, still allows 20% daylight to penetrate the clear spaces between the cells. A total of $84m^2$ of silicon photovoltaic cells have been integrated into the sealed double glazing units. In addition the south-east façade includes $46m^2$ of photovoltaics in the lower band of glazing. The total electricity production from the sun is estimated at 13,500kWh per annum, which can also be fed into the national grid. It was calculated that the photovoltaics could meet all of the electrical requirements of the building during the summer months, while about 20% could be provided in the winter.

Daylighting

The three-part façade is combined with innovative control strategies for daylight and artificial lighting to maximize the use of daylight, and improve the indoor visual and thermal climate. Venetian blind systems integrated into the double glazed units were specially developed by Lichtplanung Christian Bartenbach to redirect diffuse daylight onto the ceiling. The daylighting strategy is estimated to reduce electricity consumption when compared to a traditional lighting design for offices.

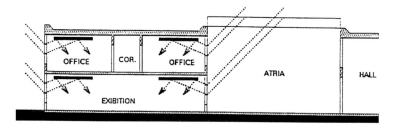

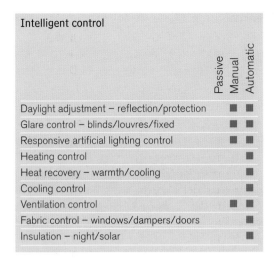

Intelligent control	Passive	Manual	Automatic
Daylight adjustment – reflection/protection		■	■
Glare control – blinds/louvres/fixed		■	■
Responsive artificial lighting control		■	■
Heating control			■
Heat recovery – warmth/cooling			■
Cooling control			■
Ventilation control		■	■
Fabric control – windows/dampers/doors			■
Insulation – night/solar			■

The upper daylighting windows incorporate a fixed array of specular louvre blades between the two layers of glass, which allows sunlight to enter the room but prevents views to the outside. A roller blind in front of the louvre system can be operated to reduce the visual discomfort caused by direct sunlight. Internally, a highly reflective microstructure is suspended beneath the exposed concrete structure to redirect the reflected daylight into the back of the room.

The central vision windows at eye level contain thin inverted venetian blinds, which can be adjusted by the central control system. They are contained in the double glazing cavity, allowing contact to be maintained with the outside and reflecting daylight onto the ceiling.

The bottom window is a normal window with manually-controlled specular venetian blinds (photovoltaics on south-east façade).

The daylighting system allows up to 75% transmission of the daylight or shading down to approximately 20%. The louvres are operated from a simple electronic control system, which can eventually be driven by a PV system. To avoid the problem of 'lights on, blinds down' the building management system is programmed to block the simultaneous closing of the solar shading and the switching on of the artificial lighting.

Artificial lighting

Specially designed uplighting luminaires (Bartenbach) with fluorescent tubes and high frequency ballasts are positioned along the window façade between the upper daylight window and the central vision window. In all rooms with the above daylighting system the artificial light can be adjusted accordingly. The user in the room only gets one switch by which they can ask for more light '+' or less light '–'. If a user presses '+', the building management system (BMS) is programmed so that whenever possible more daylight can enter via the daylight and vision windows by adjusting the tilting of the blinds, i.e. this method will be tried before switching on artificial lighting. During periods of excessive sunlight, the user might press '–', which will start the closing of the vision window blinds and the daylight window blinds giving a continuous reduction in light levels and visual discomfort.

Controls

The BMS is based on a standard system with the additional facility to monitor the energy performance. The BMS can control the roller blind in the upper daylight windows, the angle of the blinds in the vision window and the level of dimming of the artificial lighting (also influenced by occupancy sensors and photocells).

User control

As well as determining lighting levels by the '+/–' switches, the blinds can be operated individually by the users.

Performance

It is intended that the building will go through comprehensive monitoring and dissemination phases, addressing decision makers, consultants and architects throughout Europe.

Building data

Contract value	16.78m DKK
Area	1878m^2
Typical floorplate	12m
Number of storeys	2
Price per m^2	~£860/m^2
Annual energy use	38 kWh/m^{2*}
Typical energy use for building type	n/a
Annual CO_2 output	n/a
Number of sensors	n/a
Visited by authors	✗
Monitored by others	✔

*Excludes small power electricity consumption (estimated during design phase.

Delivered energy consumption

Computer simulations predicted a total energy consumption of 38kWh/m^2 per year for heating, lighting and ventilation. Overall a reduction of 72% in total energy consumption was estimated when compared with a traditional Danish office building.

Design process

Many computer simulations were used to evaluate the design, including the LT Method, tsbi3, ESP-r, Adeline/Radiance, Superlite and Superlink. They evaluated the optimum fraction of glazing for the different façades, performed various thermal simulations, calculated daylight availability and savings on electricity for lighting and produced visualizations of the daylight strategy. The simulations showed an annual saving for heating of about 60% and lighting of about 85% of the normal energy use in Danish office buildings. Lichtplanung Christian Bartenbach produced physical mock-ups of the innovative daylighting system.

The design process focused on the close co-operation between all the design team participants. The design work was initiated by a two day workshop for the whole team, discussing and analysing the design brief from the client and identifying an energy strategy for the building.

Credits

Owner/operator (client): Brundtland Center Danmark (private foundation)
Architects: KHR Architects, Virum
Service Engineer (HVAC/energy/electrical): Esbensen Consulting Engineers
Lighting Design: Lichtplannung Christian Bartenbach (Austria)
Structural Engineer: Sloth Møller Consulting Engineers
Energy monitoring: The Martin Centre, University of Cambridge

References

Architektur DK, Vol 38, No 7, July 1994
Architektur (Stockholm), Vol 95, No 6, September 1995
Bruntland Centre Denmark – Focus 21: EU Joule House Demonstration Project on Energy Efficient Office Buldings, Esbensen T, Madsen C E, Sørensen H, Givskov K, 'Solar Energy in Architecture and Urban Planning', 4th European Conference on Architecture, Berlin, 26–29 March 1996
Bruntland Centre Focus 21, The Solar House, Toftlund, Denmark, Henrik Sørensen (Esbensen)
Bruntland Centre in Toftlund Denmark – Focus 21, Madsen C E, Sørensen H, North Sun 94: Solar Energy at High Latitudes, Editors: MacGregor K, Porteous C, James and James Ltd, London
Building Research and Information, Vol 22, No 1, January/February 1994
Daylight and sunlight redirected to reflective ceiling for deeper daylight penetration, Bruntland Centre, Toftlund, Denmark
Description of Case Stories, A Working Document of Task 23 – Subtask A, Case Stories, February 1998, Edited by Christina E Madsen
World Architecture, Issue No 27, 1994
Christina E Madsen, Esbensen Consulting Engineers
Peter Høi/Bjarne A Jorgensen, Brundtland Center Danmark
Jens Christoffersen, Danish Building Research Institute (SBI)

The Green Building

The Green Building
Mixed use development
Temple Bar
Dublin
Ireland
Murray O'Laoire Associates *Architect*
Conservation Engineering Consultants *Energy*
    Consultant
Temple Bar Properties *Client*
1990–1994 *Dates*
50.11°N *Latitude*
–7°N *Primary axis of orientation*

Intelligent features

Building management system	■
Learning facility	
Weather data	■
Responsive lights	
Sun tracking facility	
Occupant override	
Self-generation – CHP/PV/wind	■
Night cooling	■
Solar water heating	■

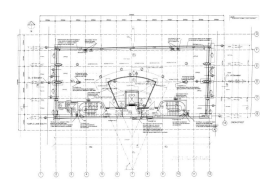

Introduction

This scheme has its origins in a THERMIE bid for a 'generic' proposal, which was made to the European Commission by University College Dublin in 1990. Sean O'Laoire and researchers at Trinity and University colleges in Dublin originally developed the idea for a low energy office building. Temple Bar Properties later commissioned the architects to design a mixed-use development on an in-fill site between Temple Lane South and Crow Street, to stimulate development in the area. This required a very different response to that considered in the 'generic' proposal, which had assumed optimum orientation on all sides. The EU support of £500,000 was continued to support the principles of the original proposal by funding the 'demonstration' elements of the revised project. The building was presented as a new benchmark for an urban building with a sophisticated energy philosophy.

The intelligence factor

The building is largely passive in its energy design features. However the central courtyard is ventilated by automatically opening roof lights that induce natural ventilation. On the roof, an array of wind turbines and photovoltaics generates enough electricity to meet the building's lighting demand. Hot and cold water is fed through microbore pipes embedded in the building's structure, a feature analogous with the human circulation system. The control software receives data directly from the Met Office and uses this together with simulation models to predict heating requirements for the following 48 hours.

Brief

Temple Bar Properties' brief called for a building of mixed-use composition in line with its own redevelopment strategy for Temple Bar. This resulted in a building that in many ways was more relevant as a European prototype than the building originally envisaged. The eight apartments are divided into two duplex units, four two-bedroom units, and two three-bedroom apartments.

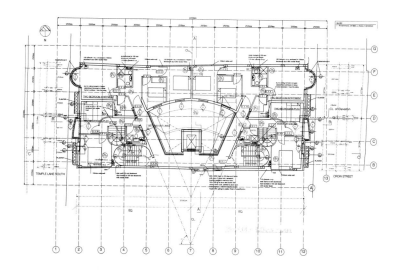

Sunpath

Latitude
53.40°

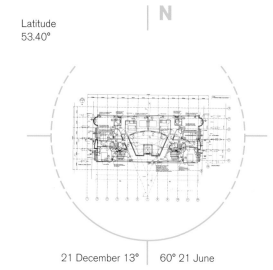

21 December 13° | 60° 21 June

12 pm

Façade transparency

North	0%
East	30%
South	0%
West	30%
Roof	25%

U-values

Walls	0.29W/m^{2}K
Slab	0.40W/m^{2}K
Roof	0.25W/m^{2}K
Windows	1.60W/m^{2}K

Accommodation

The mixed-use building comprises retail at ground and basement levels, offices at first floor level, and eight apartments on the upper three levels. The design solution for this narrow site was to place a full-height courtyard in the centre of the plan, allowing the various functions to be accommodated within the 26 m deep plan. The courtyard is covered by a glazed roof that opens automatically in warm weather and closes when it rains, and which releases smoke outside in the event of a fire (classified as open space for fire reasons). The basement is left completely open to the six-storey court and all the windows in the upper residential units open onto it. As well as providing additional lettable space, the basement accommodates plant and secure bicycle storage, instead of the more usual basement car park.

Energy strategy

The building is laid out around a six storey central courtyard, which is oriented southwards and designed to naturally ventilate and naturally light the building. Exposed thermal mass is used as a climate moderator. Electricity is generated on the roof by photovoltaic cells and wind turbines. Evacuated tube solar collectors, also on the roof, provide hot water to the apartments.

Site and climate

Temple Bar runs alongside the River Liffey, near the famous Halfpenny Bridge. Until 1987, the area was designated for demolition to make way for a new transport interchange. It has now become regarded as Dublin's cultural centre and has seen an influx of investment. The actual site is a 26m long double plot, with 11m east and west facing frontages on Temple Lane and Crow St, which are narrow streets, 5–6m and four storeys high on either side. The surrounding streets are pedestrianized, but air pollution remains problematic. The climate of Dublin is classed as 'cool maritime', with overcast skies for 65% of the day, and average solar insolation of 1046kWh/m^2. There are approximately 3073 heating degree days per year (calculated on an 18°C base).

Construction

The external walls are constructed from 215mm concrete block and recycled brick, external Rockwool insulation and coloured render on the outside face. On the uppermost storey and roof a torch-on copper membrane gives the effect of a copper roof. The frame is reinforced concrete. Internal finishes include linoleum and natural jute carpets, recycled wood and tiles, and exposed concrete soffits.

Glazing

All of the windows are softwood, sourced from managed, renewable sources, and coated with water-based, solvent-free paint. They are double-glazed with glass that has an argon gas in its cavity.

Heating

The building mainly relies on thermal mass, passive solar energy collection and good insulation values for its heating. The auxiliary heat source for the building is provided by an electric heat pump system, which uses the bedrock as a source of low-grade heat. At night, water is pumped down through a 200mm diameter borehole that goes 150m into the bedrock (mean temp of 12°C), using low-cost night rate electricity. The heated water is stored in a large tank in the basement, which acts as a short-term thermal reservoir for release during the daytime. Warm water (20–35°C) is transferred to the building's massive structure through microbore (20mm) pipes attached to the reinforcing bars and cast within the concrete floor. To maximize thermal contact with the structure, no suspended ceilings were used. The apartments are also fitted with 500W electric heaters for additional heating.

In the courtyard, two concentric heat recovery ducts made of fabric are suspended from the roof. Exhaust air passes between the outer fabric duct, and a section of the inner duct that is formed from high transmissivity foil. An axial fan pulls air in through the inner duct, past the foil section, where heat is recovered from the outgoing air. The 'fabric funnel' system provides balanced fresh air to the internal courtyard, and can be used to boost natural ventilation in winter, when carbon dioxide levels exceed pre-set limits.

Thermomax evacuated solar collectors provide heated water for the domestic hot water system. The 40 collectors mounted on the roof are able to meet 65% of the apartments' hot water needs, and an electric immersion system provides the rest.

Cooling

Summertime cooling can be promoted by circulating cool borehole water through the pipework system that is used for heating, to cool the structure at night. Cool air is drawn into the building at street level where it passes through basement planters to clean and humidify the air. The basement is cooled by evening air descending from the top of the open courtyard.

Ventilation

The strategy for natural ventilation relies on manually opening windows, supplemented by fan assistance when CO_2 levels exceed pre-set limits. The courtyard is designed as a semi-external space with the commercial, office, and residential units having access to it for lighting and ventilation. In summer, air is drawn into the courtyard from street level having passed over low level planting for cooling and humidification. Users have the choice of opening external windows both onto the street and facing the inner courtyard. The glazed roof

of the courtyard can be opened and closed by pneumatic rams under BMS control, and closes automatically in cold or wet conditions. In winter, air is introduced via a fan-assisted filter unit and heat exchanger at roof level, and directed down to basement level by a fabric funnel. The 'fabric funnel' device is powered by electric fans, and is also used to promote natural ventilation in conditions of 'heavy' air, when there is no wind or high humidity. Hanging plants in the courtyard help to clean and oxygenate the air as it rises back up through the courtyard. Mechanical ventilation units activated manually or by occupancy detectors provide forced ventilation to kitchens and bathrooms.

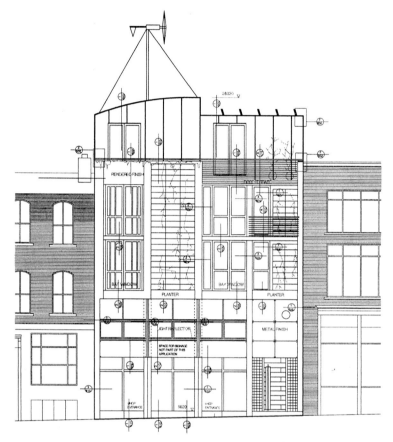

Electricity generation

Photovoltaic cells and wind generators mounted on the roof generate electricity, which is stored in 24 lead-acid batteries (fully charged capacity 2520 ampere hours) in the basement. It is converted into alternating current before linking to the lighting circuits. The batteries can also be charged by the grid at off-peak times, and are used to provide stand-by power for the fire escape ventilation system. The grid provides a back-up system. There are three wind turbines rated at 1.5kW each, and an array of photovoltaic cells rated at 3.8kW peak. The system meets 100% of the building's lighting needs.

Daylighting

The section of the courtyard narrows towards the basement, funnelling light downwards to the bottom. Glazing ratios are increased on lower floors to max-

Intelligent control

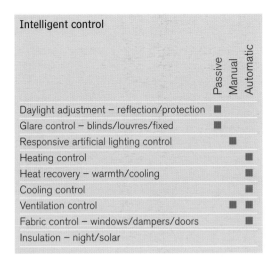

	Passive	Manual	Automatic
Daylight adjustment – reflection/protection	■		
Glare control – blinds/louvres/fixed	■		
Responsive artificial lighting control		■	
Heating control			■
Heat recovery – warmth/cooling			■
Cooling control			■
Ventilation control		■	■
Fabric control – windows/dampers/doors			■
Insulation – night/solar			

imize access to natural light. Bay windows were provided on the street façades to maximize access to natural light.

Artificial lighting

All of the artificial lighting is provided by manually controlled compact fluorescent lights (11W). Monitoring has shown that the renewable energy generated by the wind turbines and photovoltaics is sufficient to meet the lighting requirements for the building.

Solar control

The two street façades face east and west, and are adequately protected by the narrow four storey streets. The only south-facing element is the courtyard roof, which relies on the sun for passive gain. Bedrooms facing south are unlikely to be occupied during sunshine hours, and as such glare protection was not required. The maturing planting in the courtyard has provided a certain degree of shading.

Controls

The building management system (BMS) is responsible for optimizing the controls of the heat pump. The controls software receives data directly from the Met Office and uses this together with simulation models to predict heating requirements for the following 48 hour period.

User control

Occupants in the apartments have the usual degree of control in the form of opening windows and manually operated light switches. the same strategy is applied to the retail and office areas.

Operating modes

In winter, recirculated air is mixed with fresh air at roof level (roof remains closed) and then passed down the canvas duct in the courtyard to the basement, where it is heated by a heat pump and allowed to rise back up the build-

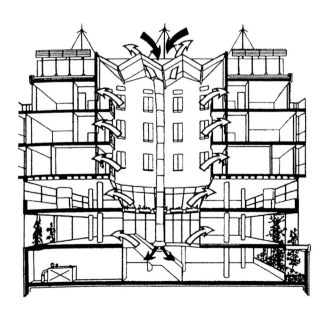

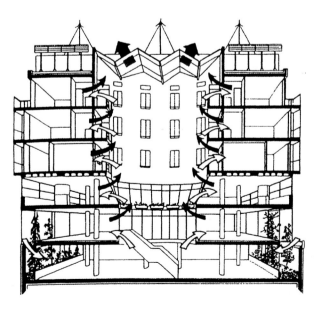

Building data

Contract value	IRL£1.5m
Area	~1500m^2
Typical floorplate	5–6m
Number of storeys	5 + B
Price per m^2	~£1000/m^2
Annual energy use	28kWh/m^{2*}
Typical energy use for building type	96kWh/m^2
Annual CO$_2$ output	n/a
Number of sensors	100
Visited by authors	✗
Monitored by others	✔

*Excludes small power electricity consumption, and lighting which is self-generated.
NB: does not include retail/office space (700m^2 residential).

ing. At night, a heat pump generates stored heat that is then distributed through small pipes in the floor.

In summer, air is drawn into the basement from above pavement level, and passed over dense planting, which both filters the air and re-oxygenates it. The air then moves to the central courtyard where it rises by stack effect, ventilating the accommodation. At night, cool water can be passed through the pipe system in the floor to provide additional cooling.

Performance

The building has been monitored by the THERMIE project coordinators, Conservation Engineering.

Delivered energy consumption

Total net energy consumption has been recorded during the initial test period at 2GJ/year (556kWh/year) for cooling, 39GJ/year (10,834kWh/year) for heating, 8GJ/year (2,223kWh/year) for hot water and 22GJ/year (6,112kWh/year) for motors. There was no net energy consumption for lighting, which was provided by the building's renewable appliances. This equates to a net energy consumption of 71GJ/year (19,723kWh/year) for the building as it was occupied during the test period, with the retail space empty, equating to a net energy consumption of 28kWh/m^2.

Design process

Computer simulations were performed on the ESP-r programme at Strathclyde University and a physical model was built to test the lighting strategy.

Credits

Client: Temple Bar Properties (partly owned state agency established to stimulate development in the Temple Bar area)
Architects: Murray O'Laoire Associates
Energy Consultants: Conservation Engineering Consultants
Service Engineer: Homan O'Brien Associates
Structural Engineer: DBFL
QS: PKS
Main Contractor: G & T Crampton
Thermie Project Manager: Tim Cooper, Conservation Engineering Consultants

References

Perspectives on Architecture, Vol 2, Issue 12, April 1995
Irish Architect, The Journal of The Royal Institute of Architects of Ireland, No 103, September/October 1994
Architecture Today, AT53, November 1994
Building Services Journal, August 1996, Vol 18, No 8
THERMIE Projects Summary Leaflets, *The Green Building, Dublin, Ireland,* Tim Cooper
Bernard Gilna, Murray O'Laoire Associates
Tim Cooper, Conservation Engineering Consultants

Heliotrop®

Heliotrop®
Residential/studio office
Ziegelweg 28
Freiburg-im-Breisgau
Germany (D-79100)
Prof Rolf Disch Architekt *Architect*
Krebser & Freyloer *Energy Consultant*
Prof Rolf Disch *Client*
Completed 1994 *Dates*
48°N *Latitude*
Variable °N *Primary axis of orientation*

Intelligent features

Building management system	■
Learning facility	
Weather data	■
Responsive lights	
Sun tracking facility	■
Occupant override	■
Self-generation – CHP/PV/wind	■
Night cooling	■
Solar water heating	■

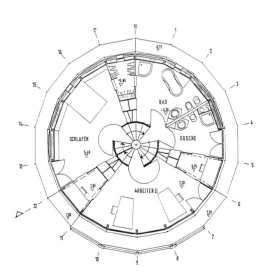

Introduction

This lightweight 'tree house' has been named after the word heliotropism, which refers to plants that grow in response to the stimulus of the sun. The wooden structure is cantilevered from a central stair shaft which can revolve the 100 ton house to track the sun, maximizing passive solar gains to the indoor spaces and active gains to the evacuated solar collectors mounted on the balustrades. Independent of the main house is a tracking photovoltaic array, which is mounted on the roof. This house was a prototype and there are now others that have been built to similar designs. The Disch office developed the energy concept and architectural planning, and Professor Disch funded the project.

Sunpath

Latitude
48.00°

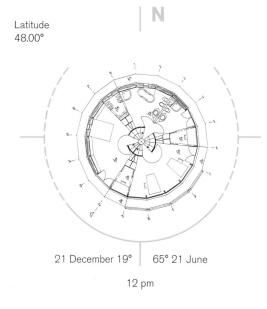

21 December 19° | 65° 21 June

12 pm

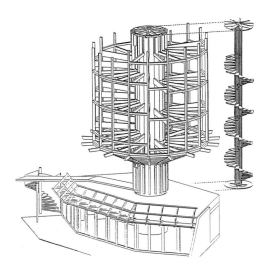

Façade transparency	
North	20%
South	100%
Roof	0%

U-values	
Walls	0.13W/m^{2}K
Slab	0.20W/m^{2}K
Roof	0.13W/m^{2}K
Windows	0.50W/m^{2}K

The intelligence factor

This is the only case study that is able to vary its orientation in response to the position of the sun. Other features include solar water heating, photovoltaics and an earth heat exchanger. The ventilation and heating input to each room is determined by an 'occupancy switch', which tells the BMS that the room is in use.

Accommodation

The office area is built into a steeply sloping bank, providing earth-sheltered accommodation at the semi-basement level. The cylindrical timber stair shaft rises from the plant room in the basement, creating a sheltered entry with the main living accommodation towering 14.5m above. The principal living spaces are arranged around the central 'trunk' within the 10.5m diameter, spiralling up the building to a roof garden at the top. One-half of the revolving living tower is highly glazed, and the other is well insulated with few window openings. The architect designed the house for himself and his wife, and he has an office in the earth-sheltered basement.

Energy strategy

The energy strategy aimed to win all of the energy for the house from the sun. It is able to adjust its position according to the need for maximum solar gain, or to turn itself out of the sun for protection. The building has a rotation capability of 400° (+20° either side). The building is programmed to follow the sun by rotating approximately 15° each hour. It stops rotating at sunset, and returns to the sunrise position at 3 am each morning. A full 400° revolution takes about one hour. The electric motor that turns the house uses about 120W (at maximum speed), equating to a yearly power consumption of between 20kWh and 40kWh.

Site and climate

Freiburg is situated at the bottom of the upper Rhine valley and lies on the edge of the Black Forest. It is the hottest place in Germany, with average temperatures of 10.3°C and 4.8 average daily sunshine hours. The typical climate is hot and moist summers and cold fogs in winter. The mean yearly global radiation on the horizontal plane is 1180kWh/m^2/a. The degree days are 3400Kd.

The steeply sloping site had previously been regarded as unusable, and the new tower utilizes the site effectively, giving beautiful views over vineyards towards the south.

Construction

The timber framework is insulated with 300mm of mineral wool insulation and the opaque elements are covered with corrugated metal cladding. The 2.6m diameter central column was prefabricated, and is made from a faceted array of 18 sheets of laminated timber panels, 111mm thick. The laminated panels are joined together with an epoxy resin and steel ties.

Glazing

Different types of glazing were used in the building for experimentation. The predominant glazing is triple glazing with krypton-filled cavities, low-e coatings and insulating blinds.

Heating

Evacuated tube collectors installed on the balustrade of the perimeter balcony provide hot water and part of the heating energy demand. The solar-heated water is fed into tanks in the basement, with up to 1200 litres of storage capacity. Underfloor heating has been laid into the 65mm screed, and is distributed at about 33°C, a temperature which can easily be achieved by the solar-heating plant in the winter. The slow response of the underfloor system can be supplemented by radiant ceiling panels of metal fins, distributing hot water at 45°C, which is also suitable for combination with solar-heated water. A back-up system for the water heating is provided by an electric heating element which is due to be replaced with a wood burning stove. Fresh air supplied mechanically to the space can be warmed in winter by the earth heat exchanger in the basement. Heating is only required between November and February.

Cooling

Ventilation air can be pre-cooled by passing it through the earth heat exchanger that is buried into the bank. The glazed side of the building can be turned away from the sun, or programmed to offset its revolution by 180° to prevent unwanted solar gain.

Ventilation

Both the basement and the top of the house can be mechanically ventilated with low level inlets and a high level extract. An earth heat exchanger in the basement that maintains year-round temperatures in the range of 8°C, ensures that

the air is pre-heated or pre-cooled depending on the season. In the winter, air is heated further by passing through heat exchangers containing solar-heated water. Outgoing air is also passed over a heat exchanger for recycling of waste heat. In summer, opening windows can be used for ventilation.

Electricity generation

A photovoltaic array on the roof is also programmed to follow the sun on a two axis tracking system (in response to azimuth and elevation), which operates independently of the house. Unlike the main living areas, the photovoltaic panels should always be positioned for maximum exposure to the sun (except during maintenance). The tracking facility is predicted to allow efficiency improvements of 30–40% over a fixed system. The 54m^2 array of mono-crystalline silicone cells has a peak output of 6.6 kilowatts, giving an estimated annual output of 9000kWh. This is five times the building's calculated electrical consumption, but this is largely offset by the increased consumption of the monitoring equipment, producing no overall net gain. Any excess electricity is sold to the grid at the same price at which it is purchased, making the grid an effective storage device instead of heavy-metal batteries. The measured annual electricity output of the PV system in 1997 was 8300kWh [Gereon Kamps].

Daylighting

All perimeter rooms are provided with windows for natural light and views. Rooms that are notionally on the south side have full-height glazing.

Solar control

Metal balconies which spiral around the perimeter of the tower allowing maintenance access and fire escape, also double as external sunshades. Internally, aluminized fabric blinds can be raised from floor level to reduce unwanted solar gain. The U-value of the triple-glazed windows is improved to 0.46W/m^{2}K when the blinds are closed.

Controls

The building is programmed to turn every ten minutes according to a calculation that determines the azimuth and elevation of the sun. Each room is fitted with a temperature sensor and an occupancy switch (activated manually) which help the computer to determine the room inputs in terms of heat and air.

User control

The rotation of the building can be manually overridden. For instance it may be desired to rotate the dining room to overlook the vineyards during a dinner party, or the building may need to be turned out of the sun when the occupants are on holiday. A manually activated occupancy switch is used to tell the computer which spaces are occupied, and the temperature of vacant rooms is kept lower.

Operating modes

In the summer, the house can be turned away from the sun to prevent overheating. By rotating the house to face northeast and opening the windows at night, room temperatures can be maintained at 25°C. In the peak of summer, the house can track the sun with an offset of 180° to avoid solar penetration to the glazed living areas.

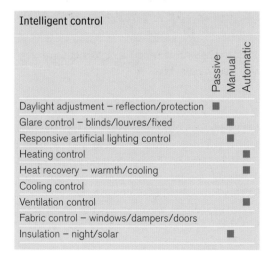

Intelligent control	Passive	Manual	Automatic
Daylight adjustment – reflection/protection	■		
Glare control – blinds/louvres/fixed		■	
Responsive artificial lighting control		■	
Heating control			■
Heat recovery – warmth/cooling			■
Cooling control			
Ventilation control		■	
Fabric control – windows/dampers/doors			
Insulation – night/solar			■

For the remainder of the year the house is rotated to take maximum advantage of passive solar gain and active solar water heating.

Performance

Continuous measurements of the house began in late 1995. In July 1996, with thermally non-optimal positioning and ventilation, the measured air temperature in the living zone lay between 21.5°C and 30.1°C, with a mean temperature of 25.5°C, and with 30°C only being exceeded once. The average ambient temperature was 18.7°C. Temperatures rose above 26°C due to absence (windows not opened). There was no ventilation or subterranean heat exchange, and no delayed tracking of the house to minimize solar gain during this test period as the occupants found the conditions agreeable.

Building data

Contract value	DM3.2m
Area	285m^2
Typical floorplate	4.2m
Number of storeys	3 + B
Price per m^2	~£3800/m^2
Annual energy use	25.3kWh/m^2
Typical energy use for building type	200kWh/m^2
Annual CO_2 output	Negative (PVs)
Number of sensors	100
Visited by authors	✔
Monitored by others	✔

It is intended to increase the storage capacity of the solar heated water by a further 6000 litres to survive longer spells of poor weather.

Delivered energy consumption

Measurements have shown that the actual heating energy demand of the Heliotrop lies close to the heating energy demand of 27kWh/m^2/a predicted by TRNSYS simulations during the design stage. A measured heating load of 25.3kWh/m^2/a has been recorded for the tower.

The typical heating energy use for domestic buildings in Germany is 200kWh/m^2 per annum. Since 1995, by law, the calculated heating energy demand of new domestic buildings has to be lower than 100kWh/m^2 (the precise value is a function of the relation between outer surface and volume of the building).

Design process

Dynamic computer simulations calculated energy lost by heat loss and infiltration, and the heat gained from internal sources and the sun. The TRNSYS simulation showed a heating energy demand of only 21kWh/m^2 for the top house and 47kWh/m^2 for the basement.

Credits

Client: Prof Rolf Disch
Architects: Prof Rolf Disch Architekt and his team
Services Engineer: Krebser & Freyler, Teningen
Structural Engineer: Andreas Wirth, Freiburg
Timber construction: Blumer AG, Waldstatt, CH

References

AIT – Intelligent Architecture 1
Der Architekt (BDA), No 1, January 1995
Deutsche Bauzeitung, Vol 129, No 6, June 1995
Deutsches Architektenblatt, Vol 127, No 5, 1 May 1995
Baumeister, October 1994
Rotatable Solar House HELIOTROP: The experience of living rotating completely around the sun, Architectural Office Rolf Disch
Energy Characterisation of the Rotatable Solar House HELIOTROP® in Freiburg Germany, First Results, Klaus Rohlffs, Andreas Gerber, Fraunhofer, Gereon Kamps, Rolf Disch, Architectural Office Rolf Disch, EuroSun 96

Villa Vision

Villa Vision
Family house
Danish Institute of Technology (DTI)
Taastrup
Denmark (DK-2630)
Flemming Skude and Ivar Moltke *Architect*
DTI Energi *Energy Consultant*
Dansk Teknologisk Institut (DTI) *Client*
1990–1994 *Dates*
55.70°N *Latitude*
0°N *Primary axis of orientation*

Intelligent features

Building management system	■
Learning facility	
Weather data	
Responsive lights	
Sun tracking facility	
Occupant override	■
Self-generation – CHP/PV/wind	■
Night cooling	
Solar water heating	■

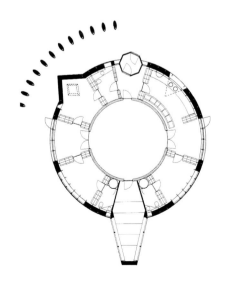

Introduction

The Villa Vision was designed as an experiment at the Danish Institute of Technology (DTI) with the intention of inspiring the Danish public to become more energy-conscious. The project involved a number of departments from the DTI, the National Energy Agency and a long list of Danish companies, institutions and foundations. Full-scale mock-ups were first erected at Building Fairs in Denmark, and a final version was built at the Institute in 1993. The Villa was opened to the public for a year in April 1994. As part of an experiment, three different families each occupied the house for periods of three months at a time.

The Intelligence Factor

The main intelligent feature of this house are the six triangular oil cloth sails that protect the central sunspace from solar overheating. The sails are programmed to close automatically like flower petals when the indoor temperature exceeds 23°C. The control system also enables the windows to open and close automatically, enabling excess heat to escape. Solar panels heat the water, and photovoltaics provide electricity.

Brief

The idea of the Villa was to create a prototype that combined minimal energy and resource use in the hope of promoting a prototype for ecological housing. The aim was for a self-sufficient house combining energy from the sun with heat from underground. The building was to be a showcase for new technologies for energy-efficient and environmentally friendly buildings. All materials specified were to be fully recyclable or easily disposable, and non-polluting during production and installation.

Façade transparency	
East	35%
West	30%
Roof	25%

U-values	
Walls	0.10W/m²K
Slab	n/a
Roof	0.10W/m²K
Windows	1.04W/m²K

Accommodation

The house is circular in plan and 16 metres in diameter. It is entered from the north side with an entrance hall leading into the main living room, which is a circular volume at the centre of the house, lit from above. There is a 'palm tree' structure that provides the residents with a platform to climb up and look out through the roof windows. The main living accommodation surrounds the central space, which is lined with a heavyweight brick wall for the absorption of solar heat. The house was designed to accommodate families of two adults and two teenagers. Villa Vision has now been converted to accommodate an engineering division of the Danish Institute of Technology. It remains open to visitors by appointment.

Energy strategy

The Villa is virtually self-sufficient in electricity and water. The accommodation has been oriented according to the compass points, with entry towards the north, dining towards the east, home work places towards the west and a television room facing south. The circular volume reduces surface area and heating loads. Surplus heat is collected by a heat pump, and stored underground for cold periods.

Site and climate

The house has been built in the municipality of Høje Taastrup, a suburb 20km west of Copenhagen. Denmark's mean annual precipitation is 60cm, spread on average between 120 and 200 days yearly. The mean temperature in the coldest month, February is 0.4°C, and in the hottest month, July, it is 16.6°C.

Construction

The house is constructed with two separated timber structures that accommodate 400mm of mineral wool insulation between them, and is clad externally with timber boards. It sits on a 100mm reinforced concrete slab, which was cast onto a bed of insulation. The roof is covered with zinc and also contains 400mm of insulation. Finishes include beechwood flooring and plasterboard made from recycled material.

Glazing

A pyramidal roof lantern is used to light the central living space. The rooflight is triple-glazed (low-e coating and krypton gas in cavity) and can be opened for ventilation. Perimeter ventilation windows are glazed with insulating glass.

Heating

Passive solar gain is collected by the brick wall and floor of the central space, and is re-radiated into the surrounding rooms. Solar panels mounted above the TV room provide hot water, and contribute to the heating. Any surplus heat is collected by a heat pump and stored underground for cold periods. An underfloor heating system circulates low temperature hot water at about 25°C. Additional heat for the underfloor system can be collected from underground by means of a 3kW propane-powered heat pump. The aerodynamic form of the building was designed to minimize wind cooling.

Cooling

The six triangular, white oil cloth sails that protect the glazed pyramidal roof serve as automatic solar shades to prevent overheating.

Ventilation

The ventilation strategy relies on a 33% fresh air supply every hour, using decentralized ventilators with heat recovery. Windows are controlled by a central computer, which opens them when the internal air temperature exceeds 25°C. If it is raining, the computer overrides this function. The glazed roof to the central space can also be opened to increase fresh air ventilation.

Electricity generation

The building obtains the electricity it needs from 40m^2 of photovoltaic cells mounted on the roof, which deliver 12V DC throughout the building. This offers a low shock risk and indistinguishable electro-magnetic forces. An additional 200kWh will be required from the national grid, equating to approximately 10% of the overall consumption.

Daylighting

All rooms are naturally lit, some from above, and all surround the top-lit central living space. The building employs low-energy lighting throughout. The triangular sails to the pyramidal roof close automatically like flower petals when the indoor temperature exceeds 23°C.

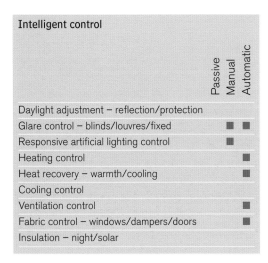

Intelligent control	Passive	Manual	Automatic
Daylight adjustment – reflection/protection			
Glare control – blinds/louvres/fixed		■	■
Responsive artificial lighting control		■	
Heating control			■
Heat recovery – warmth/cooling			■
Cooling control			
Ventilation control			■
Fabric control – windows/dampers/doors			■
Insulation – night/solar			

Building data	
Contract value	n/a
Area	200m²
Typical floorplate	4m
Number of storeys	1
Price per m²	n/a
Annual energy use	n/a
Typical energy use for building type	n/a
Annual CO₂ output	n/a
Number of sensors	n/a
Visited by authors	✗
Monitored by others	n/a

Controls

Villa Vision makes use of a full monitoring system, which is automatically fed to the central computer system to help the inhabitants to supervise a complete maintenance schedule. The fabric sails are programmed to close automatically when the indoor temperature exceeds 23°C. A windmeter retracts the sails in high winds. They are also prevented from operating in sub-zero temperatures. The sails can be operated manually if required. Ventilation and temperature are controlled without human interference. Ventilation is increased by automatically opening windows when the internal temperature exceeds 25°C.

Performance

A report of the first 3 years of operation has been produced in Danish giving detailed information on the theory and reality of the experiment.

It has not been possible to obtain delivered energy consumption figures for the building.

Credits

Client: Dansk Teknologisk Institut (DTI)
Architects: Flemming Skude and Ivar Moltke
Energy Consultant: DTI Energi
Service Engineer: Crone & Koch

References

Building, Denmark Review 2/93
World Architecture, No 36, 1995
Architektur DK, 7/94, Vol 38, No 7
Flemming Skude, The Royal Danish Academy of Fine Arts

Business Promotion Centre

Business Promotion Centre
Offices and exhibition space
Microelectronic Park, Mulheimer Strasse
Duisburg
Germany (D-47057)
Foster & Partners *Architect*
Kaiser Bautechnik *Energy Consultant*
Norbert Kaiser (Kaiser Bautechnik) *Client*
1988–1993 *Dates*
51.47°N *Latitude*
–4°N *Primary axis of orientation*

Intelligent features

Building management system	■
Learning facility	
Weather data	■
Responsive lights	
Sun tracking facility	
Occupant override	■
Self-generation – CHP/PV/wind	■
Night cooling	
Solar water heating	

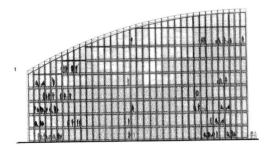

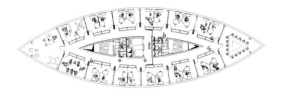

Introduction

The architects won the competition to design a centre for economic promotion in 1988. The building was conceived as providing a landmark on the edge of the masterplan for a new Microelectronics Park. Duisburg is replacing its declining heavy industries with less blighting activities, and is striving to become Europe's new nerve centre for the research and development of microelectronics. The building is to provide office space and galleries to be rented to companies which are pioneering the city's post-industrial revival. The intention was to create an energy-saving building that was electronically controlled but not artificially serviced.

The intelligence factor

The double skin surrounding the building contains computer-controlled blinds in its cavity, which automatically tilt according to information received from heat

Façade transparency

East	100%
West	100%
Roof	0%

U-values

Double skin	1.40W/m^{2}K
Slab	n/a
Roof	n/a

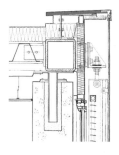

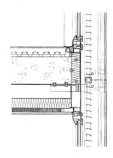

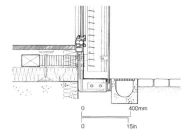

and light sensors in each room. A gas fired co-generation plant feeds an absorption chiller, providing both hot and cold water as well as electricity. The control system includes sophisticated software that analyses current and anticipated weather conditions, and uses this data to calculate the optimum heating, lighting and shading levels for the building a day or two in advance.

Accommodation

The building is lens-shaped on plan, and eight stories high. Cellular office accommodation surrounds the central lens-shaped concrete core with a radial support grid of concrete columns at 6m centres. The roof falls in a curve downwards from the 27m apex towards the fifth storey, 11m below, and creates dramatic terraced spaces underneath. The roof was to have been covered with solar water heating panels and photovoltaic cells but these were not installed.

Energy strategy

An innovative heating and air conditioning system combines passive solar gain with a co-generation engine. The building is entirely glazed around its perimeter with a dual skin envelope, separated by a 200mm air gap. Electronically-controlled blinds in the cavity are able to adjust the thermal load and the quantity of light entering the building.

Site and climate

The site of the new building is close to the city centre in the district of Neudorf, adjacent to the busy main road linking the city and the University. It is located on reclaimed land previously occupied by heavy industries. The building stands at the edge of the 89 hectare masterplan of landscaped parkland, which will house the new electronics industries.

Construction

The fully glazed double skin façade is insulated at slab level. The structural frame consists of reinforced concrete columns on a 6m grid and a load-bearing core, with 220mm concrete slabs spanning between them. The whole floor make-up amounts to only 550mm, including the structure and heating, cooling and ventilation system. The roofing membrane covers plywood decking on 100mm rigid Rockwool insulation. Internal finishes include carpeted screed, plastered walls and suspended plasterboard ceilings.

Glazing

The glazed skin is suspended from a steel ring beam at eaves level. The thermally broken aluminium profiles are suspended at 1.5m intervals with glass panels faceted on a 46m radius. The inner skin of the double wall consists of side-hung windows with thermally insulated double-glazing (6mm Pilkington K-glass with hard low-e coating, 12mm argon-filled cavity and 8mm laminated glass with soft low-e coating). The inner windows can be opened for maintenance access only. The outer skin is made up of planar glazing panels (1.5m by 3.05m) fixed to the suspended aluminium profiles (12mm armourplate toughened glass).

Heating

The circulation of hot water meets all of the heating requirements. An under-floor heating system is set into a 600mm zone at the perimeter of the floor screed, adjacent to the fresh air supply slot. Hot water is provided to the sys-

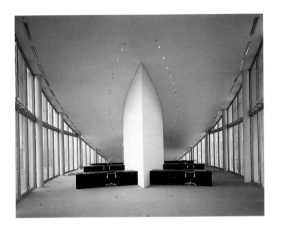

tem by a gas fired co-generation plant, which produces hot water as a by-product in the generation of electricity. It was intended to install solar water collectors on the roof to supplement the provision of hot water, but these were not executed.

Cooling

Chilled ceiling panels were developed by Kaiser Bautechnik, using a system of modified heat exchangers attached to suspended ceiling panels. The chilled water is produced by an absorption cooling machine, which is fed with waste heat from the combined heat and power unit. The water is circulated at about 13°C, and absorbs excess heat by radiation exchange. Thermal gain from the glazed façade is minimized by forced airflow through the cavity, dissipating heat collected by the metal blinds through openings at roof level.

Ventilation

The proximity of the busy main road running alongside the building's east side made the prospect of opening windows unfeasible. The building has been hermetically sealed without openable windows (openable for maintenance only). Fresh air is ducted through the suspended ceiling of the floor below, and fed into a 30mm cavity formed by PVC vacuum-formed egg crate shell used as permanent shuttering. From here it spills into the spaces through a 30mm continuous linear diffuser slot set into the floor against the glass façade. As the air escapes from the narrow perimeter slots, dehumidified and at a temperature slightly below the ambient, it forms a 'fresh air lake' across the floor, and rises naturally as contact is made with warmer surfaces, and heat is emitted by equipment and the human body. It is extracted through the luminaires, taking with it the warm and polluted air, and ducted back to the central core. Duct sizes and air velocities were kept to a minimum as all the heating and cooling requirements are met inside the space by the circulation of hot and cold water. Air is introduced into the lower parts of the glazed cavity at slightly higher than ambient pressure, and rises by a natural stack effect through the effects of warming.

Electricity generation

Electricity is generated by a gas-fired combined heat and power unit. It was also intended to install a photovoltaic array on the south-facing roof, but this has not been realized.

Daylighting

The high provision of glazing and the relatively shallow floor plan (6m deep offices) provide good levels of natural lighting, which can be controlled by the motorized blinds.

Artificial lighting

Low energy light fittings for VDUs are fitted throughout.

Solar control

Perforated metal blinds are incorporated into the cavity between the two glazed façades, and are linked to light and temperature sensors. Each of the 50,000 silver-coated slats is microprocessor controlled to tilt according to the command from the central BMS. The 7% perforations provide a view out of the building,

Intelligent control	Passive	Manual	Automatic
Daylight adjustment – reflection/protection		■	■
Glare control – blinds/louvres/fixed		■	■
Responsive artificial lighting control		■	
Heating control		■	■
Heat recovery – warmth/cooling			
Cooling control		■	■
Ventilation control			■
Fabric control – windows/dampers/doors			
Insulation – night/solar			

Building data

Contract value	~£5m
Area	4000m^2
Typical floorplate	6m
Number of storeys	8 + B
Price per m^2	~£1250/m^2
Annual energy use	n/a
Typical energy use for building type	n/a
Annual CO_2 output	n/a
Number of sensors	n/a
Visited by authors	✔
Monitored by others	✔

Credits

Client: Kaiser Bautechnik
Architects: Foster & Partners (partner in charge: David Nelson; project architect: Stefan Behling)
Service Engineer: J Roger Preston and Partners
Absorption cooling development: Dr Ofer Novick, Tel Aviv
Structural Engineer: Ingenieurbüro Dr Meyer, Kassel
Acoustic Engineer: ITA, Wiesbaden
Contractor: Hochitef

References

AJ Focus, September 1993, Vol 7, No 7
A&V Monografias de Arquitectura y Vivienda, 38 (1992)
Annual of Light and Architecture, Ingebarg Flagge, Ernst & Sohn, Berlin, 1994
Architectural Design, Vol 63, No 7/8, July/August 1993, 'Visions for the Future'
Architectural Monographs, No 20, Foster Associates: Recent Works, Academy Editions/St Martins Press, 1992
Architectural Review, February 1993, Vol CXCII, No 1152
Architecture, September 1993, Vol 82, No 9
Architecture, January 1995, Vol 84, No 1
Architecture Interieure Cree, No 258, March/April 1994
Architecture Today, AT 43
Baumeister, 1/1993
Building Design, BD 1120, 16 April 1993
Domus 754, November 1993
DBZ, 11/93, Vol 41, No 11
De Architect, The Architect (The Hague), November 1993, Vol 24, No 11
GA Document, No 29, 1991
Glass in Architecture, Michael Wigginton, Phaidon, 1996
Intelligent Glass Façades: Material Practice Design, Andrea Compagno, Birkhäuser, Basel, 1995
l'ARCA, November 1993, No 76
l'ARCA, July/August 1989, No 29
Progressive Architecture, Vol 75, No 2, February 1994
Quaderns, October/December 1990, No 191, p 66-69
World Architecture, No 33
Stefan Behling, Foster & Partners

even when the blinds are fully closed. The blinds are fixed in the lowered position, and are raised only for cleaning.

Controls

The building management system (BMS) was designed to control the building's distribution and consumption of energy micro-electronically. The building's brain is a powerful PC with sophisticated software that analyses current and anticipated weather conditions, and uses this data to calculate the optimum heating, lighting and shading levels for the building in advance. The data for these calculations arrives via a direct modem link with the regional Meteorological Office and from a rooftop weather station that measures solar radiation, temperature and wind speed. The BMS is responsible for operating the perimeter blinds according to information received from heat and light sensors in each room.

User control

Over 200 control panels that replace the conventional light switch in each room are connected via a bus link to the central BMS. These allow users to individually adjust temperature, humidity, light and shading. The blinds can also be overridden manually, but the blind position is regularly rechecked by the BMS.

Operating modes

Winter day – pre-heated fresh air is supplied to the space where it is heated further by an underfloor heating system and other occupant gains. A limited heating effect is achieved through passive solar gain, and the sealed cavity serves as a thermal buffer to the outside. The tilt of the blinds is optimized by the BMS for maximum daylighting.

Summer day – fresh air is supplied dehumidified at a temperature below ambient. Radiant cooling is provided by chilled ceiling panels. Warm, polluted air is extracted from the space, and replaced by cleaner, cooler air. The air movement through the glazed cavity, which dissipates the solar gain at roof level, also provides a limited cooling effect. The tilt of the blinds is adjusted to minimize unwanted solar gain and limit glare discomfort.

Performance

The energy performance of the building is being closely monitored by a research project at Duisburg's Gerhard Mercator University.

Figures for the delivered energy consumption are not available. A large proportion of the electricity consumption will be self-generated by relatively benign means, as a by-product of hot and cold water provision.

School of Engineering and Manufacture

School of Engineering and Manufacture
University building
Queens Building
De Montfort University
Mill Lane, Leicester
United Kingdom
Short Ford & Associates *Architect*
Max Fordham Associates *Energy Consultant*
De Montfort University *Client*
1989–1993 *Dates*
52.61°N *Latitude*
–33°N *Primary axis of orientation*

Intelligent features

Building management system	■
Learning facility	
Weather data	■
Responsive lights	■
Sun tracking facility	
Occupant override	■
Self-generation – CHP/PV/wind	■
Night cooling	■
Solar water heating	

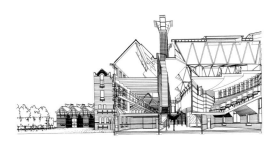

Introduction

The process of providing a new engineering teaching and research facility for De Montfort University began in 1989, shortly after the University became a freestanding corporation, formerly known as Leicester Polytechnic. The University was committed to acting as a catalyst for change in the run down inner city area in which its buildings are located. The development which was in the heart of a City Challenge area also had to fit in with Leicester's role as an Environment City. The architects developed the concept for the new building from an earlier project for a passively cooled brewery in Malta. Planning permission was gained at the end of 1989, and construction began after a long period of funding bids and environmental studies in July 1991. Teaching began as scheduled in October 1993, and the building was officially opened by HM The Queen on 9 December 1993, and named The Queens Building.

The intelligence factor

The building is naturally ventilated by a combination of simple opening windows and automatically controlled windows and vents at high level. A series of chimneys are responsible for the automatic ventilation of the two 150-seat auditoria. The lighting is automatically controlled according to occupancy. A combined heat and power (CHP) unit acts as the lead boiler, providing both heat and electricity at times when both are in high demand.

Brief

The design brief called for an innovative building of traditional construction and environmental sensitivity. As an academic institution, it was felt important that the University should challenge conventional wisdom in a creative and responsible way. The new building was located in an area with high unemployment and there was an ambition that the building would be labour-intensive and create

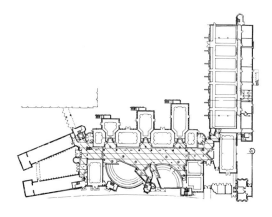

Sunpath

Latitude
52.61°

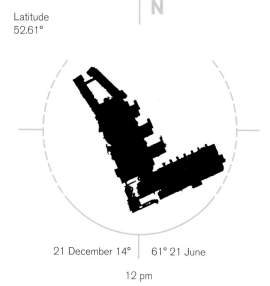

| 21 December 14° | 61° 21 June |

12 pm

Façade transparency

North	45%
East	5%
South	45%
West	5%
Roof	10%

U-values

Walls	0.32W/m²K
Slab	0.33W/m²K
Roof	0.24W/m²K
Windows	2.00W/m²K

job opportunities in its construction. It was also stated that the building should encapsulate all of the best possible features of known and potential environmental design criteria, in tune with Leicester's role as the first nominated Environment City.

Accommodation

The four-storey building lies on an approximate north-easterly axis, adjacent to a minor road running into the city. Electrical laboratories at the north-east end of the building consist of four storey wings either side of an entrance courtyard. The deep plan central building provides general purpose classrooms (nine lecture/seminar rooms), teaching staff offices, joint laboratory accommodation and two auditoria (each for 150 people). The top level accommodates drawing/design studios designed to have a combination of top- and north-light. The central building is divided by a top-lit concourse running the full height and length of the building. The mechanical laboratories are located in a double-height machine hall at the west end of the building, at right angles to the main accommodation. Large quantities of the academic offices were designed to be open plan areas, as well as many of the laboratories. The building is not simply a shell for teaching but has become a teaching object in itself. It accommodates up to 1000 students and 100 staff, with as many PCs.

Energy strategy

The energy concept relies on a highly insulated, thermally massive envelope with a shallow plan and generous ceiling heights to promote natural ventilation and daylighting. The central lightwell acts as a thermal and acoustic buffer zone, whilst permitting daylight to penetrate deep into the main building. Cross- and stack-effect ventilation minimizes the need for mechanical ventilation and cooling. Gas boilers provide the heating that is required and a small gas-driven CHP unit is incorporated for electricity and heat generation. The building has been designed to function without air conditioning despite high internal heat gains in lecture theatres and laboratories.

Site and climate

The building occupies a prominent site at the heart of the City Campus. Average temperatures in Leicester are in the region of 10.5°C (1993/94).

Construction

The building is built from load-bearing red brick, the labour-intensive technique that the University were looking for. The walls are filled with 100mm of Rockwool cavity insulation, and are fair faced internally with heavyweight 190mm concrete block. Some of the overhanging elements at high level are clad with cedar shingles. The floor slabs are precast concrete laid onto double-T beams. The pitched roofs are supported on timber rafters and steel ridge trusses, with 150mm insulation and covered in clay tiles. Finishes include exposed concrete soffits and fair-faced brickwork and blockwork partitions.

Glazing

Most of the windows are double-glazed. Triple glazing was used in the gables of the engineering workshop for acoustic isolation for the surrounding residents. In the engineering workshop, a motor that drives a shaft connected to a saw-tooth arm (greenhouse technology) is driven by temperature sensors to control the opening of high level windows. At low level windows are manually controlled, being inwardly tiltable.

Heating

Early design analysis revealed that computers and occupants would provide a significant amount of energy throughout the year. It was proposed that a Combined Heat and Power (CHP) unit and a high-efficiency boiler would meet the remaining space-heating requirement. Perimeter-mounted radiators, finned pipes and natural convectors provide the space heating. LTHW heater batteries are used in the air handling plant serving the clean rooms and welding rooms. The central concourse has underfloor heating and in the mechanical laboratories there are high level radiant panels. All heating elements are under the direct control of the building management system (BMS). The heating circuits are weather compensated, and local control is provided by two-port motorized valves and room thermostats. Hot water is supplied from central calorifiers.

As long as there is an electrical demand, the CHP unit acts as the lead boiler. The original design included a canteen, so it was envisaged that a heating demand would remain outside of the winter heating season, but this was not executed. The next boiler to be activated is a 300 kilowatt condensing boiler, which retrieves additional heat from the condensing flue gases for maximum efficiency. The two remaining boilers (300kW) are conventional appliances used in combination with the condensing boiler and the CHP unit. Monitoring has shown that the condensing boiler provided approximately 45% of the annual heat energy, the conventional boilers 41%, and the CHP unit the remaining 14% [PROBE].

There is no heat recovery in the stacks or elsewhere from exhaust air as the pressures would be too small.

Cooling

The cooling action works by a passive, natural stack-effect, unaided by fans or other mechanical means. Accumulated heat is cross-ventilated away, or removed by thermosiphonic stack-effect, promoted by chimneys distributed through the deeper parts of the plan. The large areas of exposed masonry also assist in reducing peak temperatures. During summer nights and weekends, the ventilation dampers can be opened to pre-cool the structure. This is limited to a minimum building structure temperature of 17°C to avoid discomfort and the risk of activating the heating plant. Calculations showed that the few hot days when the internal temperature was expected to exceed 27°C coincide with the long summer holidays, when the building is sparsely occupied.

The electrical laboratory wings with their intensive internal heat gains from computer equipment partially enclose a shady courtyard. The narrow plan of six metres was designed to be cross-ventilated, drawing its air from the sump of cool air which would collect in the north facing courtyard.

Ventilation

The laboratory and general teaching spaces in the compact plan of the central building are stack-effect ventilated, using a combination of manually-controlled opening windows at the perimeter and automated air exhausts via eight stack chimneys or openable roof lights at high level.

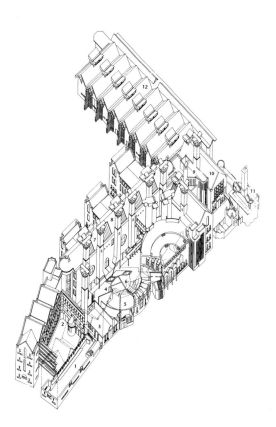

The auditoria are also stack ventilated by a thermosiphon action. Air is drawn from outside through large ventilation grilles about 8m above street level. It is passed through acoustically lined plenums and acoustic splitters to reduce the street noise with minimal pressure drop. The air enters one of the auditoriums through the seats, and the other from grilles at the front of the lecture space. Hot water heating batteries are set into the intake air path for pre-heating of outside air in cool conditions. Once inside the space, the air is warmed further by the occupants and other internal gains, rising towards high level openings in the two separate stacks. Air rises 14 metres up the acoustically lined stacks, and is expelled at the top by automatically controlled opening windows with a free area of $7.9m^2$. As a precautionary measure one stack of the two for each main auditorium is fitted with an emergency upward flow 'punkah' fan to provide minimum mechanical assistance ($1.7m^2/s$ at 10Pa) in extreme conditions. The total pressure drop from street intake to stack top with the stack louvres open is less than 5 Pascals. The air was not filtered, as this would have created too much resistance to the natural airflow. The stacks terminate approximately 3 metres above the roofline to avoid local turbulence.

The shallow section (6m) of the two entrance wings promotes cross ventilation through low- and high-level openings to give up to 50% openings to the whole façade. Some windows are electrically operated. Ventilation in the top floor design studios is provided by motor-driven rooflights under the temperature control of the BMS.

In the mechanical laboratory, ventilation air is introduced at low level through 'perforated' brick buttresses which can be manually opened via timber doors to provide cross-ventilation. Rooflights at high level also act as ridge ventilators, and are motor-driven by the BMS depending on temperature. Two small air handling units supply air to ancillary rooms and fume cupboards with mechanical ventilation (but not cooling).

Despite the overall simplicity of the building services, the complexity of the passive ventilation strategy demanded automatic control of low level inlets and stack or ridge exhaust ventilators in the majority of areas. Opening windows naturally ventilate other spaces such as offices, stairways, landings, toilets, workshops and smaller laboratories.

Electricity generation

A gas-fired combined heat and power system provides up to 38 kilowatts of electricity (three-phase) and 70 kilowatts of hot water. It is regarded as Boiler No1 in a series of three others. The system consists of a modified two-litre Ford Transit engine, which has a water-cooled reciprocating engine. Heat is reclaimed from the engine jacket, the lubricating oil and exhaust flue gases to warm the hot water via a water-to-water heat exchanger. The capital cost of £20,000 was justified more for its research potential than the economic viability, which equates to a 12-year payback at current usage. The CHP engine can only run when there is demand for both heat and electricity, and is therefore often restricted to winter operation. Monitoring data showed that the CHP unit met 21% of the building's electricity demand between August 1994 and July 1995.

Daylighting

The building is almost wholly naturally lit by a combination of perimeter windows and rooflights. The deepest part of the plan is split by a concourse, which is lit from above. Glass blocks set into the walkways ensure that daylight reaches the base of this four-storey height space.

In the electrical laboratories, daylight is controlled by light shelves beneath the high level windows which protect occupants from direct sunlight and reflect light onto the ceiling. The courtyard façades are all clad with white panels to further reflect daylight into the lower floor areas. Daylight penetrates deep into the laboratory and concourse area via rooflights and glazed gables. The drawing studios are served with glare-free northlight through glazed gables.

Artificial lighting

Lighting is generally provided by high-efficiency fluorescent tubes with high frequency electronic ballasts. Compact fluorescents are used in offices and high-pressure mercury lighting in the workshops, central concourse and large laboratories. In the offices, teaching areas and computer laboratories lighting levels were designed to give 300 lux on the working plane. In the machine hall and central laboratory, mercury lights were needed to provide 1000 lux (client requirement).

In general, the artificial lighting is switched in rows parallel to the windows to allow a response to daylight levels. Two switches in series control each light. The first is a conventional manual switch and the second is controlled via the BMS and an infrared occupancy detector (PIRs) for that space. During the core occupied period, lighting circuits are energized by the BMS and then controlled locally by manual switches. Outside normal working hours the BMS will de-energize lighting circuits unless movement is detected by the PIRs. Lighting in the machine hall and central laboratory is not controlled by occupancy detectors because of safety. Experiments have been conducted to allow external light levels to determine whether to switch off artificial lighting in certain spaces, but this has not been fully executed.

Solar control

On the south side of the central building, a series of small courtyards are created by the perimeter wall to minimise areas of south facing glazing. Roof overhangs and deep reveals in the mechanical laboratory prevent penetration of direct sunlight onto the laboratory floor. In general, most windows are shaded from direct solar heat gain by deep reveals, deep eaves and overhanging floor soffits.

Controls

A building management system (BMS) controls lighting levels, room temperatures and the amount of air entering or leaving the spaces. This is based on criteria such as fresh air requirements (based on CO_2 concentration), internal temperatures and external conditions. All control settings and temperatures can be programmed from a single computer screen. The building's daily performance is carefully monitored for optimum performance. Information regarding the heating, ventilation and lighting is continuously analysed by computer, and relayed to an Energy Management Company who have a contract to maintain the energy system. The BMS is capable of measuring over 900 variables in ten

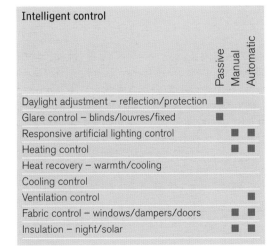

Intelligent control

	Passive	Manual	Automatic
Daylight adjustment – reflection/protection	■		
Glare control – blinds/louvres/fixed	■		
Responsive artificial lighting control		■	■
Heating control		■	■
Heat recovery – warmth/cooling			
Cooling control			
Ventilation control			■
Fabric control – windows/dampers/doors		■	■
Insulation – night/solar		■	■

different control zones. Numerous additional sensors have also been included so that students can interrogate the BMS for educational purposes.

The two lecture theatres are fitted with temperature and CO_2 sensors to determine ventilation inlet and outlet. Within each stack and each air entry plenum, there are controllable sets of dampers operated by the BMS. Proportional controllers open them when the temperature is above 19°C in the auditorium or the CO_2 concentration is higher than 25%. A printed circuit board rain sensor on top of one of the stacks prevents the stack dampers from opening more than 50% to avoid rain penetration. The BMS also monitors wind conditions with a rotating cup anemometer to determine openings at the air inlets and the top of the stacks. Air movement within the stacks is measured by in-built flow meters.

The heating system is also controlled by the BMS. Individual and averaging sensors in each room allow the BMS to monitor and record temperatures continuously. A set-point figure can be allocated to each position (normally 19°C) and the BMS controls motorized valves to the ring circuit of the appropriate space. Manually controlled thermostatic radiator valves (TRVs) can also be used at each heater.

User control

A manual override switch is provided in each lecture room to control the ventilation system. TRVs and local room thermostats provide local trimming of heating. Lights can be manually switched on and off as described.

Operating modes

Winter day – when the lecture theatres are occupied in winter, the vents are opened under the control of carbon dioxide sensors. Rain accompanied by high wind speeds will cause the exhaust dampers to close to a minimal setting. In high winds, the intake and extract dampers are closed completely, overriding the CO_2 control.

Winter night – air intakes and exhausts are kept closed during winter nights to prevent unnecessary heat loss from the unoccupied spaces.

Summer day – if the lecture theatres are occupied during the summer period, the air inlet and exhaust dampers will be fully opened when the inside temperature is higher than the outside temperature (and higher than the internal set point). If the internal temperature is lower than the external temperature, the dampers will open to a lesser degree based on CO_2 levels. As with winter operation combinations of wind and rain can close the high level exhausts and low level inlets to differing degrees, depending on the severity. A punkah fan in one of the extract stacks can be activated if the average temperature in the auditoria exceeds 25°C and is at least 2°C above the external temperature.

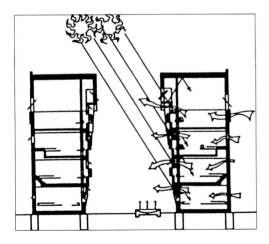

Summer night – night time ventilation is promoted in the summer by allowing external air to pre-cool the structure to a preset temperature above the dew point, and no lower than the temperature that would necessitate re-heating the next day (17°C). The punkah fan can assist airflow if necessary.

Building data

Contract value	£8.5m
Area	9850m^2
Typical floorplate	~6–12m
Number of storeys	4
Price per m^2	~£860/m^2
Annual energy use	195kWh/m^{2*}
Typical energy use for building type	260kWh/m^2
Annual CO_2 output	65kg/m^2
Number of sensors	900
Visited by authors	✔
Monitored by others	✔

*Temperature corrected figure (normalized for PROBE).
NB: energy use based on a treated floor area of 8400m^2.

Credits

Client: De Montfort University
Architects: Short Ford & Associates (Peake Short & Partners in 1989)
Service Engineer: Max Fordham Associates
Structural Engineer: YRM/Anthony Hunt Associates
Landscape Architect: Livingston Eyre Associates
QS: Dearle & Henderson
Contractor: Laing Midlands
Design Simulations: Cambridge Architectural Research Limited

References

Architecture Today, AT23, November 1991
Building Services, 'Learning Curve', October 1993
Building Services, 'PROBE 4 Queens Building', Roland Asbridge and Robert Cohen, April 1996
Natural Ventilation in Non-Domestic Buildings, Michael Fisher, Post Graduate Diploma in Architecture, Dissertation, 1997
Passive Ventilated, Daylight Optimised, Low Energy Engineering Building, De Montfort University, J W Twidell and B Howe, AMSET Centre
Queens Building – Background Information, AMSET Centre, School of Engineering and Manufacture
Queens Building, De Montfort University External Relations, 1993
The Queens Building De Montfort University – Feedback for Designers and Clients, New Practice Final Report 102, Best Practice Programme, Department of the Environment
Alan Short, Short & Associates
JJ Brown/Jim Bisgrove, Energy Manager, De Montfort University
Bart Stevens/Randall Thomas, Max Fordham & Partners

Performance

A contract was awarded by ETSU to the University's School of the Built Environment to measure actual air movement in the auditoria and to check the simulations.

A PROBE study was conducted in April 1996, including an occupant survey of the 75 staff (95% return).

The following difficulties have been observed in use [PROBE].
- opening mechanisms for glazed roof ventilators have proved problematic (some isolated after an aluminium shaft sheared off)
- delayed energizing of lighting circuits by occupancy sensors has led to this function being overridden
- in the mechanical laboratories equipment prevents the opening of internal vent doors to buttresses
- there is a tendency for users to overwind, and damage, rooflight mechanisms in computer and project rooms (because they cannot see the opening light)
- heating pipework returning through staff offices was providing unwanted heat gain

The building won the Heating and Ventilation Contractors Association (HVCA) Green Building of the Year Award in 1995.

Delivered energy consumption

The energy consumption for the first year of operation based on gross floor area was measured at 114kWh/m^2 for gas and 53kWh/m^2 electricity. Weather-corrected figures for 8400m^2 of treated floor area measured between August 1994 and July 1995 equate to 143kWh/m^2 for gas and 52kWh/m^2 for electricity. This compares well against Energy Efficiency Office 'low' targets of 185kWh/m^2 and 75kWh/m^2 respectively. Carbon dioxide emissions were calculated at 65kg/m^2 compared with Energy Efficiency Office targets of 90kg/m^2.

Design process

An Energy Design Award from the Department of Trade and Industry funded the computerized energy simulation. Two mathematical models were used to simulate the thermal performance of an auditorium space (using ESP-r) and the concourse areas (using a finite difference model) by the Environmental Computer Aided Design and Performance Group in the University's School of the Built Environment. Daylight factors were calculated using the Radiance daylight simulation programme, which was also used to test the light shelves in the computer laboratories.

Salt water modelling of the naturally ventilated auditoria was performed by Cambridge Architectural Research Limited in conjunction with the Department of Applied Mathematics and Theoretical Physics. A perspex model was immersed in a bath of water and injected with dyed salt solution to symbolize airflow patterns. A 1:50 scale model was also tested under an artificial sky and heliodon in the School of the Built Environment at De Montfort University.

SUVA Insurance Company

SUVA Insurance Company
Office building
St. Jakobs-Strasse 24/Gratenstrasse 51
Basel
Switzerland (CH4052)
Herzog & de Meuron Architekten *Architect*
W Waldhauser AG *Energy Consultant*
Schweizerische Unfall-Versicherungs-Ansalt
   (SUVA) *Client*
1988–1993 *Dates*
47.54°N *Latitude*
–45°N *Primary axis of orientation*

Intelligent features

Building management system	■
Learning facility	
Weather data	■
Responsive lights	■
Sun tracking facility	
Occupant override	■
Self-generation – CHP/PV/wind	■
Night cooling	■
Solar water heating	■

Introduction

This building is a district agency for SUVA, which is the Swiss equivalent of the UK National Insurance Service, but privately operated. The original six-storey building had been constructed in the 1950s and was typical of the period, with a regular arrangement of hole-in-the-wall windows and sandstone cladding. The architects were commissioned to overclad the existing building and improve its thermal and lighting performance. The existing sandstone façade remains intact behind a new glazed skin set 100mm in front of the original.

The intelligence factor

The new glazed outer skin consists of a tri-partite band of computer controlled windows. An upper prismatic panel is adjusted according to solar angles, a low level parapet window is closed in winter and opened in summer to create a greenhouse effect in front of the heavyweight parapet, and a central vision window can be electronically opened from inside. The building management system (BMS) measures direct and diffuse radiation, façade temperatures and wind speed. In winter, the outer skin can be completely sealed to conserve energy ($1.2W/m^2K$ when closed).

Brief

The main objective of the client and the architects had been to avoid the contradiction of blocking the sun with external blinds, meaning that artificial lighting was kept on to supplement the low light levels on bright sunny days. As most workers used visual display terminals, the quality of computer workspaces was to be improved with glare-free daylight in the offices and a feeling of contact with the outside world. The brief also called for an energy conservation strategy.

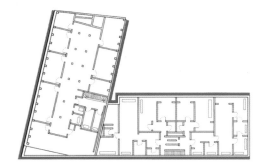

Accommodation

As the building turns the corner it continues 3 metres past the original chamfered corner to turn the glazing at right angles, leaving a small triangular volume enclosed by the new glazing. This has been occupied by a café, which spills out onto the south-facing street. An existing bas-relief sculpture depicting Daedalus and Icarus carved out of the orginal façade has been retained within this volume, just visible behind the glass. Around the corner, the architects have added a new five-storey block of apartments and conference facilities, enclosing a landscaped courtyard at the rear of the building. On the internal face of the new block a very different palette of materials has been utilized overlooking the new courtyard, with timber cladding, fabric awnings and open balconies. The renovated building provides centralized office facilities for up to 100 insurance company employees.

Energy strategy

The new skin of structural silicon glazing panels consists of a tri-partite band of operable windows at each level, designed to enhance daylight penetration with prismatic glass, allow a degree of natural ventilation with openable windows and improve the building's overall thermal performance. In summer, the lower windows are opened to cool the stone façade, whereas in winter they remain closed to build up a thermal buffer between the two façades

Site and climate

The building occupies a corner site fronting a busy main road in the centre of Basel.

Construction

The original sandstone cladding has been covered by a new framework of structural silicon glazing panels in aluminium frames. The new wing is made from a concrete frame, and includes three basement levels.

Glazing

The inner windows of the existing building were replaced with a high performance timber window, with aluminium outer facing. The new glazed façade is divided into three horizontal bands of motorized top-hinged windows at every level, each automatically controlled to perform a different function. The lower band covers the existing stone parapet, and is glazed with insulating glass, and 50% screen-printed with the SUVA logo. The central 'vision' band of insulating glass at eye level provides ventilation and a view out, situated in front of the original window openings. The upper 'daylighting' band consists of insulated prismatic glass, which adjusts its angle according to the solar altitude. The panels are driven electrically by two motors, and can be adjusted infinitely (maximum lift of motor 229mm). Glass light transmission values are between 81% and 75%, and total energy transmission lies between 73% and 58%.

Heating

The lower band of glazing is conceived as performing a solar gain function, providing a thermal buffer to the solid parapet of the original building. The insulating glass units are linked to a computerized heat-detector that signals the panels to open and close according to air temperature between the two skins. The outer skin is closed in winter to conserve and harness solar energy, creating a thermal buffer zone between inside and out. The glazing at this level is

Sunpath

Latitude
47.54°

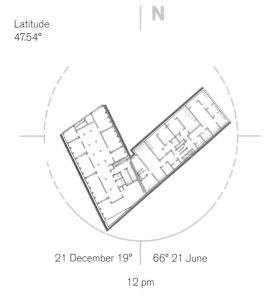

| 21 December 19° | 66° 21 June |

12 pm

screen printed with horizontal strips of the company logo, providing up to 50% shading.

The building is ventilated by a mechanical ventilation system situated in the basement. Radiators under each window provide additional heating in the offices. A district heating system that is fed by a waste incinerator supplies the heat to the building in the form of steam, piped in at 180°C, and converted for local use.

The new apartment block is provided with hot water by 70m^2 of roof-mounted solar water heating panels.

Cooling

Air conditioning is forbidden in Switzerland, and the building relies on both mechanical and natural air transfers for cooling. In addition, the parapet level glass units are linked to a computerized heat detector that signals the panels to open and close according to air temperature between the two skins. In the summer, the outer panel is opened to promote air movement around the stone parapet, and thus cool the building mass. Night time cooling is promoted by the opening of the lower panel to dissipate daytime heat from the stone façade.

Ventilation

Minimum ventilation is provided mechanically through floor inlets, and waste air is extracted at ceiling level. Occupants also have the option of natural ventilation by manually opening the inner windows of the original building. Each window has a wall-mounted switch, which controls the opening and closing of the outer glazed panels. If the outer panels are closed then the window can be fully opened inwards for ventilation from the cavity (upper prismatic panel open during day providing fresh air). However, if the outer panels are open the windows can only be tilted inwards for safety.

Façade transparency	
North	45%
East	5%
South	45%
West	5%
Roof	10%

U-values	
Walls	0.32 W/m^{2}K
Slab	0.33 W/m^{2}K
Roof	0.24 W/m^{2}K
Windows	2.00 W/m^{2}K

Electricity generation

The roof of the original building provides the base for 75m^2 of photovoltaic cells, providing a peak output of 10.2 kilowatts. The electricity generated is used to charge batteries for the uninterruptible power supply and the emergency lighting system.

Daylighting

The upper band of glazing to the new façade consists of insulated glass with prismatic plates (90° prisms) in the air space. From the inside, they are essentially translucent, but inhibit a direct view of the bright sky, refracting the direct rays of the sun. The computer system measures solar insolation and calculates the sun's azimuth and elevation on each of the three façades. A specially developed control programme adjusts the prismatic glass units at 30 minute intervals so that they are perpendicular to the solar altitude. The prismatic band can be opened to a maximum angle of 73.12°. In Basel the solar elevation varies from a winter peak of 19° to a summer maximum of 66°.

Artificial lighting

Internally, the Zumtobel lighting system is computer-controlled with sensors in the offices determining whether lights need to be on or not. The computer also

Intelligent control

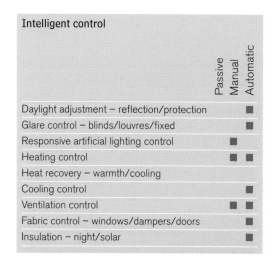

	Passive	Manual	Automatic
Daylight adjustment – reflection/protection			■
Glare control – blinds/louvres/fixed			■
Responsive artificial lighting control	■		
Heating control		■	■
Heat recovery – warmth/cooling			
Cooling control			■
Ventilation control		■	■
Fabric control – windows/dampers/doors			■
Insulation – night/solar			■

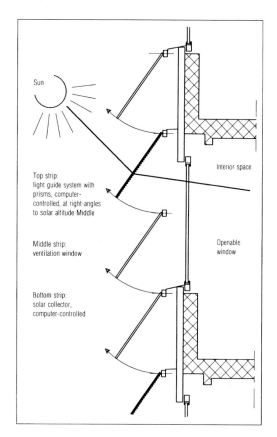

Sun

Top strip:
light guide system with prisms, computer-controlled, at right-angles to solar altitude Middle

Middle strip:
ventilation window

Bottom strip:
solar collector, computer-controlled

Interior space

Openable window

enables the management to instigate a blanket shut down of lights at the end of the working day. It was calculated that the internal light levels would be up to 130% greater than if exterior blinds had been fitted.

Solar control

The principal method of internal glare control is provided by the adjustable prismatic panels, which not only obscure a direct view of the sky vault, but also serve to refract the sun's rays into the depth of the plan. The apartments facing the courtyard are provided with external fabric blinds for additional solar protection.

Controls

The building is served by a central building management system located in the basement plant area. It controls the window operating motors, the lighting, security and plant operation. A rooftop weather station provides the computer with real time figures for diffuse solar radiation, direct solar radiation, wind speed and direction, and outside temperature. Sensors on each of the three main façades (courtyard glazing, main frontage glazing and side street glazing) give the parapet temperatures. The computer is able to calculate the solar azimuth and elevation from Basel's longitude and latitude, and the stored date and time information. The control unit consists of a PC, graphical screen output and a maintenance log printer.

Two linear drive motors drive each window panel and the computer controls and monitors the synchronism of the two motors and the specified position of the façade parts via built-in potentiometers. The computer is also able to sense if a specified threshold is exceeded, and the corresponding panel is automatically switched off and the fact displayed on the computer console. In the case of a storm, hail, rain or snow all of the panels are closed automatically.

User control

Users have control over their immediate environments with wall-switches for the external vision glazing panels, openable windows and local temperature control.

Operating modes

In winter, the closed external panels save heating energy. Between the stone façade and the insulating glass, an almost fully enclosed air volume is created, which is ensured by an airtight window cill and an airtight gusset plate in the lintel area. Direct and indirect insolation reaches the stone surface via the transparent parts of the outer glazing. The radiation energy is absorbed by the surface, is converted to heat energy and reaches the interior via the stone and concrete.

In summer, the opposite effect is required, and the panels are often fully opened. During the relatively cool night and morning hours the air movement promoted by the open panels cools the stone surface and thus the interior.

Design process

A prototype of the new façade system was created and fitted with a complete data collection system required before the design was completed. After a successful endurance test consisting of several periods of over 10,000 movements, the client agreed to the project.

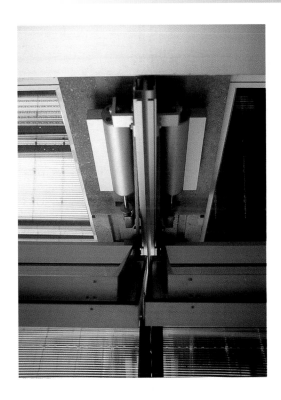

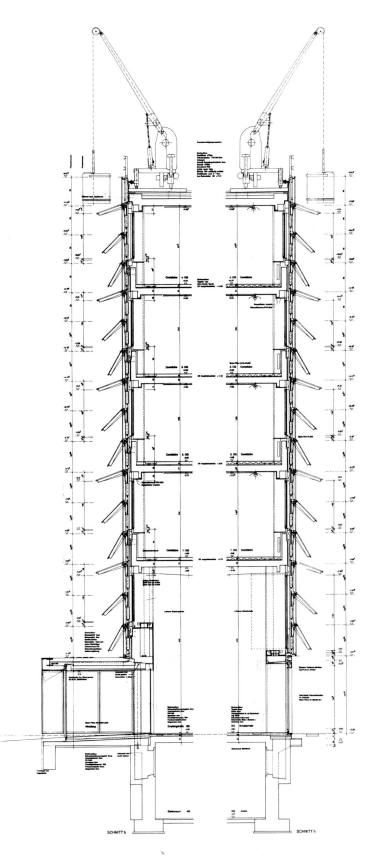

SCHNITT b

SCHNITT h

SUVA Insurance Company **141**

Building data

Contract value	n/a
Area	n/a
Typical floorplate	n/a
Number of storeys	6 ex/5+3B new
Price per m^2	n/a
Annual energy use	n/a
Typical energy use for building type	n/a
Annual CO_2 output	n/a
Number of sensors	n/a
Visited by authors	✔
Monitored by others	✗

Credits

Client: Schweizerische Unfall-Versicherungs-Anstalt (SUVA), Lucerne
Architects: Herzog + de Meuron Architekten AG, Basel CH-4056
HVAC Engineer: W Waldhauser AG, Münchenstein
Electrical Engineer: Selmoni AG, Basel
Façade Planning: Schmidlin AG, Aesch
Façade Coordination: A Müller, Basel
Contractor: Baukoslenplaner Ernst

References

Architecture (AIA), Vol 84, No 11, November 1995
Façade, 1/94, 'Light and Heat: Governing Elements of a Dynamic Façade', reprinted by Scmidlin AG
Façade in Harmony with Light and Heat, Paul Hugentobler (Schmidlin AG)
Herzog + de Meuron Das Neue Suva-Haus in Basel 1988-1993, Erweiterung und Umbau eines steinernen Geschäftshauses von 1950 (Exhibition Catalogue), Textbeitrag von Arthur Rüegg, Architekturgalerie Luzern, 1994
Reference Building SUVA Basel, No 87, Schmidlin AG
SUVA Kreisagentur Basel, SUVA Information Booklet
Mr Jacques Herzog/Andrea Saemann/A Alge, Herzog + de Meuron
Mr Hans Naf, Schmidlin AG
Martin Muller/Beat Heggli/Claudia Loosli, SUVA
Hisao Suzuk Fotógrafo

Solar House Freiburg

Solar House Freiburg
Experimental house (now used as offices/lecture room)
Christaweg 40
Freiburg
Germany (D-79114))
Hölken & Berghoff *Architect*
Fraunhofer Institute for Solar Energy Systems ISE
    Energy Consultant
Fraunhofer Institute for Solar Energy Systems ISE
    Client
1988–1992 *Dates*
48°N *Latitude*
0°N *Primary axis of orientation*

Intelligent features

Building management system	■
Learning facility	
Weather data	
Responsive lights	
Sun tracking facility	
Occupant override	■
Self-generation – CHP/PV/wind	■
Night cooling	
Solar water heating	■

Introduction

The Solar House was built by the Fraunhofer Institute for Solar Energy Systems to demonstrate that all of the energy needed in a family house could be supplied by the solar energy incident on the roof and walls. As Fraunhofer is a research institute, the project was to go through a period of continued research and monitoring. Many of the experimental technologies incorporated into the design were a realization of the state-of-the-art in solar energy systems at that time. The most sophisticated component was the hydrogen/oxygen system, which allowed the seasonal storage of solar-generated electricity. This innovative inter-seasonal storage system accounted for more than half of the overall budget.

The intelligence factor

This building is able to run almost completely on the energy of the sun. Solar collectors on the roof provide the hot water and photovoltaics produce electricity. The south-facing walls are made up of areas of a transparent insulation (TI) that maximizes passive solar gain. Both the TI walls and the solar water heating panels can be protected from the sun by automatic blinds.

Brief

The objective was to design a house in which the entire demand for space heating, hot water, electricity for equipment and appliances, and energy for cooking were met by solar energy. This was achieved by limiting the overall energy demand of the house by using energy-efficient domestic appliances, optimized ventilation heat recovery and passive solar energy collectors for space heating.

Sunpath

Latitude
48.00°

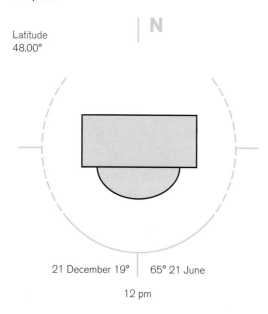

| 21 December 19° | 65° 21 June |

12 pm

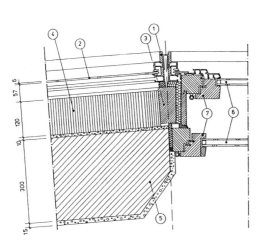

Façade transparency

North	10%
South	35%
Roof	0%

U-values

North walls	0.16W/m²K
South walls	0.51W/m²K
with blinds	0.40W/m²K
Slab	0.16W/m²K
Roof	0.18W/m²K
North windows	1.20W/m²K
South windows	0.60W/m²K

Accommodation

The two-storey building has a semi-circular plan that faces south, and all occupied rooms are oriented in this direction. A more orthogonal block to the north accommodates the corridors and staircase. The opaque elements of the south façade are insulated with transparent insulation material, and act as a form of Trombe wall. Other opaque areas are very well insulated and the window area on the north façade is kept to a minimum. The house was originally designed for and occupied by a three-person family who lived there until October 1995. It has now been converted into an office for a solar marketing company, with the downstairs living area transformed into a seminar space.

Site and climate

The self-sufficient solar house is located in Freiburg, which is one of the sunniest parts of Germany in the south-west, near to the Swiss border. The aim of the project was to demonstrate that there was enough solar energy in central European climatic conditions for complete autonomy.

Construction

The north wall is made from 300mm calcium silicate block, 240mm cellulose fibre insulation (recycled newspaper), and is faced externally with timber boarding. The south walls have an inner leaf of 300mm calcium silicate block, insulated with a transparent polycarbonate honeycomb insulation contained in a wooden support structure. Woven fabric blinds are contained in the cavity between the TI material and the outer pane of single glazing, which is held in an aluminium framework. The concrete block basement has 230mm of insulation. Inside the floors are finished with timber.

Glazing

Full-height, high performance timber windows that can be fully opened are used for the transparent elements of the south façade. The inner and outer windows are each glazed with low-e double glazing units and filled with krypton gas. The windows on the north façade are triple glazed.

Heating

The heating strategy for the house relies on good thermal insulation, controlled ventilation with heat recovery and optimized passive solar gain through the transparent insulation (TI) walls and south facing windows. A large proportion (65%) of the south-facing façade is insulated externally with transparent insulation (TI), which allows the heavyweight walls to act as solar collectors. As well as admitting solar energy the TI is able to conserve the thermal energy which is radiated into the house with a sufficient time lag (8 hours) to take over where the sun left off in heating the space. In an average year, the solar wall is able to produce a heat surplus on all but 15 days. At night the roller blinds can be lowered for additional insulation, increasing the U-value from $0.51W/m^2K$ to $0.40W/m^2K$.

Although the main heating contribution is provided by the TI wall and south-facing windows, ventilation air can also be pre-heated by a ground heat exchanger which always keeps incoming air above 0°C, or air-to-air heat recovery from the kitchen and bathroom extracts. For additional pre-heating, a hydrogen gas diffusion burner is fitted into the mechanical ventilation ductwork. This operates by the catalytic combustion of hydrogen with air, where water vapour is the only by-product. Heat for cooking is also provided by hydrogen gas diffusion burners. Four porous metallic cylinders act as a catalytic material, replacing the burners of a conventional hob.

Highly efficient solar collectors ($14m^2$) are installed on an inclined framework supported on the flat roof, and provide solar heated water to the 1000 litre storage tank. The newly developed collectors are bifacially illuminated with parabolic reflectors behind the solar plate to redirect sunlight onto both sides, and each side is also insulated with transparent insulation. Automatic roller blinds can be pulled over the collector system to protect against overheating (e.g. when the house is not occupied during the summer holidays). Hot water is provided directly to the washing machine and dishwashers to eliminate the need for electrical heating elements. The 'solar fraction' is calculated to be 86%, equal to 360kWh. Since November 1994 waste heat from the fuel cell has also been used for supplementary heating of the domestic hot water.

Cooling

The transparently insulated walls can be protected from the sun to prevent over-heating. Automatically controlled roller blinds made from aluminized polyester are positioned in front of the TI material and behind the outer glass pane. These are automatically raised at night to increase summertime heat loss. The solar water heating system on the roof can be protected from the sun with a similar roller blind system.

Cool air can be introduced into the space via the mechanical ventilation system, by utilizing the ground heat exchanger to pre-cool outside air. The ground heat exchanger consists of two pipes 16 metres in length, which are buried four metres below the surface, where temperatures remain relatively constant.

Ventilation

The building envelope is very well sealed, with air leakage restricted to 0.3 air changes an hour at 50Pa. A controlled ventilation system with heat recovery provides fresh air into the rooms through floor grilles near the windows. This produces an air exchange rate of 0.5 air changes per hour. Incoming air can be pre-heated or -cooled via the ground heat exchanger. During very cold weather, the fresh air can also be heated with a catalytic hydrogen diffusion burner (1.5kW). Warm exhaust air is drawn from the bathrooms and kitchen through cross/counter flow plate heat exchangers, and used to heat the incoming fresh air (heat recovery coefficient 0.85). Inlet and exhaust ventilators have a total power consumption of only 25 watts. The windows can also be opened for ventilation.

Electricity generation

Photovoltaic modules are also mounted on the framework supporting the solar water collectors. The 36m^2 array of mono-crystalline silicon cells (15% efficiency) can generate up to 4.2kW$_p$ during the summer months. The nominal voltage of the DC circuit is 48 Volts, which is converted to 230 Volts Alternating Current by an inverter with very low open circuit losses. A lead-acid battery system provides up to 20kWh of short-term storage. Now that the building has a change of use and the hydrogen/oxygen system has been decommissioned, it is planned to sell excess electricity back to the national grid.

In order to meet the energy demand during periods without sunshine, a hydrogen/oxygen storage system was installed. In the summer, photovoltaically generated electricity is used to convert water to hydrogen and oxygen by electrolysis. The gases are stored in pressurized tanks (300 bar) for re-conversion to electricity by a fuel cell, as well as providing a flameless combustion source for cooking and back-up heating. If there is a shortfall in electricity production from the sun, a 1kW membrane fuel cell is able to produce electricity from the reaction of hydrogen with oxygen. As the fuel cell will only be used in periods of low sunshine, the heat losses (70–80°C) from the fuel cell can be used to heat the hot water via the heat exchanger.

The household is equipped with some of the most energy-efficient electrical appliances on the market, including a TV, washing machine, freezer, fridge and dishwasher. A tumble drier was not allowed.

Daylighting

Energy-efficient lighting was used throughout. The primary influence on window sizes and location was for passive solar gain. Daylight provision is more than adequate for this domestic situation.

Solar control

The windows on the south façade can be protected from the sun on the outside by motor-driven roller blinds. A switch is located adjacent to each window for users to determine whether they are lowered or not. The blinds to the TI wall are automatically operated. In the future, it is planned to add thermotropic glazing (darkens with increasing temperature) to the facade with transparent insulation. The new glazing will act as a large-area optical switch, replacing complex mechanical shading devices and thus reducing the costs for solar heating by a third (no power).

Controls

The building can be 'run' by a computer program, but it is small enough to be operated with simple manual controls, with automatic responses provided by the responsive blind systems. The computer system was primarily used for monitoring purposes. If extremely low power consumption is to be achieved for

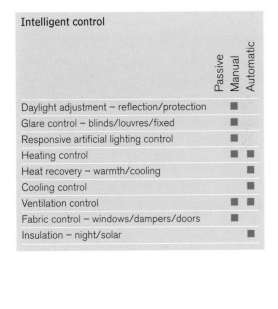

Intelligent control	Passive	Manual	Automatic
Daylight adjustment – reflection/protection	■		
Glare control – blinds/louvres/fixed	■		
Responsive artificial lighting control	■		
Heating control		■	■
Heat recovery – warmth/cooling			■
Cooling control			■
Ventilation control		■	■
Fabric control – windows/dampers/doors		■	
Insulation – night/solar			■

Building data

Contract value	DM1.5m
Area	$332m^2$
Typical floorplate	n/a
Number of storeys	2 + B
Price per m^2	~£1560/m^2
Annual energy use	8.7kWh/m^2
Typical energy use for building type	110kWh/m^2
Annual CO_2 output	n/a
Number of sensors	n/a
Visited by authors	✔
Monitored by others	✔

Credits

Client: Fraunhofer Institute for Solar Energy Systems ISE
Architects: Planerwerkstatt Hölken & Berghoff (Dieter Hölken)
Project Manager: Fraunhofer Institute for Solar Energy Systems ISE

References

Concepts in Practice: Energy, Peter Smith and Adrian C Pitts, Batsford, 1997
Press Release, Solar House: Freiburg, From the Vision to the Application, Dr Klaus Heidler, 24/7/96
Review of Ultra-Low-Energy Homes – A Series of UK and Overseas Profiles, Best Practice Programme – Report 38, David Olivier and John Willoughby, Energy Efficiency Office
Self-sufficient Solar House, BINE Projekt Info-Service, No 18, December 1994
Recent Advances in Transparent Insulation Technology, Werner J Platzer, A Goetzberger, TI Meeting, Freiburg 16/9/96
The Self-Sufficient Solar House in Freiburg – A Building Supplies Itself with Energy, K Voss, W Stahl, A Goetzberger, Solar Energy in Architecture and Urban Planning, 3rd European Conference on Architecture, Florence, May 1993
The Self-Sufficient Solar House in Freiburg – results of 3 Years of Operation, K Voss, A Goetzberger, G Bopp, A Häberle, A Heinzel and H Lehmberg
Andreas Härbele, Projektgesellschaft Solare Energiesysteme
Ursula Scheider/Dr Karsten Voss, Fraunhofer Institute for Solar Energy Systems ISE
Dieter Hölken, Hölken & Berghoff

the control and data acquisition system, hardware and software components from different manufacturers have to be used, causing various difficulties in operation and data exchange. The building control hardware installed consumes no more than 80 W_{DC}.

User control

Users are able to open the windows for additional ventilation and have manual control over the admittance of solar gain through the windows.

Performance

A three-year monitoring programme was used to investigate the house and its technology under real living conditions (occupied by a family of three). The planning, construction and measurements were funded by the German Federal Ministry for Research and Technology. Many of the problems encountered were typical of the transition from laboratory to 'real life' operation.

Delivered energy consumption

During the first two heating periods, energy autonomy was not fully achieved because of non-optimal battery management, unexpectedly high AC electricity consumption by the many visitors and TV crews, and the unreliability of the first fuel cell. The fuel cell was substituted by a provisional grid connection until a new membrane fuel cell was installed in November 1994. Except for a grid back-up during a short breakdown of the fuel cell, all energy was delivered by the stand-alone solar system during the monitoring period 1992–1995. In 1994, the total energy consumption was 800kWh.

kWh/m^2	German standard	Self-sufficient solar house		
		1993	1994	1994/95
Household	20	10.7	7.8	7.9
Ventilation		1.3	0.8	0.6
Hot water	20	–*	–*	–*
Heating	70–100	2.5	0.5	0.2
Total	110–140	12 (8–11%)	9.1 (7–8%)	8.7 (6–8%)

*DHW is heated entirely with solar collectors and the waste heat of the fuel cell

Design process

Dynamic computer simulations were carried out to assist with optimized system sizing. On the basis of the hourly weather data from the TRY for Freiburg and assumptions about the energy consumption of a four-person household, a concept for the energy supply system was developed. The program TRNSYS was applied as a powerful design tool because of its proven accuracy as well as its modular structure. Several new routines were added to model specific components.

Design Office for Gartner

Design Office for Gartner
Office building
Gundelfingen/Donau
Germany (D-89421)
Kurt Ackermann und Partner *Architect*
Büro Dr Karl Pitscheider *Energy Consultant*
NERVUS Generalübernehmer *Client*
1991–1997 *Dates*
50.11°N *Latitude*
–7°N *Primary axis of orientation*

Intelligent features

Building management system	■
Learning facility	
Weather data	■
Responsive lights	
Sun tracking facility	■
Occupant override	■
Self-generation – CHP/PV/wind	
Night cooling	
Solar water heating	

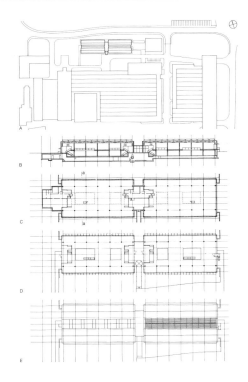

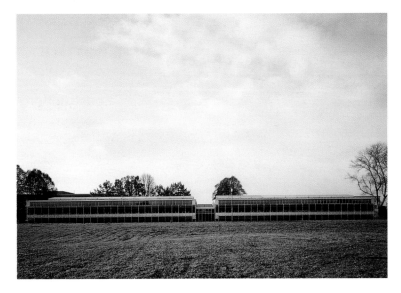

Introduction

The new design office for the Gartner cladding company was intended to serve as a testground for new developments in the fields of thermal and solar protection, and daylight illumination. The innovative curtain wall was designed to optimize and integrate thermal performance, lighting, and heating, ventilating and cooling systems.

The intelligence factor

Semi-transparent glass louvres along the north and south elevations can be adjusted by a central control system to optimum angles, which are determined by the solar angle and intensity. Dynamic shading also protects the roof glazing, clerestorey windows and the end windows.

Brief

All workplaces were supposed to have approximately the same quality and be suitable for work done on drawing boards and display screens. Accommodation was required for groups of project engineers who mostly work in small teams, which favoured an open-plan layout for communicative teamwork.

Accommodation

The building consists of two double-storey pavilions (42m long and 21m deep), connected in the centre by a glazed entrance foyer. A fully glazed rooflight runs down the centre of the building, creating a double-height atrium in the centre of each wing. The building accommodates approximately 150 staff.

Energy strategy

Effective comfort is achieved by finely adjustable protection against heat and sun, utilization of natural light and the close integration of heating and cooling

Sunpath

Latitude
48.55°

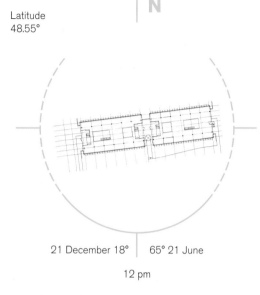

| 21 December 18° | 65° 21 June |

12 pm

Façade transparency

North	70%
East	10%
South	70%
West	10%
Roof	20%

U-values

Opaque elements	0.40W/m^{2}K
Slab	0.50W/m^{2}K
Roof	0.30W/m^{2}K
Triple glazing (argon)	0.90W/m^{2}K
Triple glazing (krypton)	0.70W/m^{2}K

systems. Strategies for daylighting, natural ventilation, and radiant heating and cooling reduce the need for overhead electric lighting, HVAC equipment and ductwork.

Site and climate

The Gartner works occupy a large industrial complex on the rural outskirts of the small provincial town of Gundelfingen in south-east Germany. A large power station is situated towards the south-east. The climate is described as 'continental', with mean daily average temperatures of −1.8°C (−4.6°C to 0.8°C) in January and 17.7°C in July (12.4°C to 23.2°C). The average solar exposure is 250W/m^2.

Construction

An intricately detailed steel frame on a 6.8m grid supports composite concrete floor slabs. The opaque elements are clad with a highly insulated aluminium curtain wall consisting of composite aluminium cladding panels sandwiching 120mm of insulation with a heat storage panel on the inner layer. A specially developed composite aluminium frame curtain walling system with double thermal separation supports the glazing and façade panels.

Glazing

The glazed elevations of curtain walling consist of triple glazing with low-e coatings on faces 3 and 5 and argon gas in the cavity. Every third unit incorporates side-bottom hung openable windows for occupant ventilation. At the east and west ends of the building, windows are triple glazed with two low-e coatings and a cavity filled with krypton gas.

Frameless glass louvres on the north and south sides of the building are fixed horizontally to the metal balconies in 1582mm lengths, and also provide maintenance and emergency exit. A special vacuum-coating treatment provides a weatherproof reflective layer and a slight tinting to the toughened glass, which is 10mm thick and 300mm deep.

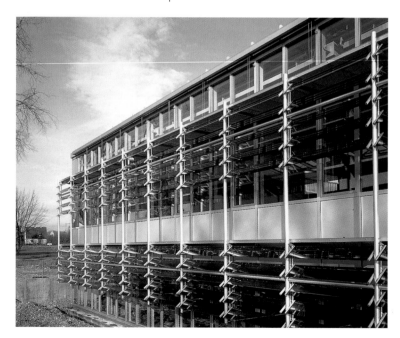

Heating

An integrated façade construction specially developed by Gartner incorporates water-carrying profiles as the 'building blocks' of a radiant heating and cooling system, which can be individually controlled. Water for heating runs through the non-structural framework of welded RHS steelwork in 100mm by 60mm sections. The heated steel frame heats both the room and the inner panes of glass, thus eliminating the risk of condensation and downdraughts, and increasing the degree of comfort near to the windows (increased surface temperature of glass). Electronically guided two-way valves control the flow of heated water. Hot water is provided by gas-fired central heating plant for the whole Gartner site.

During low external temperatures, much higher temperatures are maintained on the internal surface of the glass because of the low-e coating, which reflects infrared heat back into the space. The radiant cooling effect of cold glass is thus reduced.

Cooling

Cool water can also be circulated through the steel framework adjacent to the façade to offset solar gain at the source. In addition, chilled ceiling panels made of white, powder-coated aluminium sheets with water-conducting frames ensure an even distribution of cooling across the depth of the plan. The radiant panels work both by absorbing heat from surfaces and by convection: hot air rises, is cooled by the panels, then falls. The surface temperature of the suspended ceiling is kept below the air temperature of the room by a few degrees, resulting in radiation exchange between warmer surfaces in the room, and the ceiling. Cool water is extracted from the ground at a depth of approximately 3m and maintains 10°C–12°C all year around. The building does not rely on a night cooling strategy.

Ventilation

With a radiant heating and cooling system provided by the ceiling panels and water-filled structure, fresh air is used only for ventilation, and is supplied with minimal conditioning by a displacement system. Low velocity (0.1m/s) inlet panels beneath the windows, supply slightly cooled or heated fresh air at a temperature just below room temperature (maximum 2K). Heat from occupants and equipment causes the room air to rise, drawing the incoming fresh air upward to the breathing zone, and towards ceiling level, where it is extracted. Air extracted from the space is then passed through an air-to-air heat exchanger.

The main air inlet for the whole building is at the centre of the plan, on the north side. The air outlets are fitted along the entire length of the parapet, and supplied with fresh air through ducts at the lower level (a trench is used for the ground floor). The 'System Gartner' consists mainly of a conventional ventilation grille, which is assembled into an easily removable frame, with filter mats fitted to the back. Manually operable windows can augment the ventilation. A sensor tells the building management system (BMS) when a window has been opened, and the system adjusts the heat input to this section in winter.

Intelligent control

	Passive	Manual	Automatic
Daylight adjustment – reflection/protection			■
Glare control – blinds/louvres/fixed		■	
Responsive artificial lighting control		■	■
Heating control		■	■
Heat recovery – warmth/cooling			■
Cooling control			■
Ventilation control			■
Fabric control – windows/dampers/doors			
Insulation – night/solar			

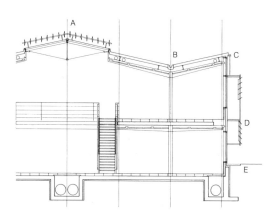

Daylighting

Adjustable glass louvres run the entire length of the north and south elevations, providing adjustable shade and light deflection. Transmission of light and radiation through the glass louvre is reduced to 14% incident light transmission. The reflecting capabilities of the glass louvres can be utilized to re-direct light onto the ceiling.

A glass roof extending the whole length of the building further promotes natural lighting in the centre of the plan.

The office ceiling on the upper level is inclined towards the daylit perimeter and the toplit atrium for maximum light penetration. The white powder-coated aluminium ceiling panels reflect light further into the depth of the plan (60% reflective). The ceiling panels which double as radiant cooling units are 20% perforated with 4mm diameter holes for increased sound absorption.

Artificial lighting

To supplement daylighting, staff can switch on task lighting. Task lighting is not controlled by the computer system, but left to individual discretion. To spread the light more evenly, typical high-efficiency fluorescent fixtures were modified with custom reflectors that diffuse the light along the almost-white underside of the suspended ceiling.

Solar control

All external shading is automatically adjusted, and can be individually overridden.

The driving shafts that adjust the tilt of the louvres are moved in a synchronized action via pivoted levers fixed to a common primary shaft. These levers are operated by driving levers, which are powered by four electric linear motors on each side of the building. By means of a central control system, the glass louvres are tilted to the best shading position, which is determined by the calculated position

of the sun, and is re-checked every 5 minutes. If the angle is adjusted properly, the windows can be shaded fully from direct sunlight, without losing visual contact with the outside (as the louvres are semi-transparent).

Aluminium louvres above the roof glazing can be automatically adjusted to provide a responsive shading system. When the sun is low, the louvres are in a vertical position, both blocking direct penetration, and reflecting low angle sunbeams. When the sun is high, the louvres are tilted slightly towards the north, blocking out direct sunlight, whilst admitting diffuse light from the north (similar to saw tooth northlights). Light transmission is optimized by the slim cross section profile (60mm) of the anodized aluminium and its diffuse, reflecting surface. Each louvre is 480mm wide with a central motorized pivot.

Fabric roller blinds (light transmission of 7%) on the inside of the windows can be used to further shade display screens from glare. The combination of external louvres and individually controlled anti-glare blinds allows light transmission to be freely adjustable between 1% and 63%.

At high level automatically-controlled, retractable louvre blinds protect the clerestorey glazing using conventional 100mm wide aluminium louvres, stored in external blind boxes.

Controls

A BMS is responsible for the control of the external glass louvres, the aluminium louvres above the rooflights, and those protecting the clerestorey glazing. The system processes information from light sensors (solar angle and intensity) and adjusts the angle of the external louvres to either a light-transmitting mode, a light-guiding mode, or a shading mode as required. The computer calculates the instantaneous angle of incidence of the sun and checks whether the glass surface will theoretically be reached by direct sunlight. At the same time, the solar intensity on the outside is measured by a solarimeter and a comparison is made against a pre-determined control level. The computer then decides whether to move the louvres into the position of their maximum light transmission, the light guidance position, or the position of shade. From the present position and the new desired position the computer calculates the necessary angle of tilt and relays the relevant signals to the linear motors. To eliminate effects of constant movement during cloud change, mean values for the intensity of the solar rays are used as deciding criteria. The façade of each pavilion is controlled as one bank and does not allow individual bay-by-bay control.

The BMS also monitors fresh air ventilation, heating and cooling systems, heat recovery, lighting, fire and security. External sensors provide details of temperature, solar radiation and wind, whilst internal sensors provide temperature information for each bay. A cable-saving Bus technique is used for data exchange between the microprocessor controls and the central computer. The BMS has been installed in the Reception of the new building, where the possibilities of the latest control techniques can be demonstrated to visitors. At the control station, diagrams of the installation can be displayed on a colour screen for instant visualization. To immediately recognize malfunctions in the system, a 'trend register' was incorporated, which offers a regular print out of the conditions of the circuits, measurements and metering of installation components. Long-term storage of process data can be used for later analysis.

Building data

Contract value	DM12.6m
Area m^2	3595m^2
Typical floorplate	7m
Number of storeys	2
Price per m^2	~£1170/m^2
Annual energy use	n/a
Typical energy use for building type	n/a
Annual CO_2 output	n/a
Number of sensors	n/a
Visited by authors	✔
Monitored by others	✔

User control

In order to meet the differing light requirements of those working at a computer screen, there are individually operable roller blinds on the inside of each window. The water-carrying profiles at the perimeter can be adjusted for local temperature control. Users are provided with opening windows in each bay for additional ventilation.

Performance

Monitoring of the lighting and thermal comfort was performed by the Fraunhofer Institute for Building Physics in Stuttgart, between March 1992 and March 1993. Thermal comfort was found to be very good.

Delivered energy consumption

No energy consumption figures have been published for the building.

Design process

Gartner conducted research into the glass louvre system between 1986 and 1990. It is now being marketed as part of its a product range. The heated steel frame curtain wall – System Gartner – was developed as part of research at the Hermann Riettschel Institute in Berlin.

Credits

Client: Josef Gartner & Co
Architects: Kurt Ackermann und Partner
Mechanical Engineer: Büro Dr Karl Pitscheider
Building Physics: Karl Gertis, Walter E Fuchs
Structural Engineering: Bernhard Behringer, Walter Müller

References

Architectural Record, October 1995, New Daylight Systems
DETAIL, 1992, Vol 32, No 6, Special Print
Fassade, No8 415/19, 43(1992), Dr Ing Winfried Heusler and Dipl Phys Christian Scholz, Translation S Wayt
MD, moebel interior design, 5 1993 mai, Vol 39 No 5, pp 64–69, English translation
Glaswelt, 'Systems to Achieve Maximum Comfort and Energy Conservation in Office Buildings', Winfried Heusler, Johann Ernst and Christian Scholz, 46 1993, Translation S Wayt
Mr Christian Scholz/Dr Fritz Gartner, Josef Gartner & Co
Professor Kurt Ackermann, Kurt Ackermann und Partner

TRON – Concept Intelligent House

TRON – Concept Intelligent House
Experimental house
Nishi-Azabu district, Minato ward
Tokyo
Japan
Professor Ken Sakamura *Architect*
The TRON Intelligent House Research Committee
  Energy Consultant
The TRON Intelligent House Research Committee
  Client
1988–1989 *Dates*
35.70°N *Latitude*
0°N *Primary axis of orientation*

Intelligent features

Building management system	■
Learning facility	
Weather data	■
Responsive lights	■
Sun tracking facility	
Occupant override	■
Self-generation – CHP/PV/wind	
Night cooling	
Solar water heating	

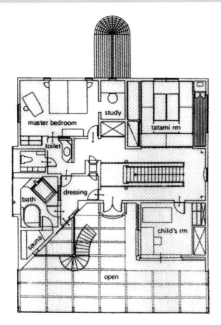

Introduction

The TRON-concept Intelligent House was a pilot project devised by Professor Ken Sakamura from the University of Tokyo. The project was financed by a group of 19 Japanese companies, who together formed The TRON Intelligent House Research Committee. TRON is an acronym for 'the real time operating system nucleus', and is concerned with creating a new computer architecture to facilitate the networking and collective response for a wide range of computerized applications. The TRON House was one of many experimental projects set up by the Department of Information Science to test the TRON concept, in this instance for its application to home automation.

The TRON house was used until March 1993 for living experiments, when it was demolished to make way for further TRON projects, such as the Hyper intelligent building (a computerized office building).

The intelligence factor

The main intelligent feature which relates to the environmental control of the house, is the automatically controlled windows, which vary their opening according to information received from external weather sensors and internal conditions. The lighting is remote-controlled, and the curtains can be automatically closed at night. In all, more than 1000 micro-processors monitor the building and its surrounding environment. There are many other novel features which make this building a truly 'intelligent home'.

Brief

The purpose of the pilot project was to carry out intensive experiments simulating living in automated dwellings. The simulations were aimed at finding out the nature of future styles of living and exploring its possibilities.

Sunpath

Latitude
35.70°

21 December 31° | 78° 21 June

12 pm

Accommodation

The exterior is a simple, two storey rectangular plan with a semi-open outdoor space to the south, incorporating a garden, a two-storey verandah and planted trees. Each room faces the semi-open area to give a sense of openness – when the windows are open it is a garden, and when they are closed it becomes a large sunspace. The house is built using natural materials and surroundings, with many traditional Japanese motifs, including a Tatami room for relaxation. It was assumed that the inhabitants would be a married couple and one child living near the centre of Tokyo, where land is limited and little scenic beauty exists. Despite the large number of sensors, actuators, and controllers the house is designed as a traditional, peaceful and functional Japanese home, where the computers are regarded as 'unseen helpers'.

Energy strategy

Apart from the bathroom and kitchen, which are both substantially automated and computerized, the main innovations are the environmental control and the integrated operating systems, covering heat, humidity, ventilation, light, video/audio, computing, external purchasing, storage and security. Computers and sensors in the Intelligent House were designed to make overall judgements on outdoor and indoor conditions, and then operate with TRON technology as an integrated system to provide maximum comfort. Energy is monitored through electricity and water meters.

Site and climate

The building is situated on a compact site in the metropolis of Tokyo. It is the high land prices that have caused the project to be demolished to make way for the next TRON project.

Construction

The walls are finished with a scraped stucco. The frame for the building is Japanese timber and reinforced concrete sections. Internal finishes include 'washi' – Japanese handmade wallpaper, and a cypress lattice suspended ceiling to hide all of the wiring.

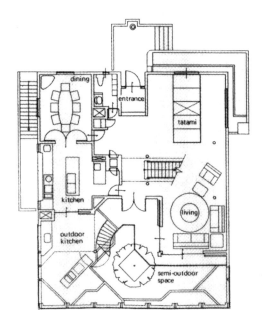

Glazing

The windows open and close automatically in response to external weather sensors and internal conditions, or by remote control. Liquid crystal glazing installed between the bedroom and bathroom provides opacity at the flick of a switch.

Heating

Heating is provided by an underfloor system and radiating panels mounted above the open ceiling grid. An air conditioning system provides a back-up source of warm air.

Cooling

The façade is opened automatically according to internal and external climate conditions. Radiant cooling panels are mounted behind the suspended ceiling. A water spray system can be activated onto the glass surfaces on the roof, providing and an added facility for evaporative cooling as well as cleaning. A variable flow air conditioning system provides cool air in extreme conditions.

Ventilation

The computer system is responsible for determining whether fresh air is best provided by automatically opening the windows, or activating the air conditioning system in periods of high humidity or wet weather. Fans can be operated to assist with natural ventilation.

Daylighting

The glazed inner court provides much of the daylight needed inside the building. The computer system controls the opening and closing of curtains according to the time of day and thermal requirements.

Artificial lighting

Lights are switched on automatically in response to movement around the building. They can also be operated by remote control units, which offer a selection from a variety of moods. This information is conveyed to the sound system, and background music is automatically matched to the lighting mood, and a sound field processor adjusts the acoustic ambience accordingly.

Controls

The building is controlled by three BTRON computers, which coordinate more than 1000 micro-processors. The separate control systems are linked over a common network that facilitates a cooperative response. External weather conditions are analysed with sensors for wind-direction, wind-velocity, air-pressure, rain and brightness. Internally, temperature and humidity sensors are installed in each room, as well as carbon dioxide concentration sensors. An indoor air-flow velocity sensor can even tell if chairs are occupied. Infrared sensors and heat sensors provide security and fire protection. The windows are opened automatically in response to a variety of sensors, which measure temperature, airflow, occupancy, humidity and rain.

The Intelligent Home also incorporates many other automated facilities, including an automatic watering system for the planting in the inner courtyard with concealed water pipes and moisture sensors that activate a solenoid valve. Tele-

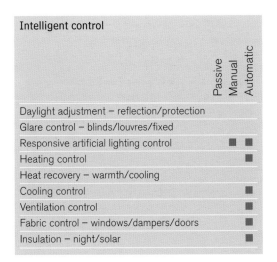

Intelligent control	Passive	Manual	Automatic
Daylight adjustment – reflection/protection			
Glare control – blinds/louvres/fixed			
Responsive artificial lighting control		■	■
Heating control			■
Heat recovery – warmth/cooling			
Cooling control			■
Ventilation control			■
Fabric control – windows/dampers/doors			■
Insulation – night/solar			■

Building data

Contract value	¥1bn ($6m)
Area m^2	372m^2
Typical floorplate	max 5m
Number of storeys	2 + B
Price per m^2	~£10,000/m^2
Annual energy use	n/a
Typical energy use for building type	n/a
Annual CO_2 output	n/a
Number of sensors	n/a
Visited by authors	✗
Monitored by others	✔

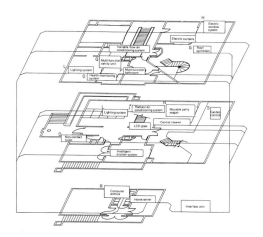

vision, audio and telephone systems are provided in every room (when the telephone is answered, the sound sources in the vicinity automatically lower their volume). Doors can be automatically opened, and locked electronically (including the front door that can be opened after a signal is received from the remote-controlled video entryphone). The bathroom and kitchen are substantially automated. The toilet has an automatic health-check, which analyses urinary sugar and protein levels. In the kitchen, touch pads are used for the taps as well as an automatic facility, and a touch-sensitive screen calls up menus and other information (including laserdisc video guides on how to prepare a meal, and a computerized link to the oven and ring controls times and temperatures). A mobile dishwasher can be taken directly to the dining table. An automatic underground storage system utilizes special containers stowed under the floor by a small elevator and conveyor. An electronic still camera installed on the ceiling photographs the contents whenever an item is retrieved or stored. An inventory list of each container can be displayed on a TV screen.

Operating modes

The computer system determines whether to open windows and skylights in order to maximize energy conservation and comfort. It is able to activate light sensitive glass into an opaque element for privacy and shading. Air conditioning is only turned on when the outside air is too hot, or in case of rain (windows have to close). The computer determines if water spray on the roof will add useful cooling system, and if fans are required to assist natural ventilation. Radiant heating and cooling systems in the floors and ceilings are activated to ensure an even temperature distribution.

Credits

The TRON Intelligent House Research Committee (Structural, mechanical engineers and general contractors): ATC, Dai-ichi Seed Co Ltd, Eiraku Electrical Co, Japan Air Lines, Mitsubishi Electric Corporation, Motoda Electronics Co Ltd, Nippon Homes Corporation, Nippon Sheet Glass Co Ltd, Nippon Telegraph and Telephone Corporation, Nisshin Steel Co Ltd, Sankyo Aluminium Industry Co Ltd, Seibu Department Stores Ltd, Sun Wave Corporation, Taikisha Ltd, Takenaka Corporation, Tokyo Electric Power Company, Toto Ltd, Yamagiwa Corporation and Yamaha Corporation.

References

AIT Special Intelligent Architecture, April 1994, page 45
Architecture Today, AT 14, January 1991
Designing the Office of the Future: The Japanese Approach to Tomorrow's Workplace, Volker Hartkopf, Wiley, New York, 1993
The Japan Architect, 9004, April 1990
Overview of the TRON Project, internet site www.is.s.u-tokyo.ac.jp
Professor Ken Sakamura, Head of Laboratory, Department of Information Science, University of Tokyo

<table>
<tr><td>CASE STUDY 21</td><td># Super Energy Conservation Building</td></tr>
</table>

CASE STUDY 21

Super Energy Conservation Building

Super Energy Conservation Building
Administration office
Kiyose City
Tokyo
Japan
Ohbayashi-Gumi *Architect*
Ohbayashi-Gumi *Energy Consultant*
Ohbayashi Corporation *Client*
1982 *Dates*
35.80°N *Latitude*
0°N *Primary axis of orientation*

Intelligent features

Building management system	■
Learning facility	
Weather data	
Responsive lights	■
Sun tracking facility	
Occupant override	
Self-generation – CHP/PV/wind	■
Night cooling	■
Solar water heating	■

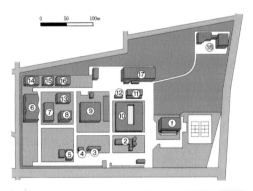

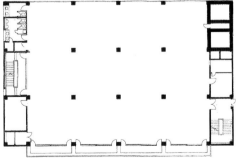

Introduction

The Ohbayashi Corporation is one of the big five Japanese General Contractors. The new building sits on a research campus of scattered buildings and test sheds, 20 kilometres from Tokyo. It was claimed at the time that it was the 'most energy-efficient building in the world', boasting as many as 98 energy-conserving technologies.

The intelligence factor

The main lighting is under photocell control depending on available daylight levels. Automatic vents at the top and bottom of the double skin allow it to be controlled for additional cooling or to act as a thermal buffer. At night, automatically controlled insulation blinds can be raised in front of south-facing office windows, which form the inner element of the double skin. A computer controlled night purge facility can be used to pre-cool the building in time for the next day.

Brief

The brief called for an office building with the smallest annual consumption of primary energy per unit area. It was intended as a showpiece exhibit for the construction company. It was designed in-house, drawing on specialist sub-contractor expertise.

Accommodation

The building is a four storey cuboid, with an inclined glass wall on its south façade. The east and west ends of the building include the access stairs, service rooms and stock rooms. These largely windowless areas protect the

Façade transparency

North	35%
East	5%
South	65%
West	5%
Roof	0%

Sunpath

Latitude
35.80°

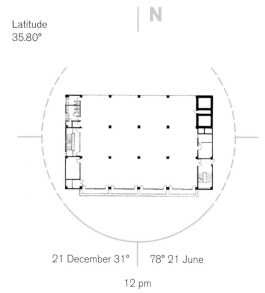

21 December 31° | 78° 21 June

12 pm

interior from the troublesome morning and evening sun, and act as a buffer to the conditioned environment. A rooftop plantroom serves as a buffer against intensive solar gain. On the south side, the ground has been excavated to form a sunken garden which allows windows to the library area in the basement. Earth berming up to the ground floor cill level was used on the east, west and north sides. The building was designed to accommodate the research institute's administration and the majority of its research scientists.

Energy strategy

The double skin glass wall on the south façade is used to preheat incoming air for the air handling units. In summer, vents at the top and bottom of the double skin are opened to create natural ventilation and thus reduce the cooling loads.

Construction

The structure of the building is pre-stressed concrete slabs in order to minimize the external surface area.

Glazing

The double skin on the south façade is used to preheat air for the air handling units. It can also be freely ventilated to reduce internal cooling loads, and closed up to act as a thermal buffer for the internally conditioned environment.

Heating

A hot water storage tank is incorporated into the eastern core of the building, providing $70m^3$ of storage in stratified tanks that stand the full height of the building. In winter, the high temperature tank is fed by over $200m^2$ of evacuated solar collectors mounted on the roof. Water bound for the solar collectors is pumped up from the bottom of the storage tank. When it has been heated by the sun, it returns to the tank's upper level, and is pumped to the air handling units (AHUs) where its surplus heat is transferred to the air. The water is then returned to the lower levels of the tank for recycling. A photovoltaic solar cell is used to drive the circuit pump. Water from the bottom of the tanks is also used as a source by the heat pump when in operation. Any excess heat is discharged to the cooling tower.

Buried beneath the building are two coils of plastic piping, which are used to store surplus solar energy, and to provide a low-grade source of energy for the heat pumps. For much of the heating season this warm ground serves as a thermal blanket to counter the basement's heat loss. There is a useful time lag of one or two months.

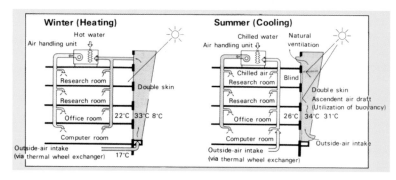

A computer controls air intake to the dual skin, which is pre-heated up to about 33°C, and then led through the air handling units that distribute it through the building by a system of fans and ducts. The double skin also serves as a thermal buffer to the internal conditioned environment. There are also automatically controlled insulation blinds that descend at night to reduce heat loss from the office area.

Domestic hot water is provided by the array of 126 evacuated tube solar collectors mounted on the roof of the building.

Cooling

Also located in the eastern core is a chilled water storage tank of a similar volume. In the summertime condition, the solar collectors are used to drive an absorption chiller and it is now the chilled water storage tanks that feed the AHUs. The solar collectors feed a smaller 8m^3 tank, which is used to store solar-heated water at temperatures up to 85°C. This is enough to power the building's absorption chiller which can chill water in the cool water storage tank from 15°C to 10°C. On really hot days, the system is augmented by an electrically powered chiller which lowers the water temperature to 8°C.

Vents at the top and bottom of the double skin can be opened to create natural ventilation and thus reduce the internal cooling loads. A computer-controlled night purge facility can be employed to exploit nighttime cooling.

Ventilation

The building is fully air conditioned with a variable air volume system. External windows cannot be opened. Opening vents in the double skin ensure adequate ventilation of this glazed cavity in summer. In winter, they are opened to admit fresh air, which is pre-heated prior to passing through the air conditioning plant. Fresh air inlets on the north side of the building feed the roof-mounted AHUs in summer.

Electricity generation

A photovoltaic array on the roof is utilized to drive the circuit pump for the solar water heating system, providing a peak output of one kilowatt.

Daylighting

The building has a relatively deep plan, with windows provided more for views than the provision of daylight. Restrooms and stairways in the east and west cores are provided with windows to minimize lighting requirements in these areas.

Artificial lighting

The main lighting strategy relies on low powered ambient lighting and task lighting on individual desks for brighter working conditions. The main lighting is under photocell control, with dimming control of lights in the perimeter section. A computer controls lighting in restrooms and stairs depending on daylight levels, and also turns the lighting off during lunch hour. Emergency exit signs are deactivated during daytime and holiday periods to conserve energy.

A tablet type switch has been installed as a way of ensuring that lights in conference rooms are only used when they are needed. Workers bring the switch

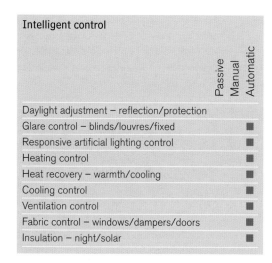

Intelligent control

	Passive	Manual	Automatic
Daylight adjustment – reflection/protection			
Glare control – blinds/louvres/fixed			■
Responsive artificial lighting control			■
Heating control			■
Heat recovery – warmth/cooling			■
Cooling control			■
Ventilation control			■
Fabric control – windows/dampers/doors			■
Insulation – night/solar			■

Building data

Contract value	n/a
Area m^2	3776m^2
Typical floorplate	n/a
Number of storeys	3 + B
Price per m^2	n/a
Annual energy use	112kWh/m^2
Typical energy use for building type	441kWh/m^2
Annual CO$_2$ output	n/a
Number of sensors	300
Visited by authors	✗
Monitored by others	✔

Credits

Client: Ohbayashi Corporation

References

Building Design, 4 June 1982, No 597
Building Services, Vol 5, No 10, October 1983
Energy in Buildings, September 1985

to the room they intend to use, like a key, and insert it to turn on the lights. On leaving the room they remove the switch.

Floodlights within the double skin illuminate the ceilings inside the office space itself. The resultant heat load is kept out of the conditioned zone, and also contributes to the preheating of ventilation air.

Solar control

The east and west walls are largely windowless ancillary spaces. The main office areas are protected from direct solar gain during summer by louvred blinds on the outside of the office windows, within the dual skin cavity.

Controls

The switching of circuits between seasonal modes and occupational modes is under the control of a building management system (BMS). The computer is used to operate the heating, cooling and ventilating plant in accordance with weather conditions and usage conditions of the building, optimizing operation and minimizing energy consumption. The BMS uses dispersed micro-computers with a mass-produced micro-computer as an operating console located in the rooftop plant area. The software has been designed for easy adaptation to allow operator experience to be incorporated. Over 300 sensors are used for measurement and control and 200 additional sensors are used for the scientific monitoring of the building.

There are 18 separate modes of operation and optimal manual control of the building was seen to be impossible

Operating modes

In the winter mode, the south-facing cavity is flushed with fresh air, preheated from a thermal wheel heat exchanger. This air is then further heated by any available solar gain before it rejoins the recirculated air from the occupied space entering the air handling unit.

In the summer cooling mode, the cavity is closed off from the fresh air intake, and blinds on the cavity side of the interior glazing provide solar protection. The whole cavity is then ventilated by stack effect through vents on the ground floor and at the roof level.

Performance

An occupant survey by the Ohbayashi Corporation led to the modification of the CO$_2$ levels that determine the fresh air intake.

Delivered energy consumption

During the first year, the actual energy use was 86.7Mcal/m^2 (approx 102kWh/m^2). This figure increased to 95.9Mcal/m^2 (112kWh/m^2) in the second year because of more overtime, additional office equipment and extreme weather. A conventional Japanese office building at the time consumed 378Mcal/m^2 (approx 442kWh/m^2).

CASE STUDY 22

Occidental Chemical Center

Occidental Chemical Center
Corporate office building
360 Rainbow Boulevard
Niagara Falls, New York
USA
Cannon Design *Architect*
Professors John Yellott and Richard S Levine, Burt Hill
Kosar Rittelman Associates *Energy Consultant*
Hooker Chemicals and Plastic Corporation *Client*
1978–1981 *Dates*
43.00°N *Latitude*
0°N *Primary axis of orientation*

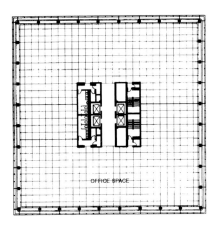

OFFICE SPACE

Intelligent features

Building management system	■
Learning facility	
Weather data	
Responsive lights	■
Sun tracking facility	■
Occupant override	■
Self-generation – CHP/PV/wind	
Night cooling	
Solar water heating	

Introduction

The 'Oxy Building' is located in the heart of downtown Niagara Falls on the American side of the world-renowned waterfalls. The architects wanted to take advantage of the magnificent views of the Falls without adopting the standard design response of the time, which seemed to prescribe restricted window areas to limit energy loss. The prospect of daylit interiors seemed to offer much greater opportunities for energy savings, and a double envelope was proposed to counter the excessive heat losses and gains that would be incurred by a fully glazed building.

The Intelligence Factor

Time- and temperature-activated sensors operate dampers at the top and bottom of the cavity to vent the double skin. In the cavity, photocell sensors on each building face activate the motorized louvres. The computerized control system includes security, alarm and fire alarm systems as well as energy management. A two-stage lighting control allows for maximum daylighting benefits.

Brief

The initial brief called for a corporate office building to consolidate disparate company facilities, with the provision of additional facilities for sub-letting. The client wanted a building that signified its commitment to reviving the urban core of Niagara Falls. It was also fortuitous that the architects chose to push the idea of an energy-conserving building, which was embraced by the oil company client.

Accommodation

The square plan is diagonally on axis with the Rainbow Bridge that links America with Canada over the Niagara River Gorge. It provides views of the Gorge, including the famous waterfalls, in three directions. The nine-storey build-

Sunpath

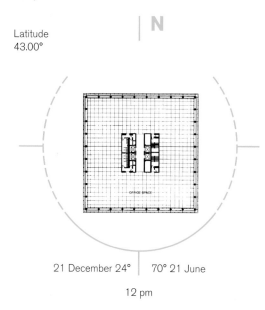

Latitude
43.00°

N

21 December 24° | 70° 21 June

12 pm

ing provides up to 161,150ft^2 (14,971m^2) of column-free office space around a central core for 500 Occidental employees. An additional 41,300ft^2 (3836m^2) of commercial and office rental space was provided for sub-letting. A second skin was wrapped around the inner glazing, creating a perimeter cavity of 1500mm the full height of the building. This is broken only at the entrance point, where it draws people through the thick glazed skin into a double-height foyer space. The new office building provided a consolidated base for the company's local administrative operations, accommodating approximately 500 staff.

Energy strategy

The double skin performs as an unconditioned thermal zone that changes the energy performance characteristics of the building from heating-load dominated to cooling-load dominated. It virtually eliminates infiltration and reduces the impact of extreme external temperatures. The cavity acts as a thermal buffer in winter (heat demand condition), allowing for lateral re-distribution of solar heated air. It can also be automatically opened in summer (cooling demand condition) to vent away convective warm air. Louvres within the void are adjustable for solar control, and can be closed at night to increase insulation. They provide an effective balance between daylighting, solar shielding and thermal conditioning demands. It was estimated that the building would consume less than one-third of the energy required for a conventionally designed office building.

After the building footprint was established, three alternative design solutions were developed, each representing an incremental response to energy conservation objectives.

Site and climate

The 2.3-acre site overlooks the Niagara River Gorge and Falls. It is located in a cold and cloudy area, experiencing many of the secondary climatic effects from the colder northern areas of Canada.

Construction

The main structure is a steel frame encased in concrete on a 4586mm grid (15ft). Composite concrete floors are cast onto metal decking.

Glazing

The outer skin is a white aluminium curtain walling system with blue-green tinted insulating glass. It transmits up to 80% of visible light. The inner skin consists of clear single glazing. Louvres in the cavity void were selected 'off-the-shelf' (normally used as HVAC dampers for high velocity applications). A mock-up that was made at Arizona State University determined the U-value of the double skin as 0.27Btu/°F ft^2 h, which equates to about 1.54W/m^{2}K.

Heating

The building was originally designed to be heated by a 2 million Btu gas-fired boiler. A change of use whereby one floor was dedicated to a 24-hour central computer facility for the whole corporation led to a much higher cooling load than was originally anticipated. This led to the chillers being run all year round, and the waste heat being used during the heating season. Domestic hot water is preheated through a 'shell and tube' heat exchanger by heat rejected from the chiller condenser.

Façade transparency

North	100%
East	100%
South	100%
West	100%
Roof	0%

U-values

Double skin	1.54W/m^{2}K
Slab	1.14W/m^{2}K
Roof	0.29W/m^{2}K

The double skin serves to reduce the impact of severe outside temperatures by limiting the effect of infiltration on the conditioned interior to an insignificant level. In the winter, a degree of solar collection offsets subfreezing external conditions by acting as a thermal buffer to the internal conditioned environment. Some convection will occur around the building, with warm air flowing from sunnier sides to cooler, more shaded exposures. Under extreme conditions (sunny, very cold, windy), it has been shown that the temperature in the buffer space varies 5.5°C from bottom to top. Convection currents around the building hold the temperature differential between north and south to 8.3°C. At night when the building is unoccupied, it was intended that the cavity louvres would be closed up completely to retain conditioned air from daytime operation. In practice the louvres are often not closed except during rare weekends when the computers are shut down and when the weather is very cold.

A heat wheel on the exhaust air extract achieves between 10% and 15% heat recovery for preconditioning ventilation air.

Cooling

Two electrically driven centrifugal chillers meet the predominant cooling load with heat recovery, which provides chilled water to the air handling units. These are supported by three cooling towers, with one dedicated to heat rejection from the computer space. When the building is in a net heat gain, heat is rejected through the closed circuit cooling towers. The system therefore acts as a 'hydronic heat pump'.

The double skin reduces the impact of outside temperatures and in summer, the cavity can be vented at top and bottom to increase airflow, and reduce solar build-up.

Ventilation

The heating, ventilating and air conditioning needs are met by two low-pressure variable air volume (VAV) air handling units. Minimum ventilation air is preheated/precooled through an air-to-air heat exchanger from toilet room exhaust

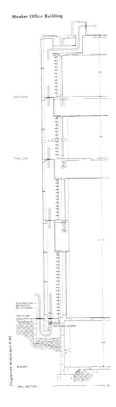

Hooker Office Building

air. The inner zone is served by VAV only, whereas the outer zone has fan-assisted VAV with heating coils.

Electricity generation

The building is located in an area that is well served by huge hydroelectric generating plant on the adjacent Niagara River.

Daylighting

The design was driven by a desire for maximum transparency to preserve outward views of the Niagara Falls and to maximize internal daylighting. The white aerofoil louvres in the double skin cavity reflect daylight deep into the internal spaces. Even with the louvres in their fully shaded position, sufficient light will be refracted by the white louvre surfaces. More than 50% of the usable floor area benefits from daylighting.

Artificial Lighting

Immediately inside the inner skin is a 15 foot (4586mm) perimeter lighting zone, with two-stage lighting controls to allow for maximum daylighting benefits, and reduced power use. Two light sensors per exposure allow the building control system to dim the artificial lights concentrically inward in accordance with light levels from outside. Task lighting is employed for localized adjustments to ambient light levels.

Solar Control

Horizontal louvres in the glazed cavity normally used for HVAC applications were adapted to provide adjustable solar control. There are 12 aluminium louvres for each floor, spanning the full distance of 4.5 metres between columns at vertical spacings of 200mm. Motorized screw shaft rods provide the power drive for each segment to respond to ambient sunlight conditions. During the occupied daytime period, the louvres track the sun, virtually eliminating solar heat gain in the occupied zone, whilst still allowing the penetration of diffuse daylight. Each

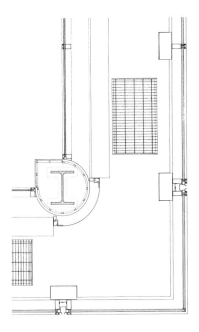

building face is fitted with two photocell sensors which when shaded stop the movement of the louvre, i.e. when the photocell is in shade, the angle of the louvre is sufficient to shade the interior of the building. The louvres were designed to be fully adjustable between the horizontal position and 45° for full shade.

Controls

The computerized building management system (BMS) includes facilities for security, alarm and fire alarm systems as well as energy management of the HVAC system. It has control over dampers, fans, chillers, boilers and air handling units. The perimeter lighting system and louvres are also controlled by the BMS to respond to ambient daylight levels. When heat is not required in the double skin cavity, time- and temperature-activated sensors will operate venting dampers at the top and bottom of the cavity, releasing the convective warm air at the top.

Sensors were placed inside the concrete slabs at many points around the building perimeter so that data about the thermal performance of the building could be monitored and analysed on a continuing basis. The system was fully equipped with data collection capabilities to provide information on energy usage patterns throughout the building.

User control

Wall-mounted switches within each of the corner offices (approximately 10%) can locally override the position of the louvres. The remainder of the louvres are always under automatic control. Temperature control thermostats are under occupant control.

Operating modes

In summer and winter, the operable louvres in the glazed cavity are automatically adjusted to prevent direct solar radiation from entering the building by means of a photocell controller.

At night and during other unoccupied hours, the louvres are closed for increased insulation, retaining the conditioned air from daytime operation.

Performance

Due to corporate policies, no actual energy use or monitoring information has been released to the design team. An independent analysis of the design was conducted by Dr Vladimir Bazjanac from the University of California, Berkeley. He developed a computerized model of the building's energy performance, by applying mathematical values to those variables that affect energy consumption. Evaluations were performed that analysed the demands for heating, cooling, lighting and occupant-operated equipment. The study found that the predominant energy characteristic of the building was the louvred double skin, which optimized energy performance. The building was found to maintain unique energy demand stability, particularly when compared to a conventional office design. At the time of completion, it was believed to be the most energy-efficient building in its particular climatic zone.

Intelligent control

	Passive	Manual	Automatic
Daylight adjustment – reflection/protection	■		
Glare control – blinds/louvres/fixed		■	■
Responsive artificial lighting control			■
Heating control		■	■
Heat recovery – warmth/cooling			■
Cooling control			■
Ventilation control			■
Fabric control – windows/dampers/doors			■
Insulation – night/solar			■

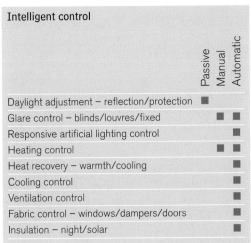

Building data

Contract value	$12.5m (1980)
Area m^2	18,808m^2
Typical floorplate	13m
Number of storeys	9 + B
Price per m^2	~£420/m^2 (1980)
Annual energy use	104kWh/m^{2*}
Typical energy use for building type	316kWh/m^2
Annual CO_2 output	n/a
Number of sensors	16
Visited by authors	✔
Monitored by others	✗

*Estimated during design phase (actual figures not available due to corporate policies).

Poor quality circuit boards for the louvre control system were changed in 1984. The operating team for the building has taken to blocking off the cavity vents at top and bottom with plywood boards to minimize winter air infiltration.

Delivered energy consumption

The target energy consumption for the building was set at a maximum of 55,000 Btu/ft^2/yr (174kWh/m^2 per year) during the design phase. Three alternative schemes were developed, each representing a different response to the energy conservation objectives and cost/benefit performance. The dynamic skin concept proved the most energy efficient, and was selected as the preferred solution. The energy performance of this design was calculated at 39,000Btu/ft^2/yr (123kWh/m^2 per year). Figures as low as 33,000Btu/ft^2/yr (104kWh/m^2 per year) have been quoted for the predicted consumption rates.

Design process

Computer based simulations of predicted energy use were performed for each of the three alternative schemes. A variety of computer tools were used by the energy consultants, Burt Hill Kosar Rittelman Associates, to determine heating and cooling requirements and solar shading. Additional energy analysis was performed at University of California Berkeley, using the DOE-2 program and TRY weather data for nearby Buffalo. The heating load was estimated at 2% of that for a conventional building and cooling loads 19% of normal.

The calculations were confirmed with mock-ups of the double skin. A full-scale mock-up of one module of the double skin design was erected in Tempe at the College of Architecture, Arizona State University. It was instrumented and tested by Professor John Yellott to determine the skin's shading coefficient, U-values and light transmission characteristics. The mock-up demonstrated that a substantial airflow was induced by chimney action when the outer glazing and the louvres were heated by solar radiation.

Credits

Client: Hooker Chemicals and Plastics Corporation (now Occidental Chemical Corporation), Dallas
Architects: Cannon Design Inc, Grand Island, NY
Early planning: Hellmuth Obata & Kassabaum (consulting architects)
M/E: Cannon Design Inc, Grand Island, NY
Energy Consultants: Professor John Yellott (Phoenix, AZ), Professor Richard S Levine (Lexington, KY), Burt Hill Kosar Rittelman Associates (Cambridge, MA)
Structural: Gillum Consulting Engineers
General Contractor: Siegfried-Scrufari Joint venture

References

Architecture, March 1989, Vol 78, No 3
Architecture d'Aujourd Hui, December 1980, No212
At the Rainbow's End, Anon
The Building Systems Integration Handbook, Richard D Dush (Ed), Wiley, Chichester, NY 1986
Glass in Architecture, Michael Wigginton, Phaidon, 1996
Marketing Material provided by Cannon Design Inc
Progressive Architecture, 4:80
Progressive Architecture, 4:83
Mark Mendell/Frank Smaak/Millard Berry, Cannon Design Inc
Mr Victor Snyder, Occidental Chemical Corporation

Selected bibliography

AIT (Architektur Innenarchitektur Technischer Ausbau) Spezial: Intelligente Architektur, Issues 1–12, October 1995 to April 1998.

Atkin, Brian, ed. (1988), *Intelligent Buildings: Applications of IT and Building Automation to High Technology Construction Projects*, Kogan Page.

Baker, N.V. *et al.* (1993), *Daylighting in Architecture*, James and James.

Banham Reyner (1969), *The Architecture of the Well Tempered Environment*, The Architectural Press.

Barker, Tom, Sedgewick, Andy, Yau, Raymon (1992), From Intelligent Buildings to Intelligent Planning, *Arup Journal*, Autumn 1992.

Barnett Howland, Matthew (1994), A Wall That …, *Architectural Design*, Vol. 64, No. 9/10, September/October 1994.

Battle, G. and McCarthy, C. (1992), *The Intelligent Building Façade*, Intelligent Buildings and Management, Conference, Unicom Seminars, Uxbridge, 28–29 January 1992.

Battle, Guy and McCarthy, Christopher (1992), The Façade as a Climate Moderator, *Intelligent Buildings and Management*, Conference, Unicom Seminars, Uxbridge, 28–29 January 1992.

Battle, Guy and McCarthy, Christopher (1994), Multi Source Synthesis: Intelligent Cities – A Climate for Change, *Architectural Design*, Vol. 66, No. 9/10, March/April 1994.

Behling, Stefan and Behling, Sophia (1996), *Sol Power: The Evolution of Solar Architecture*, Prestel.

Bhatnager, Kaninika, Gupta, Ashok and Bhattacharjee, B. (1997), Neural Networks as Decision Support Systems for Energy Efficient Building Design, *Architectural Science Review*, Vol. 40, June 1997, pp. 53–59.

Bothwell, Keith, *Towards a Common Specification for Case Studies*, Discussion Paper, BRE Note N12/96.

Boumann, Ole (1995), The Story So Far … , *Archis*, 12/95.

Boyd, D. (1992), *What is an Intelligent Building?*, Intelligent Buildings and Management, Conference, Unicom Seminars, Uxbridge, 28–29 January 1992.

Boyd, D. and Jankovic, L. (1992), Building IQ - Rating the Intelligent Building, *Intelligent Buildings and Management*, Conference, Unicom Seminars, Uxbridge, 28–29 January 1992.

Boyd, David (1993), What Are Really Intelligent Buildings?, *Intelligent Buildings Today and in the Future*, Proceedings of Conference (Jankovic, L., ed.), UCE, Birmingham, 7 October 1993.

Boyd, David ed. (1994), *Intelligent Buildings*, Alfred Waller Ltd, Henley on Thames in association with Unicom.

Bradshaw, Vaughan (1993), Building Control Systems, 2nd edn. John Wiley, New York.

Brister, Andrew (1990), Buildings with Gumption, *Building Services*, Vol. 12, No. 12, December 1990.

Building with Intelligence, *Architects Journal*, 8 July 1992.

Buildings and the Environment: Proceedings of the First International Conference, BRE, Watford, 16–20 May 1994.

Cohen, Robert, Ruyssevelt, Paul, Standeven, Mark, Bordass, Bill and Leaman, Adrian (1997), *The PROBE Method of Investigation*, TIA Workshop, Oxford, 14 June 1997.

Compagno, Andrea (1995), *Intelligent Glass Façades: Material Practice Design*, Birkhäuser, Basel.

Connolly, Simon (1995), Toward the Transparent Envelope, *Architects Journal*, 15 June 1995, Vol. 201, No. 21.

Connolly, Simon (1994), Nothing ventured … , *Building Design*, 15 April 1994, BD1168.

Daniels, Klaus (1995), *The Technology of Ecological Building: Basic Principles and Measures, Examples and Ideas*, Birkhäuser Verlag, Basel.

Daniels, Klaus (1998), *Low-tech, Light-tech, High-tech: Building in the Information Age*, Birkhauser, Basel.

Davey, Peter (1995), Who's Responsible?, *Architectural Review*, July 1995, Vol. CCII, No. 1205.

Davies, Mike (1981), A Wall for all Seasons, *RIBA Journal*, Vol. 88, No. 2, February 1981.

Davies, Mike (1987), *Intelligent Buildings*, Pidgeon Audio Visual.

DTI (1997), *Energy Consumption in the United Kingdom*, Energy Paper 66, The Stationery Office.

Duffy, Frank, *The Intelligent Building*, Owlion Audio Programme, Surveyors Publications, RICS and College of Estate Management.

Edwards, Brian (1996), *Towards Sustainable Architecture: European Directives & Building Design*, Butterworth Architecture Legal Series, Oxford.

Energy Advisory Associates (1992), *Energy Efficiency and Renewables: Recent experience on Mainland Europe*, Credenhill.

Environmental Design: An Introduction for Architects and Engineers, E. & F.N. Spon, 1996.

Farmer, John (1996), *Green Shift: Towards a Green Sensibility in Architecture*, Butterworth Architecture/WWF UK, Oxford.

Fiast, A.P. (1998), *Double Skin Walls*, Institute of Building Technology, Department of Architecture, Lausanne.

Foster, Sir Norman ed. (1993), *Solar Energy in Architecture and Urban Planning: Third European Conference on Architecture*, H.S. Stephens Associates, Bedford.

Gardner, Gareth (1998), Skin-tight Genes, *Building Design*, BD1364, 11 September.

Gardiner, Peter and Bailey, Stuart (1992), Smart Materials, *Design*, June 1992.

Gertis, Karl (1999), A Critical Review of Double Glazing Facades Under Aspects of Building Physics, *Bauphysik*, No. 21, pp. 54–66.

Gonin, Michelle D. and Cross, Thomas B. (1986), *Intelligent Buildings: Strategies for Technology and Architecture*, Dow Jones-Irwin, USA.

Goulding, John R., Lewis, J. Owen, Steemers, Theo C. (1992), *Energy in Architecture: The European Passive Solar Handbook*, CEC, Batsford.

Gregory, D.P. (1986), *Adaptive Building Envelopes*, BSRIA, Bracknell, TN3/86.

Greig, Jonathan (1988), Celebrating the Cerebral, *Building Design Supplement*, BD884, May 1988.

Hall, Andrew (1996), Heralding the Intelligent Wall, *Building Design*, BD1257, 22 March 1996.

Hans, DuMoulin (1994), Energy for the Future: An Environmentally resilient Strategy, *Renewable Energy*, Vol. 5, Part II, pp. 1254–1261, 1994.

Harris, Jude (1994), *Dual Skins: A Review of Double Envelope Buildings*, BSc dissertation, University of Wales, January, 1994.

Harrison, Andrew (1994), Intelligence Quotient: Smart Tips for Smart Buildings, DEGW, *Architecture Today*, AT46, March 1994.

Hartkopf, Volker (1993), *Designing the Office of the Future: The Japanese Approach to Tomorrow's Workplace*. John Wiley, New York.

Hawkes, Dean (1996), *The Environmental Tradition: Studies in Architecture of the Environment*, E. & F.N. Spon.

Herzog, Thomas ed. (1996), *Solar Energy in Architecture and Urban Planning*, Prestel, Munich.

In Finite State Machines, *Architectural Design*, Vol. 66, No. 9/10, September/October 1994.

Infotheque: A Showcase for Intelligent Buildings, *Architecture Today*, AST53, November 1994.

Integrating Hi-Tech, *Architects Journal*, Vol. 185, No. 13, 1987.

Intelligent Architecture through Intelligent Design, *Futures*, August 1989, pp. 319–333.

Intelligent Buildings International, IBC Business Publishing, London, 1990/1.

Intelligent Buildings: Proceedings of the Business Strategy Conference held in New York, June 1986, Online, New York, 1986.

Jankovic, L. (1993), Steps Towards Greater System Intelligence, *Intelligent Buildings Today and in the Future*, 7 October 1993, University of Central England.

Jankovic, L. ed. (1993), *Intelligent Buildings Today and in the Future: Proceedings of a Conference Organised by the UCE in Birmingham*, 7 October 1993, University of Central England, Birmingham.

Kerr, Philip, *Gridiron*, Chatto & Windus.

Kim, Jong-Jin and Jones, James (1993), *A Conceptual Framework for Dynamic Control of Daylighting and Electric Lighting Systems*, IEEE Industry Applications Society, Ontario, 2–8 October 1993.

Kim, Jong-Jin (1996), Intelligent Building Technologies: A Case of Japanese Buildings, *The Journal of Architecture*, Vol. 1, No. 2, Summer 1996.

Kroner, Walter M. (1997), An Intelligent and Responsive Architecture, *Automation in Construction*, 200, 1997.

Kroner, Walter M, *Intelligent Design for Intelligent Façades: Towards Responsive Building Enclosure Systems*, USA, Unpublished.

Krueger, Ted (1994), Like a Second Skin, Living Machines, *Architectural Design*, Vol. 66, No. 9/10, March/April 1994.

Lerner, Steve (1997), *Eco-pioneers: Practical Visionaries Solving Today's Environmental Problems*, MIT Press, Boston, MA.

Littlefair, P.J., Cooper, I., McKennan, G. (1988), *Daylighting as a Passive Solar Energy Option: An Assessment of its Potential in Non-domestic Buildings*, BRE, Watford.

MacInnes, Katherine (1994), Is Intelligent the Opposite of Clever?, *Architectural Design*, Vol. 64, No. 3/4, March/April 1994.

McLelland, Stephen ed. (1988), *Intelligent Buildings: An IFS Briefing*, IFS Publications, Bedford, 1988.

Murphy, Ian (1988), Working in Harness, *Building Design Supplement*, BD884, May 1988.

Murphy, Ian (1988), Prospects for the Smart Set, *Building Design Supplement*, BD884, May 1988.

Murphy, Ian (1988), The Art of Slick Skins, *Building Design Supplement*, BD884, May 1988.

Murphy, Ian (1990), Putting the Brains into Buildings: How Intelligent Can Buildings Become, *Architecture Today*, AT6, March 1990.

Nutt, B.B. (1994), The Use and Management of Passive Solar Environments, *Renewable Energy*, Vol. 5, Part II, pp. 1009–1014.

O'Cofaigh, E., Olley, J.A. and Lewis, J.O. (1995), *The Climatic Dwelling*, James and James.

Olgyay, V. (1992), *Design with Climate: Bioclimatic Approach to Architectural Regionalism*, Von Nostrand Reinhold, New York,.

Olivier, David and Willoughby, John (1994), *Review of Ultra Low Energy Homes: Phase I and II*, BRECSU.

Owens, P.G.T. (Pilkington), (1992), Intelligent Skins for Buildings, *Building Control*, No. 52, June 1992.

Permasteelisa (1999), *Active Facades and Environmental Systems – A Design Primer*, Permasteelisa Research and Engineering, Italy

Robathan, D.P. (1992), *The Future of Intelligent Buildings, Intelligent Buildings and Management*, Conference, Unicom Seminars, Uxbridge, 28–29 January 1992.

Robathan, Paull (1988), *Intelligent Buildings Guide*, IBC Technical Services Ltd.

Robathan, Paull (1989), *Intelligent Buildings International*, Paull Robathan, IBC Technical Services Ltd.

Sala, Marco (1994), The Intelligent Envelope: The Current State of the Art, *Renewable Energy*, Vol. 5, Part II, pp. 1039–1046.

Sheehan, Tony (1995), Advanced Construction Materials, *Architects Journal*, 13 July 1995, Vol. 202, No. 2.

Shorrock, L.D. and Henderson, G. (1990), *Energy Use in Buildings and Carbon Dioxide Emissions*, Building Research Establishment Report, Watford.

Smith, Peter and Pitts, Adrian C. (1997), *Concepts in Practice: Energy*, Batsford.

Spiller Neil (1994), When is a Door not a Door?, *Architectural Design*, Vol. 64, No. 7/8, July/August 1994.

Stake, Robert E. (1995), *The Art of Case Study Research*, Sage Publications, Thousand Oaks.

Stephens, H.S. ed. (1996), *Solar Energy in Architecture and Urban Planning: Proceedings of an International Conference*, Berlin, Germany, 26–29 March 1996, H.S. Stephens Associates, Bedford.

Swann, Dick (1985), Le Corbusier on Controlling the Environment, *RIBA Journal*, Vol. 92, No. 2, February 1985.

The Building Breathes, *Architectural Record*, October 1995.

The ECD Partnership and the Commission of the European Communities (1991), *Solar Architecture in Europe: Design, Performance and Evaluation*, Prism Press.

Tombazis, Alexandros N., *On Skins and Other Preoccupations in Architectural Design*, Unpublished.

Tumm, Othmar and Toggweiler, Peter (1993), *Photovoltaics in Architecture*, Birkhäuser Verlag, Basel.

Vale, Brenda and Vale, Robert (1991), *Towards a Green Architecture*, RIBA Publications.

Vale, Brenda and Vale, Robert (1991), *Green Architecture*, Thames and Hudson.

van Paassen, A.H.C. and Lute, P.J. (1993), *Energy Saving Through Controlled Ventilation Windows*, Third European Conference on Architecture, Florence, 17–21 May 1993.

van Paassen, A.H.C. (1988), Passive Solar Energy in Intelligent Buildings, *ASHRAE Transactions*, Vol. 94, No. 1.

Vincent, Gordon and Peacock, John (1985), *The Automated Building*, The Architectural Press.

von Weizsäcke, Erst, Lovins, Amory B. and Lovins, L. Hunter (1997), *Factor Four: Doubling Wealth, Halving Resource Use*, Earthscan.

Walker, Bryan (1990), A Building Aware of our Needs, *Building Services*, Vol. 12, No. 12, December 1990.

Wigginton, Michael (1995), *The Intelligent Façade: A Research Proposal*, Unpublished.

Wigginton, Michael (1992), Response and Responsibility: How Clever can a Building be Today, *Architecture Today*, AT 25, February.

Wigginton, Michael (1996), *Glass in Architecture*, Phaidon, Oxford.

Wigginton, Michael, *Do We Need Intelligent Buildings?*

World Commission on Environment and Development (1987), *Our Common Future*, Oxford University Press, Oxford.

Yannas, Simos (1994), *Solar Energy and Housing Design*, Volume 2: Examples, AA Publications for DTI.

Yeang, Ken (1990), The Idea of the Intelligent Building, *South East Asia Building*, April.

Yeang, Ken (1995), *Designing with Nature: The Ecological Basis for Architectural Design*, McGraw-Hill, New York.

Yeang, Ken (1994), *Bioclimatic Skyscrapers*, Artemis, London.

Definitions

The Intelligent Building

There follows a selection of various definitions related to the intelligent building and the intelligent skin found during the research for this book. They are recorded here to highlight the many different perceptions of what the 'intelligent' building actually constitutes, and the variety of definitions with a different emphasis to that proposed in this book.

The term intelligent building has been around since the early 1980s. Early definitions focused almost entirely on technology related to building automation. After 1985 the concept of adaptability crept in – a building had to be able to respond to organisational change and adapt to new tasks.
Andrew Harrison, DEGW

Any building which provides a responsive, effective and supportive environment within which the organisation can achieve its business objectives.
DEGW Report

A building that creates an environment that maximises the efficiency of the occupants of the building while at the same time allowing effective management of resources with minimum life-time costs.
Intelligent Buildings International (IBC)

A truly intelligent building would be one that can anticipate conditions and forces acting on the building. Such a building may change its colour, envelope configuration, orientation and composition … .
Professor Walter Kroner, Rensselaer Polytechnic Institute

An intelligent building is one that is fully let!
Tom Cross, Consultant and Author

A building becomes an intelligent building as soon as it is fully rented.
New York Developer

A building that responds to its function and environment through technology.
Rab Bennetts

Buildings (automatic) that take some initiative in their own operation.
James Madge

Where buildings are designed and constructed to be flexible instruments that will be adaptable over the years according to the demands foreseen in the wake of the development of IT.
Piero Sartogo

A building that provides a productive and cost-effective environment through optimization of its four basic elements – structure, systems, services and management – and the interrelationship between them. Intelligent buildings help business owners, property managers and occupants to realize their goals in the areas of cost, comfort, convenience, safety, long-term flexibility and marketability.
Dr Jong-Jin Kim, University of Michigan (Intelligent Buildings Institute Definition)

The Intelligent Building (*continued*)

Buildings that have advanced features that promote occupants' productivity and the efficient use of energy and resources.
Dr Jong-Jin Kim, University of Michigan

A term blessed with instant credibility and instant attraction.
Frank Duffy, Owlion Audio Programme

Intelligent Buildings have telecommunications equipment, office automation and smart building services providing a 'responsive, effective and supportive environment in which the organisation can achieve its business objectives.
Barrie Evans, AJ 1/7/92

An environment that maximises the efficiency of the occupants of the building and at the same time allows effective management of resources.
Intelligent Buildings Group

Buildings which predict the user demands upon it and its plant systems, rather than simply reacting to them.
Dr Dave Leifer, Architecture Australia, May 1989

The intelligent building is the inert, passive, well-adjusted responsive building; the building which adjusts and uses biomorphic systems to optimise.
Michael Wigginton, Butterworth correspondence

An intelligent building is a house with no style, It is possible that such a building would be positively unsightly, or that there might not even be anything to see.
Ole Bouman, Archis, December 1995

Intelligence to a building owner is a good business decision [image].
Alan Abramson

A building that is organised and regulated by means of artificial intelligence.
Modo 122

A building in which a tenant can enjoy common information and communications equipment that will increase productivity and which also has a very human environment suited to the needs of the information society.
Tadashi Tomano, 1987

Intelligent office buildings provide for unique and changing assemblies of recent technologies in appropriate physical, environmental and organizational settings, to enhance worker speed, understanding, communication, and overall productivity.
Intelligent Buildings Institute, Washington, Intelligent Facilities Management Conference

An intelligent building is one that helps an organisation function.
David Boyd

Buildings which 'provide information' for an intelligent operator to act upon.
Fagan, 1985

Buildings which have fully automated building service control systems.
Cardin, 1983

Buildings which are 'more than ordinarily responsive' to changes in security, external environment, tenant demand and which offer shared tenant services.
Duffy, 1986

Buildings where the fabric is used to serve as 'half of the building services'.
Building Services, 1985

An intelligent building is one that maximises the efficiency of the occupants while at the same time minimising the costs associated with running the building.
David Boyd, 1994

Buildings that contain high levels of advanced industrial technology and that can also adapt their internal environments in response to external conditions and forces hav been termed intelligent buildings.
David Boyd, 1987

An intelligent building is one which has an information communication network through which two or more of its services systems are automatically controlled, guided by predictions based upon knowledge of the building usage, maintained in an integrated database.
Dave Leifer, November 1987

The type of building which harnesses and integrates all levels of IT from data processing to environmental control and security.
David S Brockfield, 1989

Intelligent building as an ideal system 'means an automated enclosural and support servicing system that is capable of responding both environmentally and physically to the activities, needs and requirements of its users, to the external environment, and to exchanges between the system and its environment.'
Ken Yeang

An intelligent building is one that creates an environment that maximises the efficiency of the occupants of the building while at the same tiome allows effective management of resources with minimum lifetime costs.
Robathan, 1989

An Intelligent Building incorporates the best available concepts, materials, systems and technologies. These elements are integrated together to achieve a building which meets or exceeds performance requirements of the building stakeholders. These stakeholders include the building's owners, managers and users as well as the local and global community.
European Intelligent Building Group

A building may be considered intelligent if "it creates an environment which allows the organisation to achieve its business objectives, while maximising the effectiveness of its occupants and achieving minimum lifecycle costs.
EIBG

The Intelligent Skin

Smart skin – a series of manipulative layers which can respond either individually or cumulatively, to external climatic variations or internally generated functional changes.
Ian Murphy, 'The Smart Set'

Polyvalent wall – will remove the distinction between solid and transparent, as it will be capable of replacing both conditions and will dynamically regulate energy flow in either direction depending upon external and internal conditions, monitor and control light levels and constant ratios as necessary at all points in the envelope.
Mike Davies, 'A Wall for All Seasons'

The Intelligent Skin (*continued*)

Smart materials – materials which can automatically adjust their properties (reflectance, thermal conductivity, physical form, ventilation) in response to environmental changes. Stimuli such as temperature and strain can produce effects such as change in colour and electrical signature.
Peter Gardiner and Stuart Bailey, Design

Smart or 'intelligent' materials are able to detect changes in their present state, and to take some action following this detection
Tony Sheehan, Materials Adviser, Ove Arup & Partners

Slick skins – balanced skins which are specifically tailored to building functions and geographical (and hence climatic) location
Ian Murphy, 'Working in Harness'

Intelligent Glass Façade – makes use of self-regulating thermal protection and solar control measures to adapt in a dynamic, 'living' way to changing light and weather conditions; interaction between façade and building services.
Andrea Compagno

Smart Skin – a dynamic surface that balances outside and inside climates through changes of colour.
AJ 1/4/87

Intelligence – capable of intelligent analysis and processing of the physical quantity being sensed.
J Wilkins and S Willis

Intelligence – an ability to respond to the changing environmental conditions according to the time of day or year, in such a way as to reduce primary energy needs for heating, cooling, and lighting, and thus make a contribution to environmental conservation.
Andrea Compagno

Smart Skin – a building fabric that changes its thermal properties in accordance with internal demand and external environment.
Building 17/7/87

Smart materials – materials which have the ability to respond to external stimulation in a predictable way and thus have additional functionality.
EPSRC

Intelligent façades … incorporate variable devices whose adjustability and control adaptability is used to further enhance the façade's role as a climate moderator. This capacity gives the façade the ability to accept and reject free energy from the external environment and thus reduce the amount of energy required to achieve a comfortable internal environment.
Mark Skelly, University of Bath

Intelligent skin – should be able to tune itself to provide the ideal thermal response to any given set of external climatic conditions, occupancy requirements, orientation and building type.
Battle and McCarthy [AD]

Index

Acoustic dampers 36
Arizona 45
Artificial
    intelligence 17–18
    lighting, responsive 39–40
    neural networks 18
Atkin, Brian 22
    Intelligent Buildings 22
Australia 9
Autonomic action 18–19, 29

Behling, Stefan 33
Bennetts Associates 38
'Bioclimatic design' 24
Biological metaphors 3–4, 22–23, 43
Biotechnology 12
Blood vessels 28
Brain 17, 18, 24, 29, 39
BRECSU's Normalized Performance Indices
    47
Bruder/DWL Architects 99
Brundtland Centre, The 103
Brundtland, Gro Harlem 8–9
Budget 3
Building
    design for low energy 12
    fabric 4, 41
    façade 38
    management systems 3, 39
    Regulations 9–10
    services 3, 46
    skin 27, 28, *see also* Double skin system,
        Human Skin
Business Promotion Centre 125

Canada and greenhouse gas emissions 9
Cannon Design 3, 163
Capital cost 3
Carbon dioxide 8
Central building management system
    24
Chameleon 29
Chicago office buildings 11
China, People's Republic of 11
Chlorofluorocarbons (CFCs) 8, 9
Chromogenic devices 31
Churn 30
City Place 20–21
Climate 19
    change 7
Club of Rome 7
    The Limits to Growth 7
Cognitive science 22, 31
Commerzbank Headquarters 21, 59
Congress of the UIA/AIA (1993) 14

Cooling 13
    devices 41
Curtains 30

Darwinian principles 25, 30
Davies, Michael 30
Daylight 36
    controllers 40
Debis Building 37, 55
DEGW 21
Dermis 28
Design Office for Gartner 149
Design team 13–14
Developing world, 10–11
Dinosaurs 43–44
Disch, Prof Rolf, Architekt 115
Double skin system 41–42
Dynamic
    membrane 27
    response mechanisms 4

Earth Summit 9
Ecological goals 14
Economics 34–35
Electrical
    autonomy 33, 40–41
    power 8
    services 3
Electricity
    generation by fuel source 10
    generators 40–41
Electro-solar technology 43–44
Energy
    consumption 46
        by building type 12
        for non-transport uses 12
        levels 10
        per capita 11
        inland 12
    costs 11–12
    efficiency 10
    embodied 13
    flows 23–24
    sources, renewable 9–10
    use 7–9, 32–33
Environmental
    Building, The 75
    burden 34–35
    data 39
    services 3
Epidermis 3–4, 27, 28
Essen 38
European
    Charter 14
    Intelligent Building Group 22

Union and greenhouse gas emissions 9
Evolution 43–44, *see also* Darwinian
    principles
Evolutionary time scales 22–23
Existing building stock 13

Façade of a building 3, *see also* Intelligent
    Façade Programme 4, 7, 39
Fault logging 34
Feilden Clegg Architects 75
Flemming Skude and Ivar Moltke 121
Fossil fuels 8, 13
Foster & Partners 59, 125
Fuel
    consumption 10
    sources 10
Fuzzy logic 39

Gartner 149
Genetic model 4
GlaxoWellcome House West 71
Glazing 30–31
    electrochromic 31
    intelligent 13
Global
    impact 7
    pollution 10–11
    warming 19, 43–44, *see also* Greenhouse
        effect
Götz 93
'Green' agenda 44
Green Building, The 109
Greenhouse effect 7–9
GSW Headquarters 37, 49

Hartford, Connecticut 20
HCFCs 9
Headquarters of Götz 93
Heating 41
Helicon 83
Heliotrop® 115
Herzog & de Meuron Architects 13
Hölken & Berghoff 143
Hooker Building 3
Hormones 29
Human
    body and intelligence systems 26
    endocrine system 29
    eye and its adaptability 29
    skin 3–4, 27–28
        biological metaphor of 3–4
        see also Multifunctional skin
Hypothalamus 29

Iceland 9

Igloo 24–25
Insulating shutter 31
Intelligence 17
'Intelligent building' 3, 29
    attributes of 22
    evolving models 20
    first 20, 21
    instincts 32
    need for 19
    redefinition of 23
Intelligent
    Building Programme 3, 4
    glazing systems 13
    design 24–25
    façade 23, 36–37
    Façade Programme 4, 7, 39
    skin 23
    Skin Study 3, 5
Interactive Building Envelope study 44
Intergovernmental Panel on Climate Change
    (IPCC) 8
Iris of the eye, action of 29

KHR Architects 103
Kroner, Walter 21, 24, 25
Kruger, Ted 28
Kurt Ackermann und Partner 149
Kyoto Summit 9

Learning abilities 31, 39
'Life-cycle costing' principle 13
Lighting and appliances 13
Lovins, Amory 12
Low energy
    design 12
    buildings 32–33

Maintenance 33–34
    scheduling 34
Manual override 40
McHarg, Ian 14
Mechanical services 3
Metabolism 23
Methane 8
Montreal Protocol 9
Morris, William 12
Motorized windows 41
Multifunctional skin 30
Murray O'Laoire Associates 109

Nanometric functions 30
Nanometric technologies 44
Natural
    analogies 29
    intelligence 18
    stack effect 41–42
Nerve endings 28
Neural networks 18, 39
New Zealand 9

Nitrous oxides 8
Non-survival of the unfit 43–44
Norway 9
Nuclear energy 43–44

Occidental Chemical Building 3, 163
Occupancy patterns 19–20
Occupant control 20, 40, 31–32
Office equipment. energy load 13
Ohbayashi-Gumi 159
Oil
    as an energy source 7
    crises 7
Opening window 23
Overdiek and Partners 38
Ozone 8

Passive
    architecture 4
    approaches 19, 23, 27, 32, 33, 37, 39
Personal control 40
Petzinka Pink und Partner 65
Phoenix Central Library 99
Photovoltaics 12, 32, 36, 43–44
Pneumatic dampers 41
Powergen Building 38
Protein collagen 28

Rain forests 9
Renewable Energy in Architecture and
    Design (READ) Group 14
Rensselaer Polytechnic Institute 21
Renzo Piano Building Workshop 55
Resource management 43–44
Retractable roofs 41
Rio de Janeiro 9
RMJM 71
Royal Institute of British Architects' Code of
    Conduct 14
Russia 9
Ruurd Roorda, Government Building
    Agency 87
RWE Building 38

Sakamura, Ken, Professor 155
Sauerbruch & Hutton 49
Scandinavia 45
School of Engineering and Manufacture 129
Sense receptors 28
Sheppard Robson 83
Short Ford & Associates 129
Shutters 23–24, 31, 36
Skidmore Owings and Merrill 20, 21
Sky Lab 16
'Smart'
    materials, concept of 3
    technologies 34
Solar
    collectors 36

electricity generation 12
    energy 32
    House Freiburg 143
    radiation 30–31
Somatic response 18–19, 23, 29
Space heating 13
Stadttor (City Gate) 65
Sun controllers 40
Sun
    effects of 32
    see also Solar
Sunpath programme 46
Super Energy Conservation Building 159
SUVA Insurance Company 13, 137

Tax Office Extension 87
Technibank 21
Technology
    and buildings 4
    transfer 43
Temperature controllers 41, see also
    Thermoregulation
Thai village house 11
Thermochromics 31
Thermophysical properties 30
Thermoregulation 18, 28
Transport 9, 10
TRON – Concept Intelligent House 155

United Nations
    Conference on Environment and
        Development 9
    Convention on Climate Change 9
    Environment Programme 8
    World Commission on Environment and
        Development 8–9
    Our Common Future 8–9
United States and greenhouse gas emissions
    9
User expectation 31–32
U-values 46

Variability 30
Venetian blind 23, 30
Ventilation 3, 12, 19, 25, 33, 36
    chimneys 36
    controllers 41
Villa Vision 121
Vitruvius 12

Water heating 13
Watson, Donald 12
Webler + Geissler 93
Wind turbines 40–41
World Meteorological Organization 8
World population 43–44

Zero-energy operation 33